INSTRUCTOR'S M

LITERATURE
AND THE
WRITING PROCESS

FIFTH EDITION

ELIZABETH McMAHAN
Illinois State University

SUSAN DAY
University of Illinois

ROBERT FUNK
Eastern Illinois University

PRENTICE HALL, *Upper Saddle River, NJ 07458*

CONTENTS

v

PART III   WRITING ABOUT POETRY

ANTHOLOGY OF POETRY

vii

PART IV   WRITING ABOUT DRAMA

ANTHOLOGY OF DRAMA

PART I   COMPOSING: AN OVERVIEW

Chapter 1   The Prewriting Process   [pp. 3-16]

In this opening chapter, we focus on analytical reading—on giving careful attention to the literary text and asking pertinent questions about it in order to derive a thorough understanding of the meaning. At the same time, we assume that students will be writing about this work, so we introduce them to several useful invention techniques that will help them discover what they want to say about the piece when they get ready to write.

Prewriting Exercise (letters to and from Eveline)   [p. 7]

The purpose of this activity is to teach students the concept of audience. But from reading or hearing the students read their letters, you will also be able to see how well they understand the characterizations in the story.

Prewriting Exercise (about purpose)   [pp. 8-9]

These four assignments may prove too taxing for students to complete individually. Instead, you may want to assign this section to groups of three or four students to complete as a project—checking, revising, and approving one another's work.

Self-Questioning (inventing ideas)   [pp. 9-10]

Here are some possible responses to the invention questions:

1. Eveline's home life is dreary, routine, and oppressive.
2. In her new life with Frank, Eveline expects to gain freedom, respect, adventure—and maybe love.
3. Since Eveline apparently knows very little about Frank or Buenos Ayres, her expectations seem to be based mainly on hopes and wishes.
4. The dust is a symbol of the dry stagnation of Eveline's life.
5. Dusty cretonne, a yellowing photograph of a priest, a broken harmonium, a "coloured print of the promises made to the Blessed Margaret Mary Alacoque" (which would be promises of lifelong virginity): all of these suggest decay and the denial of a vital life.
6. Eveline is "over nineteen." Probably she is around twenty years old, a time when one usually reaches adulthood and is making life decisions.
7. Eveline's father is an alcoholic, selfish, demanding tyrant, who—like most of his kind—has moments of tenderness. His being in "a bad way" means that he is drunk.

1

Organization, which requires hard, clear thinking, is one of the most difficult elements of the writing process for students to handle. Most writing specialists agree that compiling a formal outline is unnecessary, but most also agree that devising some plan is essential. Students should understand, though, that the plan can always be modified as the writing proceeds.

The plan can be as simple as recording the main points of the essay in the order to be followed. But we feel strongly that these points should be stated as sentences, not merely as topics, in order to make clear the direction of the writer's thoughts (as well as to make sure that those thoughts *have* some direction). Students who merely jot down topics sometimes experience difficulty in keeping their essays unified because, as they write, their ideas veer off in directions not relevant to the thesis.

In this chapter we suggest ways to organize an essay about a literary work and offer advice about how to develop the ideas in this plan.

Writing Rituals May Help in Getting Started

Most experienced writers perform—perhaps unconsciously—little rituals that help them get started. Some people, for instance, always write in the same place—in a comfortable chair, at a desk, at the kitchen table, perhaps lying on the living room rug. It matters not where a person writes, but having an established place may help to get the process going when writing needs to be done. Some people sharpen pencils before they start or find a favorite pen. Some always compose at the keyboard. Some get themselves a cup of coffee or a soft drink to keep their strength up during this arduous undertaking. You may want to discuss writing rituals with your students. If they have none, suggest that they try to establish some just in case these preparations may help to spark the writing process.

Questions for Consideration (using adequate detail) [p. 20]

We think the sample paragraph is adequately developed. Here are the details used to support the main point (the topic sentence):
  —Eveline's brothers and sisters are grown.
  —Her mother is dead.
  —Her father will be alone.
  —He has a drinking problem.
  —He is getting old.
  —She thinks he will miss her.
  —She feels she is abandoning her father.
  —She has written to him to ease the blow.
  —The letter soothes her conscience.

Students may mention the following additional details as possible support for the main idea of the paragraph:
    —Tizzy Dunn and the Walters (possibly former friends of her father) are gone; also gone is the priest who was his school friend.
    —". . . latterly he had begun to threaten her"; she apparently forgets this fear—or discounts it, even though "now she has nobody to protect her."
    —"Sometimes he could be very nice"; she remembers when he took care of her one day when she was sick and when he played with the children on a picnic long ago.

The writer introduces personal opinion in the final sentence: "Eveline *seems to* feel. . . ."

Most students will probably agree that the interpretation is valid, but some may disagree about whether Eveline's younger brothers and sisters (entrusted to her care by her dying mother) are indeed "grown up" by the time she considers leaving with Frank. Some might argue also that Eveline writes the letter to her father, not out of consideration for his feelings, but as a means of avoiding a bitter confrontation with him.

Class Activity on Introductions and Conclusions [pp. 20-23]

You will want to be sure your students understand all of the material in this chapter—especially the section on distinguishing critical details from plot details so that they can successfully maintain a critical focus in their papers. But since an effective opening and closing are crucial to the success of an essay, you may want to give your students extra practice in writing these special kinds of paragraphs.

Ask your students to devise a thesis statement for paper about a work of literature they have read recently. Then have them write only the introduction and conclusion for such a paper. After they have completed their paragraphs, you could have them exchange papers and do peer evaluation. Write the following questions on the board and ask your students to respond (concerning a fellow student's paper) in writing.

ABOUT THE INTRODUCTORY PARAGRAPH:
    1. Is the main point of the (intended) paper made clear?
    2. Is the topic introduced gracefully? Or is it too bluntly stated?
    3. Is the thesis itself interesting? Or is it too obvious?
    4. Would you want to continue reading a paper that began with this introduction?

ABOUT THE CONCLUSION:
    1. Does it simply repeat the introduction?
    2. Does it convincingly establish the main point of the paper?
    3. Does it have an emphatic final sentence?

Peer Evaluation Checklist [p. 25]

These questions are designed to help students learn to evaluate their own or another student's papers. We have found that learning to be good editors helps students to become good writers.

You might find it helpful to duplicate this checklist, leaving spaces so that your students can write directly on the sheets during peer evaluation sessions.

Suggestions for Writing [pp. 26, 30]

After studying these opening chapters, your students should be able to write a first draft of a literary analysis focusing on character. We suggest Kate Chopin's "Story of an Hour" as a story that lends itself well to this approach.

If you do not think your students are ready to tackle a conventional analysis, you can let them choose instead from the list of "Ideas for Responsive Writing," which also focus on character but allow more individuality in style and approach. Chapter 3, which follows in the text, provides the instruction they will need for revising these first drafts. (Other stories in the Anthology of Short Fiction that might provide students with interesting characters to analyze or respond to are Richard Wright's "The Man Who Was Almost a Man," Sherwood Anderson's "Hands," Tillie Olsen's "I Stand Here Ironing," John Updike's "A & P," and Bessie Head's "Life.")

Chapter 3   The Rewriting Process   [pp.31-50]

Nancy Sommers's award-winning article, "Revision Strategies of Student Writers and Experienced Adult Writers" [*College Composition and Communication* 31 (Dec. 1980): 378-88], reveals that student writers typically do little revising—even when they *think* they have. Their alterations fall into the category of editing—cosmetic changes—rather than a true re-visioning of the writing. So, you will probably need to monitor your students' revising process by looking at drafts and suggesting improvements if you want to be sure that they learn to revise in a meaningful way.

The sample student paper that appears in its first draft in Chapter 2 and in its revised version at the end of this chapter provides a good model of an essay that is much improved by revision. Our student Wendy outlined her first draft and discovered that she had a paragraph that lacked support and a couple of points out of place. Making these changes produced a far better paper, and the effort proved well worth her time, raising her grade considerably.

We are sold on outlining after the writing. Since many writers won't take the time to plan carefully before they begin, the after-the-writing outline lets them see whether their first draft is orderly and coherent or whether it wanders around, has underdeveloped paragraphs, and repeats ideas.

The exercises in this chapter concern revision at the sentence level—perhaps not as crucial as global revision but still essential for effective writing.

Rearranging for Conciseness: Sentence Combining Exercise   [pp. 37-38]

Responses will vary, of course.

1. The second common stereotype, usually symbolizing sexual temptation, is the dark lady.
2. As the title suggests, Kate Chopin's short story "The Storm" shows how the characters react during a cyclone.
3. Because Emily Dickinson's poetry can be extremely elliptical, readers often have difficulty discovering the literal meaning.
4. There are three major things to consider in understanding Goodman Brown's character: what the author tells us about Brown, what Brown himself says and does, and what other people say to and about him.
5. Most of the humorous incidents that inspire Walter Mitty's fantasies fall into two groups, the first illustrating his desire to be in charge of the situation.

Varying the Pattern [pp. 38-39]

Emphasis is usually achieved when the most important information is placed near the end of the sentence. Advise your students to shift less important modifiers (whether words, clauses, or phrases) to the front of the sentence. For example, in the first sentence of the exercise, "when she was a child" should be moved out of the emphatic or "stress" position at the end and placed somewhere earlier in the sentence. The most important information (and the most surprising) is that Wharton was "not allowed to have paper on which to write" and that should be placed at the end of the sentence.

Exercise on Style [p. 39]

Students will be able to combine sentences in several ways; here are some likely constructions:
1. Edith Wharton, who was born into a rich, upper-class family, was, as a child, not allowed to have paper on which to write.
   Or: Born into a rich, upper-class family, Edith Wharton, as a child, was not allowed to have paper to write on.
2. Because her governesses never taught her how to organize ideas in writing, she had to ask her friend Walter Berry to help write her book on the decoration of houses.
3. When she was twenty-three years old, Edith married Teddy Wharton, who always carried a one-thousand dollar bill in his wallet—just in case she wanted anything.
4. Although her good friend Henry James helped her to improve her novels, Wharton's books invariably sold far more copies than his.
5. Following World War I, she was presented the highest award given by the French government—the Legion of Honor—for her refugee relief activities.

Exercise on Word Choice [p. 40]

Responses will vary, of course; here are some possibilities:
1. The narrator's overactive sense of humor marks him as an unusual character.
2. His constant practical joking finally disgusts the reader.
3. The readers of the story realize that some people enjoy the misfortunes of others.
4. The narrator decides that Jim deserved his fate.
5. Since Whitey narrates the whole story, we know only what he tells us.

Exercise on Passive Voice [p. 41]

Answers may vary somewhat.
1. Creon brutalizes Antigone because of her struggle to achieve justice.
2. Antigone's tirade against his unbending authority did not convince Creon.
3. The play pitted male against female.
4. Society may experience considerable benefit if someone wins even a small point against a tyrant.
5. Creon's exercise of iron-bound authority caused the tragedy.

PART II WRITING ABOUT SHORT FICTION

Chapter 4   How Do I Read Short Fiction?   [pp.53-58]

Although you may not have time to assign all of the papers suggested in the following chapters on fiction, poetry, and drama, we think it advisable to assign your students to read every chapter in order to receive an adequate understanding of all the fundamentals of literary analysis. Each chapter also presents a practical approach to writing about literature and includes explanations of various revising and editing techniques.

On page 58, at the end of this brief introduction to the study of short fiction, your students will find the useful list of "Critical Questions for Reading the Short Story." These questions can serve as an invention heuristic to develop material for writing about any of the stories included in the anthology

9

Bloom, Harold, ed. *Alice Walker*. Modern Critical Views. New York: Chelsea, 1989.

Byerman, Keith E. *Fingering the Jagged Grain: Tradition and Form in Recent Black Fiction*. Athens: U of Georgia P, 1985. 142-46.

Byrne, Mary Ellen. "Welty's 'A Worn Path' and Walker's 'Everyday Use': Companion Pieces." *Teaching English in the Two-Year College* 16.2 (May 1989): 129-33.

Christian, Barbara. "Alice Walker: The Black Woman Artist as Wayward." *Black Women Writers (1950-1980): A Critical Evaluation*. Ed. Mari Evans. Garden City: Doubleday, 1984. 457-77, specifically 462-63.

Winchell, Donna H. *Alice Walker*. New York: Twayne, 1992.

Chapter 6   Writing About Imagery and Symbolism   [pp. 71-93]

Interpreting Symbols   [p. 80]

1. The townspeople know that the unlucky person who draws the black dot will be killed, but whether they understand the social purpose of the ritual is left vague. The implication is that the people don't want to face the cruelty of their actions. The ritual seems to be re-enacted out of fear and a blind adherence to tradition.

2. The uncertain history of the lottery suggests that the violent ritual has been around for a long time and that the townspeople don't care to examine their behavior, and its origins, too closely. The precise meaning of the lottery is not important to the townspeople; what is important is the tradition that binds them together and focuses their repressed aggression on a single object. That Mr. Summers asks a question that everybody knows the answer to underscores the mindless nature of the ritual: they go through the motions without reflecting on what they're doing and why they're doing it. A stylized question-and-response formula is part of many religious rituals.

3. The black box is a symbol of the tradition the townspeople follow. The color black conventionally signifies evil. The box is clearly an icon (i.e., a sacred or revered image), as the details of its history suggest.

4. The stones mentioned at the story's opening foreshadow the ending and add an unspecified but threatening note to the early description. Historically, stoning was the fate of outcasts from a community (as in the Christian story of Mary Magdalene, who was saved by Jesus from being stoned as a harlot). Though the outcasts had supposedly violated the community's rules or laws, many times they served as scapegoats. Mrs. Hutchinson is an extreme example of a scapegoat, since she has not transgressed.

5. Although the characters are not fully developed, they do present a variety of viewpoints. (The fact that few of them have first names suggests that they are types.) Old Man Warner (who is always called "Old Man") serves as a rigid conservative who doesn't approve of any change in the traditional ritual (perhaps partly because he has escaped the black dot for 77 years). Mr. Summers, whose sunny name is surely ironic, is a civic booster who enjoys his priestlike role in the ritual; he represents the dutiful liberal who bends the rules a little but never questions the value of tradition. Mr. and Mrs. Adams can be seen as ineffectual radicals who point out that some communities are giving up the lottery but who do nothing to change their own community. Mrs Hutchinson, ironically, is a well-liked, cheerful woman who seems to enjoy the ritual (until the end), though she forgets about the date and arrives late (which also seems ironic). The name *Hutchinson* may be significant for its association with Anne Hutchinson (1591-1643), a religious liberal who became one of the founders of Rhode Island after her banishment from Massachusetts Bay Colony. Hutchinson stressed individual intuition in finding salvation; she also criticized the Massachusetts Puritans for their narrow concepts of morality. Although Tessie Hutchinson does not stand up to her community, it is interesting that her name recalls a New Englander who was once tried and banished for speaking out against established authority. This historical association may also suggest parallels between "The Lottery" and the Salem Witch Trials.

13

Exercise on Thesis Statements   [p. 81]

This exercise works well in small groups of three or four because the discussion of each revision will bring up criticisms and suggestions beyond what each individual could generate alone. Answers will vary, but here are some possible revisions:

1. Shirley Jackson's "The Lottery" presents a compelling indictment of the practice of blaming innocent people for society's ills.
2. The ritual of the lottery itself serves as a symbol of a society dominated by unexamined tradition.
3. The impact of Shirley Jackson's "The Lottery" depends largely on the contrast between the placid, ordinary setting and the horrifying conclusion.
4. The characters in "The Lottery" symbolize the conflict between tradition and progress.
5. Shirley Jackson's "The Lottery" explores the dangers of conformity and mob action.

Ideas for Writing   [pp. 81-82]

The responsive writing suggestions ask students to examine their understanding of and experience with two key concepts in the story—traditional rituals and scapegoats. These assignments can be used to stimulate discussion and generate material for further writing.

Each of the critical writing assignments calls for a general statement (thesis) supported by analyzed examples. You may want to talk through a sample essay or outline of this type before your students begin to write (see Chapter 3).

Sample Student Paper   [pp. 83-93]

Here are some possible responses to the questions in the margins of the finished version:

Todd dropped "incongruities" from the thesis because he discusses only one incongruity, and it's a supporting detail rather than the main point.

The opening sentence was revised for conciseness and exactness.

"Jackson does this" was vague and general; "Jackson creates tension" uses more precise language and makes a definite point.

Todd improved the opening sentence of the second paragraph by identifying the black box as the "controlling image" and specifying the connection of the box to death. Both of these revisions sharpen the point of the topic sentence.

Changing "grew" to "growing" makes the series of three modifiers ("faded," "splintered," "growing shabbier") grammatically parallel (they're all participles).

Adding the information about the townspeople's failure to see the need for change makes this sentence more relevant to the general thesis.

14

The elimination of sarcasm is an improvement because the opening had not prepared the reader for a sarcastic tone; thus, the passage was confusing in the uncorrected draft.

The word "selfishness" narrows the focus of the paragraph to a specific aspect of human nature.

Todd moved the last paragraph of the draft because it was one more example of Jackson's use of symbols, not a conclusion.

Todd replaced the informal phrase "in a nutshell" to keep the tone consistently serious.

The last two sentences in the final version refine and reflect the thesis from the opening paragraph, bringing the analysis full circle and giving it a sense of unity.

Video: "The Lottery." 18 minutes, color, 1969. Available from Filmic Archives.
"A Discussion of the Lottery." With Dr. James Burbin. 10 minutes, color, 1969. Available from Filmic Archives.
"The Lottery" and "A Discussion of the Lottery" together on laser disc. Available from Filmic Archives.

Audio: "The Lottery." Read by Shirley Jackson and Maureen Stapleton. 1 cassette. Available from Caedmon Records.

Suggestions for Further Reading on "The Lottery"

Friedman, Lenemaja. *Shirley Jackson*. Boston: Twayne, 1975. 63-67.
Hall, Joan W. *Shirley Jackson: A Study of the Short Fiction*. New York: Twayne, 1993.
Jackson, Shirley. "Biography of a Story." *Come Along with Me*. Ed. Stanley Hyman. New York: Viking, 1968. 211-24.
Nebeker, Helen E. "'The Lottery': Symbolic Tour de Force." *American Literature* 46 (Mar. 1974). 100-07.
Oehlschlaeger, Fritz. "The Stoning of Mistress Hutchinson: Meaning and Context in 'The Lottery.'" *Essays in Literature* 15.2 (Fall 1988): 259-65.
Schaub, Danielle. "Shirley Jackson's Use of Symbols in 'The Lottery.'" *Journal of the Short Story in English* 14 (1990). 79-86.

(much as Robert did in *The Awakening*). This detail gives Alcée some moral standing, within the value structure of the story. Since Calixta is now married and sexually experienced, Alcée feels no need to flee to protect her.

d. When Alcée rides off, he and Calixta are smiling, beaming, and laughing. She lifts her head (in contrast to hanging it in shame). This parting conveys the lack of guilt or remorse felt by the characters. To most readers, it also suggests that they have no future plans to cheat again, since there is a sense of closure to their leave-taking. (However, some readers believe that Alcée's letter to Clarisse suggests that he intends to repeat the adultery while she is conveniently in Biloxi.)

e. An audience in 1898 would find the lack of terrible consequences shocking. The idea that marriage could be unaffected—or even improved—by an unfaithful act would be surprising. Readers today, even if not agreeing with this idea, would not find it totally unfamiliar. The popular novel *Bridges of Madison County* promotes the same point of view. On the other hand, the modern film *Fatal Attraction* reflects the opposite point of view, and this work was also immensely popular. At any rate, the question is today a public one, as it was not in 1898.

Improving Style: Sentence Modeling Exercise [pp. 114-15]

Because sentence modeling may be new to your students, you can help them get the idea by writing one of the sample sentences on the board and marking the parallel elements. Also let them know that they need not imitate the sentence structure precisely but should try to come close enough to catch the cadence of the balance that makes the model sentences impressive.

Suggested Further Readings on "The Storm"

Baker, Christopher. "Chopin's 'The Storm.'" *Explicator* 52.4 (1994): 225-26.

Berkhove, Lawrence I. "'Acting Like Fools': The Ill-Fated Romances of 'At the 'Cadian Ball' and 'The Storm.'" *Critical Essays on Kate Chopin.* Ed. Alice Petry. New York: Hall, 1996. 184-96.

Johnson, Rose M. "A Ratio-nal Pedagogy for Kate Chopin's Passional Fiction: Using Burke's Scene-Act Ratio to Teach 'Story' and 'Storm.'" *Conference of College Teachers of English Studies* 60 (1996): 122-28.

Toth, Emily. *Kate Chopin.* New York: Morrow, 1990. 318-22.

Seyersted, Per. *Kate Chopin: A Critical Biography.* Baton Rouge: Louisiana State UP, 1969. 164-69.

Chapter 9   Writing About Theme   [116-38]

Students often have more difficulty in *stating* theme than in *understanding* theme. Many common literary themes can be expressed in familiar maxims (like, "People who live in glass houses shouldn't throw stones" or "You should practice what you preach"); but in writing about literature students need to learn to phrase themes in a more mature and thoughtful manner. They usually need practice in order to master the technique.

Every time you begin the study of a literary work, you might try having your students write in class a statement of the theme in a sentence or two. At the start of the semester, you can have them compose their theme statements after having discussed the selection, but later in the semester, have them write before the class discussion—in order to judge how well they are learning to understand and express the theme of a work on their own. Collect these impromptu writing samples and read them aloud to the class, asking the students to discuss the virtues and shortcomings of each one. At the end, reread the two or three that everyone agrees are the most effective. In these exercises, stress the importance of precise word choice and clear sentence structure.

Figuring Out the Theme   [p. 131]

Leading questions on the story elements will vary; here are some possibilities:

1. What does "country people" mean in this story? Does the title apply to all the characters in the story? Are they all "good"? Is it an ironic title?
2. Why is Hulga still living at home? How well off are the Hopewells? Does their economic status affect the way they live and think?
3. Why does Joy want to be called Hulga? Why does Mrs. Freeman call her Hulga even though her mother doesn't? Is Manley Pointer's name a sexual pun? Why does Mrs. Hopewell tolerate Mrs. Freeman? Are Mrs. Hopewell and Mrs. Freeman parallels or foils? Why are Mrs. Freeman's daughters mentioned but never seen? Why does Hulga dress the way she does? Why does the author describe Manley's clothes in such detail? What does this description convey about him? What does Mrs. Freeman's name suggest about her character? Is she free in a way that Hulga and her mother are not?
4. Is Hulga's leg symbolic of her artificial or incomplete character? Is it the cause of her personality problems? Is there some symbolic connection between her artificial leg and her heart problem? Is Manley's Bible a symbol of hypocrisy? Is it meant to parallel Hulga's leg? How sincere is Mrs. Hopewell when she says that "Everybody is different. . . . It takes all kinds to make the world. . . . Nothing is perfect"? How well does Mrs. Hopewell actually tolerate differences and imperfections?
5. What does it mean that Hulga shows interest in Manley? Why does Hulga want to seduce Manley? Why is Manley obsessed with Hulga's artificial leg?

ANTHOLOGY OF SHORT FICTION

The following brief analyses and suggestions may prove useful to you in teaching the stories included in this anthology and in formulating writing assignments derived from them.

YOUNG GOODMAN BROWN by Nathaniel Hawthorne   [pp. 140-48]

Hawthorne himself once wrote, "I am not quite sure that I entirely comprehend my own meaning in some of these blasted allegories." Certainly this story is one of his most ambiguous. *Goodman* (meaning, in effect, *Mr.*) Brown represents the archetypal young man on a quest to discover some significance about the meaning of being human. In fact, since he searches for knowledge of good and evil, some critics equate him with Adam. The devil (in the form of Brown's father, thus suggesting the existence of original sin) is clearly an allegorical figure, and Faith's name indicates her allegorical role. The minor characters are less easy to label except as they represent facets of organized religion (Sunday school teacher, minister, deacon).

Critics have endlessly debated whether Goodman Brown's adventures actually took place or whether he fell asleep and dreamed it all. Probably it makes little difference since Hawthorne's theme is one of his favorites: human beings must maintain a common bond of love and trust in order to make life worth living. When Brown loses that trust, he becomes "a stern, a sad, a darkly meditative, a distrustful, if not a desperate man" whose "dying hour was gloom."

Questions for Discussion and Writing
1. What is the significance of Goodman Brown's name?
2. As you read the story a second time, make a list of all the qualifying words that Hawthorne uses to suggest that the events described may or may not be actually happening—words like *seem, appear, fancied, as it were, as if, perhaps.* What does Hawthorne achieve through this word choice?
3. Consult an encyclopedia to find out exactly what the meaning of a *Witches' Sabbath* is. Is Hawthorne's description accurate?
4. Can you decide what causes Goodman Brown's tragedy? What is it that ruins his life?
5. What, then, might Hawthorne's major theme be in this story?
6. Write an essay focusing on symbolism in "Young Goodman Brown." Be sure to consider the symbolic significance of the setting.

Video: "Young Goodman Brown." 30 min., color, 1973. Available from Pyramid Film & Video.

Suggested Readings
Connolly, Thomas E. "Hawthorne's 'Young Goodman Brown': An Attack of Puritanic Calvinism." *American Literature* 28 (1957): 370-75.

Gallagher, Edward J. "The Concluding Paragraph of 'Young Goodman Brown.'" *Studies in Short Fiction* 12 (1975): 29-30.
Newman, Lea Bertani. *A Reader's Guide to the Short Stories of Nathaniel Hawthorne.* Boston: Hall, 1979.
Robinson, E. Arthur. "The Vision of Goodman Brown: A Source and Interpretation." *American Literature* 35 (1963): 218-25.
Tritt, Michael. "'Young Goodman Brown' and the Psychology of Projection." *Studies in Short Fiction* 23 (1986): 113-17.
Von Frank, Albert J., ed. *Critical Essays on Hawthorne's Short Stories.* Boston: Hall, 1991.
Whelan, Robert W. "Hawthorne Interprets 'Young Goodman Brown.'" *Emerson Society Quarterly* 62 (1971): 3-6.

THE CASK OF AMONTILLADO by Edgar Allan Poe [pp. 149-53]

Poe's stories are written not to express a theme but to produce an effect of horror on the reader. Often his stories depict the disintegration of a human psyche or, as is the case in "The Cask of Amontillado," the behavior of a man already mad. Setting is crucial in most Poe stories. The "supreme madness of the carnival season" is important in allowing the narrator to find his victim already drunk and costumed as a fool. The descent into the dank, moldering, bone-filled catacombs beneath the palazzo increases our horror as we realize Montresor's fiendish intentions. The narrator's skill in using reverse psychology is one of Poe's most effective touches. Because Montresor plays on Fortunato's pride in judging wines, the victim hastens his own destruction

Questions for Discussion and Writing
1. Why is the first person point of view particularly effective?
2. Why does Poe not tell us the nature of the insult or describe any of the "thousand injuries" that the narrator suffered?
3. Why does the narrator consider an insult worse than an injury?
4. Why is Luchresi mentioned? What other examples of reverse psychology does the narrator employ?
5. After reading the story a second time, write a character sketch of Montresor in which you thoroughly analyze the kind of person he is.

Audio: "The Cask of Amontillado." A reading of the work. Available from Caedmon Records and Spoken Arts Records.
"Edgar Allan Poe: Short Stories." Edward Blake reads 7 stories and some poetry. 2 cassettes. Available from Filmic Archives.

Video: "The Cask of Amontillado." 19 min., color, 1979. Available from Films for the Humanities & Sciences, and from Filmic Archives.
"The Cask of Amontillado." 29 min., b&w, 1965. American Short Story Classics Series. Available from Michigan Media.
"Edgar Allan Poe: Terror of the Soul." 1 hour, color, 1995. Biography conveying Poe's genius and personal experiences through dramatic re-creations of important scenes from his works. Available from PBS Video.

Suggested Readings
Gargano, James W. " 'The Cask of Amontillado': A Masquerade of Motive and Identity.".
Studies in Short Fiction 4 (1967): 119-26.
Engel, Leonard W. "Victim and Victimizer: Poe's 'The Cask of Amontillado.'"
Interpretations 15 (1983): 26-30.
May, Charles E. *Edgar Allan Poe: A Study of Short Fiction.* Boston: Twayne, 1990.
White, Patrick. " 'The Cask of Amontillado': A Case for the Defense." *Studies in Short
Fiction* 26 (1989): 550-55.

THE STORY OF THE BAD LITTLE BOY by Mark Twain [pp. 154-55]

A discussion of "The Story of the Bad Little Boy" demands clarifying terms such as *irony, satire, sarcasm,* and *parody.* As most of Twain's writing does, this piece depends on these types of humor. Your students can read the definitions in the Glossary of Literary and Rhetorical Terms at the back of the text.
     Many of the students may have never seen the "Sunday-school books" lampooned in this story, yet they will probably be able to imagine what such books are like. Ask for some descriptive terms that might apply, and the class will come up with words such as *preachy, simplistic, wimpy,* and even *stupid.* You might encourage students who have seen materials like this to describe them, or you might have to turn to television for examples of moralism for children.
     Twain's technique in this story consists of turning the traditional moral tales upside down, showing the dire punishments that do *not* befall the bad little boy. In this version, the good little boy George Wilson is unfairly accused and punished, while Jim gloats. In fact, the ending of the tale teaches that "all manner of cheating and rascality" are amply rewarded, including a seat in the legislature.

Questions for Discussion and Writing
1. What type of material is Twain ridiculing? Have you ever seen a "Sunday-school book" or something like it? What is the purpose of giving children these materials?
2. Do moral tales work on children? Do you remember one that worked on you? Assuming that Twain considers these tales useless, what would be his reasons for thinking so?
3. What view of the world does Twain promote instead of the "Sunday-school book" version?
4. Find elements of *irony, sarcasm, parody,* and *satire* in "The Story of the Bad Little Boy." What are some qualities of the "Sunday-school book" that are ridiculed through these techniques?
5. When Twain refers to Jim's experiences as "very strange," "a charmed life," and "a streak of luck," are you supposed to take the words at face value? How can you tell?

Audio: "The Best of Mark Twain." 6 cassettes, 5+ hours, 1975. Includes unabridged version of "The Story of the Bad Little Boy." Available from Listening Library.
     "Mark Twain Short Stories." 11 stories read by Jack Whitaker. 2 cassettes, 2 hours. Available from Filmic Archives.

THE AWAKENING by Kate Chopin [pp. 156-242]

This novella by Chopin is a perfect vehicle for teaching students about several elements of a literary work. The symbols Chopin uses, for instance, are not obtrusive, but because they tend to represent archetypes, students can see and understand them easily. The sea, as the controlling symbol, serves to incorporate both aspects of Edna Pontellier's awakening: her awakening to sexuality ("the sea is sensuous, enfolding the body in its soft, close embrace") and her awakening to selfhood ("the sea speaks to the soul . . ."). Edna's learning to swim in that sensuous sea functions also to signal the duality of her awakening. The bird imagery also relates to the changes in Edna. In the opening scenes, the birds (like Edna) are caged; her reverie (while listening to Adele Ratignolle play the piano) of the bird winging its way from the naked man on the rocky shore prefigures her separation from Robert, who is far too conventional to keep up with the changing Edna; the bird with the broken wing circling down into the sea at the end is clearly symbolic of Edna's fate and ties directly in with the earlier scene in which Mlle. Reisz feels Edna's shoulder blades and warns, "the bird that would soar above the level plain of tradition and prejudice must have strong wings." The flower motif functions similarly: in the opening scenes appears white jasmine, whose tiny blossoms suggest Edna's innocence of true sexuality; in the dinner scene we see full-blown red and yellow roses, archetypal symbols of female sexuality; and at the end, as Edna's childhood flashes before her, the small flowers associated with these presexual years are delicate pinks

The novella also serves perfectly to illustrate how foil relationships enrich our understanding of a fictional work. Edna has two foils, Mme. Ratignolle and Mlle. Reisz. Adèle serves to show how unlike the traditional "mother-women" Edna is, while her contrast with Mlle. Reisz lets us see that she will never become a true nonconforming artist either, despite her desire to do so. Students often think that Robert and Léonce, Edna's husband, are foils, but indeed the two are very much alike, not different. Robert's foils are his brother Victor and Alcée Arobin, neither is a gentleman.

Edna's suicide at the end should be seen not as a defeat but as her only means of evading her "soul's servitude." She has no better alternative. Suicide provides her escape from returning to her role as wife and mother, a life she now considers intensely restrictive. The imagery in the final scene clearly supports this affirmative interpretation: the sunlight is gleaming on the water; she feels like a "newborn creature" as she stands naked on the beach; the water is inviting, as Chopin repeats her earlier descriptions of the sea as sensuous and soul-nourishing. And the little waves, curling like serpents about her ankles, represent, through their phallic associations, the patriarchal nineteenth-century society whose restrictive codes governing suitable feminine behavior undermine Edna's attempts to be her own person. In The Awakening Chopin shows her readers that marriage and motherhood are not roles suitable for every woman; that marriage in her day made selfhood difficult for a woman to achieve; and that most women, like Adele Ratignolle, were not even aware of what they were missing.

Questions for Discussion and Writing
1. How do you respond to Edna? Do you like her and feel sympathy for her, or do you consider her selfish?
2. What sort of person is Léonce? What kind of father is he?
3. Why does Robert go to Mexico without even telling Edna?
4. What is Chopin's attitude toward the "mother-women" at Grand Isle?
5. Why is Edna's father in the novella? How does his role help to illuminate the theme?
6. What is the symbolic significance of the woman in black, constantly telling her beads and dogging the footsteps of the young lovers?

27

7. Why does Edna feel faint and unable to breathe when she goes to church with Robert on the island?
8. What does Robert mean by his poignant note, "Goodbye—because I love you"?
9. Choose a key scene from the novella—perhaps the one in which Léonce comes home tipsy from his club, wakes the boys, and quarrels with Edna; or the dinner party scene; or the scene in which Edna learns to swim—and analyze it in detail. Conclude by showing how the scene contributes to developing the theme.
10. Compose an imaginary conversation between Adele and Dr. Mandelet in which the two try to make sense of Edna's suicide. Be sure that each stays in character.

Suggested Readings

Bloom, Harold, ed. *Kate Chopin.* Modern Critical Views. New York: Chelsea, 1987.

Dyer, Joyce. The Awakening: *A Novel of Beginnings.* Twayne's Masterwork Studies. New York: Twayne, 1993.

Koloski, Bernard, ed. *Approaches to Teaching Chopin's* The Awakening. New York: MLA, 1988.

Martin, Wendy, ed. *New Essays on* The Awakening. American Novel Series. New York: Cambridge UP, 1988.

Petry, Alice Hall, ed. *Critical Essays on Kate Chopin.* Critical Essays on American Literature Series. New York: Hall, 1996.

Thorton, Lawrence. *"The Awakening:* A Political Romance." *American Literature* 52 (1980): 50-66.

Toth, Emily. *Kate Chopin.* New York: Morrow, 1990. 328-62.

THE STORY OF AN HOUR by Kate Chopin [pp. 242-43]

Chopin's *The Awakening* is captured in miniature in "The Story of an Hour"—but with an ironic twist at the end. Brilliantly crafted to entice readers into empathizing with Mrs. Mallard, this brief work is a tour de force. Chopin makes it clear that the widow who rejoices in her new freedom did not consciously arrive at this perception. Instead, in a state of "suspension of intelligent thought," this "thing" came to her even as "she was striving to beat it back with her will—as powerless as her two white slender hands would have been." The ironic ending is also foreshadowed in the first line by the reference to Mrs. Mallard's "heart trouble," a trouble that acquires a double meaning as the story progresses. The major theme is the same as that of *The Awakening*—the constriction of a woman's life by marriage in the late nineteenth-century.

Questions for Discussion and Writing
1. What is the double meaning of Mrs. Mallard's "heart trouble," mentioned in the first line of the story?
2. Discuss the function of the imagery in paragraphs 4, 5, and 6.
3. How does Chopin maintain our sympathy for Mrs. Mallard?
4. Discuss the dual irony of the final line.
5. Does this exceedingly short story have a theme? If so, can you state one?

Video: "The Joy That Kills." 56 min., color. Available from Films for the Humanities & Sciences.

"Kate Chopin: Five Stories of an Hour." Five versions of the story. 26 min., color. Available from Films for the Humanities & Sciences.

Suggested Readings
Bender, B. "Kate Chopin's Lyrical Short Stories." *Studies in Short Fiction* 11 (1974): 257-66.
Seyersted, Per. *Kate Chopin: A Critical Biography.* Baton Rouge: Louisiana State UP, 1969. 57-59.

THE REVOLT OF 'MOTHER' by Mary E. Wilkins Freeman [pp. 244-54]

Though the setting and era may be alien, Sarah and Adoniram's struggle is familiar to families everywhere. The opening scene, in which Sarah insists on knowing why the men are digging a foundation in the field, sets up the conflict between the conventional patriarch and matriarch, both of whom are sure that they have worked hard enough in their own spheres to deserve reward. Unfortunately, each has a heart set on a reward that supplants the other's.

The communication gap between the sexes, a popular topic in the 1990s, is amply demonstrated in this story. Adoniram's "speech was almost as inarticulate as a growl," but Sarah understands it as "her most native tongue," while he does not respond to her eloquence at all. This difference reflects what sociologists call the "muted group theory," which basically says that the less powerful group will always understand the language and culture of the more powerful group better than vice versa. The livelihood of the less powerful depends on their sensitivity to those with more. In her solution to the barn problem, Sarah shows insight into "the right besieging tools" to use on Adoniram, who crumbles still protesting that he had not known Sarah "was so set on't as all this comes to."

The dynamics between the Penns and their almost-grown children show the parents' sincere devotion to tradition as far as sex roles. Sarah does not see herself as the enemy of a sexist family structure; she simply insists on what is her due for a lifetime of fulfilling her part in it.

Questions for Discussion and Writing
1. At what point do you notice the male-female conflict in the story? How is this conflict continued throughout? In other words, in what different ways is it manifested?
2. What is different about the way Sarah talks to Nanny and what she says to Adoniram? What does this difference show about the family power structure?
3. Sarah uses both appeals to emotion and appeals to reason when she first confronts Adoniram fully about the barn. To what emotions does she try to appeal? What reasoning does she attempt to use? Why do her efforts fail?
4. What do the townspeople think about Sarah's move to the barn? Does the author seem to share their opinion? How do you know?
5. Why does Sarah win the last confrontation? Does Adoniram undergo any character change over the course of the action? Does Sarah?

Video: "The Revolt of 'Mother.'" 60 minutes, color. Available from Filmic Archives.

29

Suggested Readings
Cutter, Martha J. "Frontiers of Language: Engendering Discourse in 'The Revolt of Mother.'" *American Literature* 63 (1991): 279-91.
McElrath, J. R., Jr. "Artistry of Mary E. Wilkins Freeman's 'The Revolt.'" *Studies in Short Fiction* 17 (1980): 255-61.
Pryse, M. "An Uncloistered New England Nun." *Studies in Short Fiction* 20 (1983): 289-95.
Reichardt, Mary R. *A Web of Relationships: Women in the Stories of Mary Wilkins Freeman.* Jackson: UP of Mississippi, 1992. 48-53.

ROMAN FEVER by Edith Wharton [pp. 255-63]

Like Faulkner's "A Rose for Emily," Wharton's story is masterfully crafted to build to the climax of a startling ending. Both stories involve a complex of ironies—all related to the central irony on which the plot turns. The setting in "Roman Fever" is essential to the plot, but the view of the city below—"the great accumulated wreckage of passion and splendor"—also neatly reminds us of the wreckage of passion that is revealed in the final line. The richness of the story lies in the accumulation of ironies that appear upon second reading. These two "ripe but well-cared-for" ladies are quite different in personality, but each has lived a life in which her own personal value was judged according to the wealth and accomplishments of her husband and the relative brilliance and charm of her daughter. The irony extends even to the title in which "Roman fever" or malaria—a dangerous, sometimes fatal disease in the nineteenth century—comes to mean the fever of flaming sexual passion which gives life to Mrs. Ansley's daughter Barbara.

Questions for Discussion and Writing
1. What was "Roman fever" in the time of Mrs. Slade and Mrs. Ansley's youth? Does the term take on a metaphoric meaning by the end of the story?
2. As you read the story a second time, take note of all the times Grace Ansley hints at her secret. For example, on the first page of the story, Mrs. Slade praises the glory of Rome,
   "After all, it's still the most beautiful view in the world."
   "It always will be, to me," assented her friend Mrs. Ansley, with so slight a stress on the 'me.' . . .
   How does this foreshadowing contribute to the effectiveness of the story?
3. Contrast the characters of Mrs. Slade and Mrs. Ansley. What sort of lives have these ladies led before their widowhood? Which one do you respond to more favorably and why?
4. What is the source of Mrs. Slade's resentment of Grace Ansley?
5. Explain the implications of the last line of the story.
6. Write an essay focusing on the function of setting in "Roman Fever."

Suggested Readings
Berkove, Lawrence I. "'Roman Fever': A Mortal Malady." *CEA Critic* 56 (1994): 56-60.
Lewis, R. B. W. "A Writer of Short Stories." *Modern Critical Views: Edith Wharton.* Ed. Harold Bloom. New York: Chelsea, 1986. 9-28.

Petry, Alice Hall. "A Twist of Crimson Silk: Edith Wharton's 'Roman Fever.'" *Studies in Short Fiction* 24 (1987): 163-66.

PAUL'S CASE by Willa Cather   [pp. 264-76]

The very title of this story puts Paul in the position of a specimen or example, a "case" as a doctor, police officer, or social worker would call him. In the opening scene, the high school faculty scrutinizes his behavior and appearance and finds him a disturbing misfit. They even have a juvenile urge as a group to torment him, since he has caused them so much discomfort individually.

We soon discover the huge disparity between Paul's imaginary, ideal life and his real situation, which he sees as depressingly trivial, sordid, and dull. The sensory images used to describe his two worlds show how he has polarized his experiences. He feels that he is living a lie except when swept away by the concert hall or theater, and that he is being watched for clues to his oddity (which, in fact, is true—otherwise, he would not be a "case"). Many readers put together evidence that Paul is a young, confused gay man, which is a plausible explanatory frame for his distress. It also helps explain the "singularly cool" parting with the Yale freshman after a drunken night out.

Paul's choice to commit suicide after eight perfect days in New York seems inevitable. Though at the last minute, he feels his folly, it is hard to imagine what else could happen to this sensitive, imaginative soul. Like Paul, we can hardly picture his return to Cornelia Street with its stale cooking smells. An interesting comparison "case" is Connie in "Where Are You Going, Where Have You Been?" who chooses certain danger and harm over her mundane teenaged existence.

Questions for Discussion and Writing
1. What do you make of the title, "Paul's Case"? What kind of people refer to other people as "cases"?
2. What makes Paul a misfit at school? Why do the teachers have an urge to torment him when they get together? Were you surprised that he made a perfect usher at the concert hall?
3. Sensory imagery figures strongly in Paul's perceptions. Compare the patterns of imagery associated with the concert hall, theater, and New York with the patterns associated with Cornelia Street, his home, and his school.
4. Do you think that Paul's lively imagination is more helpful or more harmful to him? How does it affect his view of reality? Why does Paul feel that he is constantly lying?
5. What do you believe happened during the drunken night out in New York with the Yale freshman? Why was the parting "singularly cool"? Can you think of more than one possible explanation?
6. How soon did you realize how Paul's time in New York would end? Or was his suicide a surprise to you? Why did Paul himself consider his suicide inevitable? Why did he reject the revolver as a method?

Video: "Paul's Case." 52 minutes, color. Introduction by Henry Fonda; with Eric Roberts. Available from Filmic Archives.

Audio: "Paul's Case." 54 minutes, 1 cassette. Performed by Carole Shelley. Available from Filmic Archives.

Suggested Readings

Arnold, Marilyn. *Willa Cather's Short Fiction.* Athens: Ohio UP, 1984.

Daiches, David. *Willa Cather: A Critical Introduction.* Ithaca: Cornell UP, 1951. 144-47.

Rubin, Larry. "The Homosexual Motif in Willa Cather's 'Paul's Case.'" *Studies in Short Fiction* 12 (Spring 1975): 127-31.

Salda, Michael N. "What Really Happens in Cather's 'Paul's Case'?" *Studies in Short Fiction* 29 (1992): 113-19.

Summers, Claude J. " 'A Losing Game in the End': Aestheticism and Homosexuality in Cather's 'Paul's Case.'" *Modern Fiction Studies* 36 (1990): 103-19.

Wasserman, Loretta. *Willa Cather: A Study of the Short Fiction.* Boston: Twayne, 1991. 21-26.

HANDS by Sherwood Anderson   [pp. 277-80]

You may want to explain the story's context when your class begins to discuss "Hands." It comes from *Winesburg, Ohio,* a collection of twenty-three stories held together by a common small town location. Characters from one story appear in the others, as George Willard appears in this one.

"Hands" is relevant today, as ever, when communities are roused to point accusing fingers at individuals whom they perceive as dangerous to young people. Like Adolph Myers/Wing Biddlebaum, these individuals might well be gifted eccentrics who have not mastered the codes of ordinary social behavior. The fact that even Wing never seems to understand what he was accused of (homosexual advances toward his students) certifies his innocence of such aggression. His actual sexual orientation is not really important, though students may find evidence in the comparison of Wing to "the finer sort of women" and in his dream of young men at his feet.

The action of the Pennsylvania men and its repercussions in Wing's life are the substantial issues of the story. The first rumor started in an enamored student's dreams, which the half-witted boy could not distinguish from reality, and the first action against Wing came from a saloon keeper, whose view of human nature could understandably be negatively distorted. Wing finds himself in exile, ridiculed by the young people he loves and hiding his talents except from George Willard (who is the voice of broad-mindedness in Winesburg in several stories).

Questions for Discussion and Writing

1. Reread the first paragraph of the story closely. How does the imagery of the scene forecast themes developed later?

2. Why does the author say more than once that the story of Wing's hands is material for a poet? In what ways do you think a poem is different from a story?

3. What did the men of the Pennsylvania town decide about Adolph Myers? Why did they have such a rabid reaction? What is the significance of the source of the rumors? Why do you think the first confrontation came from the saloon keeper? Have you ever witnessed a situation like this?

4. What is Wing trying to tell George in their talks? What does he mean by "You must begin to dream"? Why do you think the content of Wing's teachings are left vague?

5. How do you reconcile the final image of Wing with the rest of the story? What emotional tone does it convey to you?

Suggested Readings

Brown, Linda. "Anderson's Wing Biddlebaum and Freeman's Louisa Ellis." *Studies in Short Fiction* 27 (1990): 413-14.

Bucco, Martin. "A Reading of Sherwood Anderson's 'Hands.'" *Colorado State Review* 1 (Spring): 5-8.

Burbank, Rex. *Sherwood Anderson.* Twayne's US Authors Series. New York: Twayne, 1964. 64-66.

Crowley, John W., ed. *New Essays on* Winesburg, Ohio. New York: Cambridge UP, 1990.

Phillips, William L. "How Sherwood Anderson Wrote Winesburg, Ohio." *American Literature* 23 (1951): 7-30.

White, Ray Lewis. Winesburg, Ohio: *An Exploration.* Twayne's Masterwork Studies. Boston: Twayne, 1990.

A JURY OF HER PEERS by Susan Glaspell [pp. 281-94]

This story is based on the author's one-act play *Trifles*, which was written in 1916 for the Provincetown Players (see Part IV in this manual). Glaspell, who lived in Iowa for the first part of her life, said that the idea for the play (and hence the short story) was suggested by an experience she had while working as a reporter for a Des Moines newspaper.

The story contrasts the world of men with the world of women. The longer non-dramatic version emphasizes the loneliness and isolation of the Wright farm. Minnie Foster was a lively young woman whose youth ended when she married John Wright, a hard, taciturn man. But the conflicts between the murdered husband and his suspected wife are not as important as the conflicts that Mrs. Hale and Mrs. Peters have with themselves and with the men in the story. Convinced of the importance of their own work, the men laugh at the "insignificance of kitchen things," believe that "women are used to worrying over trifles," and doubt that the women would "know a clue if they did come upon it." Ironically, of course, it is the women's familiarity with the details of running a house and being a farm wife that enables them to discover the clues that the men cannot find.

The story centers on the conspiracy formed between Mrs. Hale and Mrs. Peters. Recognizing that "the law is the law" and that "the law has to punish crime," the two women tacitly decide to conceal evidence that they feel would be used by a male-run legal system to condemn and execute a female suspect. As a true jury of Minnie Wright's peers, the women render a compassionate and understanding verdict about the nature of her crime. (It is worth noting that at the time the story was published [1917] women did not have the right to vote and could not serve as jurors.)

Questions for Discussion and Writing
1. What do Mrs. Hale and Mrs. Peters surmise about Minnie Wright's life and her motives for killing her husband? Why are they able to grasp the truth of the situation when the men cannot?

2. Why do Mrs. Hale and Mrs. Peters decide to conceal the evidence of the strangled bird? Have they done the "right" thing?
3. What does it mean that Mrs. Peters is "married to the law"? What is significant and ironic about that description?
4. In what ways do Mrs. Hale and Mrs. Peters act as a "jury" in this case? Whom do they convict and whom do they exonerate?
5. Write an essay in which you discuss the strangled bird as the story's central symbol.

Video: "A Jury of Her Peers." 30 min., color, 1980. Available from Films Inc. and Michigan Media.

Suggested Readings

Alkalay-Gut, Karen. "Jury of Her Peers: The Importance of Trifles." *Studies in Short Fiction* 21 (1984): 1-9.
Carpentier, Martha C. "Susan Glaspell's Fiction: Fidelity as American Romance." *Twentieth Century Literature* 40.1 (1994): 92-113.
Hallgren, Sherri. "'The Law Is the Law—and a Bad Stove Is a Bad Stove': Subversive Justice and Layers of Collusion in 'A Jury of Her Peers.'" *Violence, Silence, and Anger: Women's Writing as Transgression.* Charlottesville: UP of Virginia, 1995. 203-18.
Hedges, Elaine. "Small Things Considered: Susan Glaspell's 'A Jury of Her Peers.'" *Women's Studies* 12 (1986): 89-110.
Mustazza, Leonard. "Generic Translation and Thematic Shift in Susan Glaspell's 'Trifles' and 'A Jury of Her Peers.'" *Studies in Short Fiction* 26 (1989): 489-96.

ARABY by James Joyce [pp. 295-98]

The tension in "Araby" stems from the disparity between the boy's romantic illusions of love and the drab reality of his world. The descriptive details of the first few paragraphs delineate the dinginess of Joyce's "dear, dirty Dublin," especially as these details contrast with the excitement and energy of the boys playing in the "dead-end" street. The first-person narrator is, of course, an adolescent boy, but clearly the story is being told from an adult's somewhat jaundiced perspective. The boy has scarcely spoken to Mangan's sister, yet he undertakes a lover's quest in order to bring her a token of his love. As he bears his "chalice through a throng of foes," reality provides the numerous obstacles met by those who quest, and the bazaar turns out to be not a place of exotic, Eastern enchantment but a tawdry, money-making church bazaar. When he hears in the flirtatious banter carried on by the girl and the two young men in the serving stall a parody of his own ecstatic love, the boy's disillusionment is complete. Ironically, the epiphany of the boy's insight occurs just as the lights are extinguished. The theme of the story is a familiar one: the disillusionment resulting from a conflict between illusion and reality.

Questions for Discussion and Writing
1. Why do you think Joyce left the boy in this story unnamed?
2. What details make clear that the narrator now feels differently about the events being described than at the time they occurred?

34

3. Note all the religious images and terminology used throughout the story, and explain how they complement the meaning.
4. Describe the tone of this story—the attitude of the narrator toward the events he describes.
5. Write an essay in which you contrast the way you perceived a person or an event as a child and the way you see it today.

Audio: " 'The Dead' and Other Stories from *Dubliners*." Read by Danny Huston and Kate Mulgrew. 2 cassettes. Available from Audio Editions.

Suggested Readings

Beck, Warren. *Joyce's* Dubliners: *Substance, Vision, and Art*. Durham: Duke UP, 1969. 96-109.

Brandabur, James Edward. *A Scrupulous Meanness: A Study of Joyce's Early Work*. Urbana: U of Illinois P, 1971.

Brugaletta, J. J., and M. H. Hayden. "Motivation for Anguish in Joyce's 'Araby.'" *Studies in Short Fiction* 15 (1978): 11-17.

Dolch, Martin. *James Joyce's* Dubliners: *A Critical Handbook*. Ed. James R. Baker and Thomas F. Staley. Belmont: Wadsworth, 1969.

Hart, Clive, ed.. *James Joyce's* Dubliners: *Critical Essays*. New York: Viking, 1969

Leonard, Garry. *Reading* Dubliners *Again: A Lacanian Perspective*. Syracuse: Syracuse UP, 1993. 73-94.

Morrissey, L. J. "Joyce's Narrative Struggles in 'Araby '" *Modern Fiction Studies* 28 (1982). 54-52.

THE ROCKING-HORSE WINNER by D. H. Lawrence [pp. 299-308]

This story has fairy tale elements and an age-old theme: wealth does not equal love or happiness. The family atmosphere Lawrence builds is one charged with damaging values, such as the attribution of failure and success to luck, the son's belief that his mother's love is something he must acquire, and the "whispering voices" that insist there is never enough money, even after Paul begins to bring in his winners.

In the midst of such a family, a child is likely to take blame and responsibility upon himself or herself, often in unrealistic ways. Thus, Paul decides that he will acquire luck by an act of will, and thereby gain the love and happiness he has mistakenly connected to luck. He finds himself undertaking a series of tasks to win the prize, just as it happens in fairy tales, and the tasks become more difficult. The final one kills him.

The real prize, the love and happiness of his mother, is never achieved. Lawrence suggests that some inherent defective in the mother has set off the fatal course of events, and in the end her heart "turned actually into a stone." Today's students may remark on the sexist assumptions of the story—the cold mother, rather than the ineffectual father or the other exploitative adult men or some systemic family failure, is the villain.

Questions for Discussion and Writing
1. How did you respond to the supernatural elements of "The Rocking-Horse Winner"? If you were able to suspend your disbelief as you read the story, what do you think

35

allowed you to do so? If the unbelievable elements impaired your acceptance of the story, why? Why do you think the supernatural elements are used in the story?
2. What happens when Paul manages to present some money to his mother? Why do the voices become louder, rather than softer, over the course of the story? What does money represent to Paul and to his mother?
3. The story seems to criticize both people who think that success and failure are purely a matter of luck and those who pursue control zealously, as Paul does. How can these two criticisms be reconciled?
4. Why must Paul die in the end?
5. Most readers see the cold-hearted mother as the villain of the story. However, Oscar and Bassett take meaningful roles, too. Can you present a feminist reading of the story, in which the unfit mother is not the source of all evil?

Videos: *The Rocking-Horse Winner*. 30 min., color, 1977. With Kenneth More. Adapted by Julian Bond. Directed by Peter Modak. Available from Learning Corp. of America.

The Rocking-Horse Winner. 91 min., b&w, 1949. With John Mills, Valerie Hobson; directed by Anthony Pelessier. Available from Films for the Humanities & Sciences.

Suggested Readings

Consolo, Dominick P. *The Rocking-Horse Winner*. Merrill Casebooks. Columbus: 1969.
Harris, Janice. *The Short Fiction of D. H. Lawrence*. New Brunswick: Rutgers U P, 1984.
Koban, Charles. "Allegory and the Death of the Heart in 'The Rocking-Horse Winner.'" *Studies in Short Fiction* 15 (1978): 391-96.
Marks, W. S. "The Psychology of the Uncanny in Lawrence's 'The Rocking-Horse Winner.'" *Modern Fiction Studies* 11 (1966): 381-92.
San Juan, Epifanio, Jr. "Theme Versus Imitation: D. H. Lawrence's 'The Rocking-Horse Winner.'" *The D. H. Lawrence Review* 3 (1970): 136-40.
Turner, John F. "The Perversion of Play in D. H. Lawrence's 'The Rocking-Horse Winner.'" *The D. H. Lawrence Review* 15.3 (Fall 1982): 249-70.
Watkins, Daniel P. "Labor and Religion in D. H. Lawrence's 'The Rocking-Horse Winner.'" *Studies in Short Fiction* 24.3 (Summer 1987): 295-301.
Wilson, Keith. "D. H. Lawrence's 'The Rocking-Horse Winner': Parable and Structure." *English Studies in Canada* 13.4 (Dec. 1987): 438-50.

THE JILTING OF GRANNY WEATHERALL by Katherine Anne Porter   [pp. 309-14]

Porter's brilliantly executed stream-of-consciousness narrative makes "Granny Weatherall" difficult for novice students on first reading. You might want to tell them when you assign the story that the point of view shifts from the dying Granny's bedside to thoughts running through her disoriented mind to flashbacks from her past. Those with Catholic backgrounds may be more likely than others to be aware that the second "bridegroom," whom Granny expects to appear at her bedside, is Christ. In her forceful, assertive way, Granny demands, "God, give a sign!" Porter's perfect final paragraph records Granny's response when, again, no bridegroom appears. The blowing out of the light—in effect, deciding herself to end her life—is quite in keeping with the strong, independent nature of the woman whose life is sketched in the flashbacks, a woman who "weathers all."

Some parts of the story are difficult for even experienced readers to figure out. Hapsy, for instance, has died before her mother—perhaps in childbirth, for she has "a baby on her arm" in Granny's memory. Critics speculate that Hapsy was the child Ellen "really wanted" because she was the last—by which time perhaps Ellen had come to love her husband John. But clearly Ellen never got over loving George, the man who first jilted her. She decides she wants, after all, to see George just in order to tell him that her marriage to John gave her even "Better than I hoped for even. Tell him I was given back everything he took away and more." But then she cries, "Oh, no, oh, God, no, there was something else . . . . Something not given back . . . ," suggesting that she never recaptured the passion she felt for George. Notice also that her sons are named George and Jimmy—no John.

Questions for Discussion and Writing
1. Describe the point of view in this story and try to explain its effectiveness.
2. What kind of person is Granny Weatherall? If you could choose just one adjective to describe her, what word would you select?
3. Why do you think Porter named Granny's solicitous, caring daughter *Cornelia*?
4. Do you think Ellen Weatherall completely recovered from being jilted by George?
5. Who jilts her again in the final scene?
6. Write an essay discussing Granny Weatherall's peculiar brand of Catholicism.

Video: "The Jilting of Granny Weatherall." With Geraldine Fitzgerald. 57 minutes, color. Available from Filmic Archives.
"Katherine Anne Porter." Dramatizations combined with comments by Eudora Welty, Robert Penn Warren, and Joan Givner. 56 minutes, color. Available from Films for the Humanities & Sciences.
"Katherine Anne Porter: The Eye of Memory." Hosted by Joanne Woodward. 60 minutes, color, 1988. Available from Filmic Archives.

Suggested Readings
Brinkman, Robert H. *Katherine Anne Porter's Artistic Development*. Baton Rouge: Louisiana State UP, 1993. 134-39.
DeMouy, Jane K. *Katherine Anne Porter's Women: The Eye of Her Fiction*. Austin: U of Texas P, 1983. 45-54.
Hoefel, Roseanne. "The Jilting of (Hetero)sexist Criticism: Porter's Ellen Weatherall and Hapsy." *Studies in Short Fiction* 28 (1991): 9-20.
Lamar, Barbara. "Porter's 'The Jilting of Granny Weatherall.'" *Explicator* 48 (1991): 279-81.
Welty, Eudora. "The Eye of the Story." *Katherine Anne Porter: A Collection of Critical Essays*. Ed. Robert Penn Warren. Englewood Cliffs: Prentice, 1979. 72-80.
Wisenfareth, Joseph. "Internal Opposition in Porter's 'Granny Weatherall.'" *Critique* 11.2 (1969): 47-55.

A ROSE FOR EMILY by William Faulkner [pp. 315-20]

Commentators have discussed "A Rose for Emily" in terms of conflict between the North (Homer Barron) and the South (Emily Grierson). But, if indeed there are allegorical implications, the story seems more reasonably to present the crumbling of the old aristocracy as it is absorbed by the new mercantile society. The story can profitably be approached through its structure, since without the deliberate disruption of the time scheme, Faulkner would lose the impact of the final line. But the character of Miss Emily is clearly important, as is an understanding of the title. Faulkner revealed that ". . . here was a woman who had had a tragedy, an irrevocable tragedy and nothing could be done about it, and I pitied her and this [story] was a salute, . . . to a woman you would hand a rose." Her father, by driving away her suitors, has deprived her of the only role in life allowed her by society. Thus, when she finds another man, she wants to keep him. Faulkner explained it this way:

> She picked out probably a bad one, who was about to desert her. And when she lost him she could see that for her that was the end of life, there was nothing left, except to grow older, alone, solitary; she had had something and she wanted to keep it, which is bad—to go to any length to keep something; but I pity Emily [because] her life had probably been warped by a selfish father.

Thus, though Miss Emily Grierson is patently insane (insanity runs in her family, remember), we nonetheless admire her dignity, her pride, her endurance—and can perhaps see her, not just as a "fallen monument," but as a tragic heroine.

Questions for Discussion and Writing
1. What does Faulkner achieve by disrupting the chronology of Miss Emily's story?
2. How would you describe the point of view here? Do you find it effective? Why or why not?
3. What kind of person is Emily Grierson? Why does she live in the past? How do the townspeople feel about her? How do you feel about her?
4. What kind of person is Homer Barron? Why do the townspeople consider him not good enough for Miss Emily?
5. Explain the function of dust and decay in the story.
6. Write an essay focusing on Emily Grierson's relationship with her father as contributing to her tragedy.

Video: "A Rose for Emily." 27 min., color, 1983. Available from Pyramid Film & Video.

Suggested Readings
Allen, Dennis W. "Horror and Perverse Delight: Faulkner's 'A Rose for Emily.'" *Modern Fiction Studies* 30 (1984): 685-95.
Heller, Terry. "The Telltale Hair: A Critical Study of William Faulkner's 'A Rose for Emily.'" *Arizona Quarterly* 28 (1972): 301-18.
McGlynn, Paul D. "The Chronology of 'A Rose for Emily.'" *Studies in Short Fiction* 6 (1969): 461-62.
Moore, Gene M. "Of Time and Its Mathematical Progression: Problems of Chronology in Faulkner's 'A Rose for Emily.'" *Studies in Short Fiction* 29.2 (1992): 195-204.
Page, Sally R. *Faulkner's Women: Characterization and Meaning.* DeLand: Everett/Edwards, 1972. 99-103.
Scherting, Jack. "Emily Grierson's Oedipus Complex: Motif, Motive, and Meaning in Faulkner's 'A Rose for Emily.'" *Studies in Short Fiction* 17.4 (1980): 397-405.

HILLS LIKE WHITE ELEPHANTS by Ernest Hemingway [pp. 321-24]

This story consists mainly of dialogue, which often seems trivial, even pointless. We learn practically all we know of the characters (which is really very little) through what they say. But the understatement is so subtle that we only gradually realize that beneath the small talk lies a very serious argument: the unnamed male speaker wants the woman (Jig) to have an abortion, which she resists. In the end, the man manipulates "the girl" (as Hemingway insists on calling her) to agree to the operation, although it appears that she is not completely swayed by his words. The speeches, if read carefully, do reveal a difference in personalities: the man seems literal-minded, irritable, unthinking; the woman seems more sensitive and emotional.

The description outside the dialogue is highly suggestive. The landscape seems to mirror the two choices that the woman faces: a dry, sterile landscape ("no shade and no trees") on one side of the train tracks and a peaceful fecundity ("fields of grain and trees along the banks of the Ebro") on the other side. The setting of a railroad junction serves to reinforce the crossroads motif.

Questions for Discussion and Writing
1. While the near-total dependence on dialogue moves the story quickly forward, the lack of explicit explanations may be bothersome. What problems does Hemingway's terse, rigidly objective style pose for the reader?
2. The number *two* is used ten times in the story. What is the significance of this repetition? (Note especially the two parallel train tracks and the two strings of beads that do not intersect: do they suggest anything about the characters' lives?)
3. What is the main point or theme of the story? Is the abortion the central issue? Or is the lack of communication between the lovers more important?
4. What is a "white elephant"? Explain the story's title.
5. Write an essay in which you speculate on what will happen to the couple. Will Jig get an abortion? Will they remain lovers?

Video: "An Introduction to Ernest Hemingway's Fiction." Lecture, 45 min., color. Available from Filmic Archives.

Suggested Readings
Benson, Jackson. *New Critical Approaches to the Short Fiction of Ernest Hemingway.* Durham: Duke UP, 1990.

Flora, Joseph M. *Ernest Hemingway: A Study of the Short Fiction.* Boston: Twayne, 1989.

Johnston, Kenneth G. "'Hills Like White Elephants': Lean, Vintage Hemingway." *Studies in American Fiction* 10 (1982): 233-38.

Kozikowski, Stanley. "Hemingway's 'Hills Like White Elephants.'" *Explicator* 52 (1994): 107-09.

O'Brien, Timothy D. "Allusion, Word-Play, and the Central Conflict in Hemingway's 'Hills Like White Elephants.'" *Hemingway Review* 12.1 (Fall 1992): 19-25.

Renner, Stanley. "Moving to the Girl's Side of 'Hills Like White Elephants.'" *The Hemingway Review* 15.1 (Fall 1995): 27-41.

Weeks, Lewis E., Jr. "Hemingway's Hills: Symbolism in 'Hills Like White Elephants.'" *Studies in Short Fiction* 17 (1980): 75-77.

THE GILDED SIX BITS by Zora Neale Hurston   [pp. 325-32]

This story treats two of the main problems among newly married people: sex and money. Both topics hold an unexpected spin for the playful Missie May and Joe, as they avert disaster in the face of crisis.

Students will probably express surprise and puzzlement about Joe's initial reaction to and ultimate forgiveness of Missie Mae's adultery. They may read the story assuming that Joe belongs to a macho male culture which would require at least desertion and at most murder of an unfaithful wife. However, looking closely at the text, we see evidence that Joe has a good sense of humor and a sound idea of what is really genuine and what is false—what is a "gilded six bits," so to speak. Holding a grudge is not his style, and in the end he even brags about making a fool of Slemmons rather than the other way round. Missie May, too, is good natured and well grounded in the realities of everyday life (notice her cooking and cleaning), not prone to remaining guilt-ridden forever.

The cycles of sun and moon, day and night, water running downhill and birds nesting reinforce the inevitability of Joe and Missie Mae resuming their life together and procreating. Only Joe's addition of six more genuine silver dollars to his weekly throw is a teasing reminder of Missie May's misstep.

Questions for Discussion and Writing
1. What can you infer about the relationship between Joe and Missie May from the first description of their Saturday ritual? What qualities do you see in their relationship? How do these qualities come into play later in the story?
2. How do you react to the use of dialect in the characters' speech? Do you find it racist or demeaning? Why or why not? Did you have trouble understanding the slang expressions used?
3. What are some of the sources of humor in the story?
4. Trace the sun and moon imagery throughout "The Gilded Six Bits." Look at other nature imagery as well. Can you relate the imagery to what happens in the human matters?
5. We frequently expect infidelity to have serious, negative consequences. How do you account for the resilience that Joe and Missie May show? Do you approve of their ability to recover their relationship?

Video: "Zora Is My Name!" A tribute, with Ruby Dee and Louis Gossett, Jr. 90 minutes, color, 1989. Available from Filmic Archives.

Suggested Reading
Baum, Rosalio M. "The Shape of Hurston's Fiction." *Zora in Florida*. Ed. Steve Glassman and Kathryn Seidel. Orlando: U of Central Florida P, 1991. 101-04.
Howard, Lillie P. "Marriage: Zora Neale Hurston's System of Values." *CLA Journal* 21 (1977): 256-68.
Jarrett, Mary. "The Idea of Audience in the Short Stories of Zora Neale Hurston and Alice Walker." *Journal of the Short Story in English* 12 (1989): 34-35.
Lupton, M. J. "Zora Neale Hurston and the Survival of the Female." *Southern Literary Journal* 15 (1982): 45-54.

A SUMMER TRAGEDY by Arna Bontemps [pp. 333-38]

This story, rich in detail and characterization, is deceptive in its simplicity. The reproduction of the black dialect gives the impression that we are listening to the conversation of the old black couple. The narrative gradually increases its tension: Jeff and Jennie Patton are nervous about their journey, and their anxiety grows as bits of information are inserted into the lyrical descriptions of the old homestead. The long-standing concerns and rivalries of the couple are fleshed out as they inspect their beloved home for what is, we begin to realize, the last time. Despite their half a century of marriage, they still avoid telling each other their feelings for fear that the additional emotional burden will overwhelm their determination to commit suicide.

By recounting many personal events in their lives, Bontemps is able to make his characters come alive; he draws the reader into caring about them in a very short tale. The couple's decision soon becomes apparent, though the chosen means is carefully left unexplored until the very end. The author explores the value of the elderly to a society by narrating this event. The theme of the abandonment of hope in the elderly is all the more poignant for people who have never considered the consequences of living to old age.

Questions for Discussion and Writing
1. Consider the contradictory title: how do the words "summer" and "tragedy" define and control the paradoxical mood of this story?
2. What are the main themes? What is the author suggesting about the effect of social and economic forces on people's lives?
3. At what point did you become aware that the old couple had decided to commit suicide? Analyze how the foreshadowing influenced your reactions to the story.
4. How you feel at the end of the story? Write an essay about the thoughts and feelings that the story aroused in you.
5. Write an obituary for Jeff and Jennie Patton.
6. Compare this story to Eudora Welty's "A Worn Path," focusing on the question of whether endurance is always a virtue.

Suggested Readings
Gaudet, Marcia. "Images of Old Age in Three Louisiana Short Stories." *Louisiana English Journal* 1.1 (1983): 62-64.
Kuperman, David. "Dying: The Shape of Victory in 'A Summer Tragedy.'" *MELUS* 5.1 (1978): 66-68.

THE CHRYSANTHEMUMS by John Steinbeck [pp. 339-45]

Elisa Allen is good with flowers, like her mother before her, but she is vaguely anxious and unfulfilled. Elisa is strong and mature, at the height of her physical strength, but there is no appropriate outlet for her energies. She is like the Salinas Valley she lives in: a "closed pot," shut off by the fog from the sky and from the rest of the world. Her urge to fulfill her nature is directed into the chrysanthemums, which bloom profusely (in contrast to her own barrenness—she has no children).

The men in the story feel none of Elisa's unfulfillment. They take the opportunities of the male world for granted. Henry Allen has sold his cattle for a good price and is celebrating by taking his wife out to dinner. The itinerant repairman is temporarily down on his luck, but he recognizes an easy mark when he sees one. He flatters Elisa and hands her a line about chrysanthemums for a lady he knows down the road. Both men disappoint Elisa. Her husband's reward of a trip to town is just a concession to allow her to accompany him for his entertainment. After Elisa does her hair and puts on make-up and her prettiest dress, the only compliments that her husband can offer is that she looks "nice" and "strong" and "happy." And when Elisa sees that the tinker has cruelly discarded her chrysanthemum sprouts, she is too disheartened even to attend the prizefights (where she might get some satisfaction of seeing men hurt each other, as they have hurt her). At the end of the story, Elisa is "crying weakly—like an old woman"; her strength and energy have been completely depleted.

Questions for Discussion and Writing
1. The chrysanthemums are a symbol—that is, they stand for something more than what they are (flowers). Are they Elisa's "children"? Do they represent the earthy, sensuous part of her nature? Or do they perhaps stand for her untapped talents and frustrated energies? Write an essay that explores the symbolism of the chrysanthemums.
2. Discuss the interactions between Elisa and the two males in the story. How do the men manipulate her? How does she try to manipulate them?
3. Does Elisa encourage the tinker's sexual insinuations?
4. Compare Elisa, as a woman in a man's world, to Life, the title character of Bessie Head's story.
5. Two different ways of life are presented in this story. Identify and discuss them.

Video: "The Chrysanthemums." Film guide with purchase. 24 min., VHS. Available from Pyramid Film & Video.

Suggested Readings
Marcus, Mordecai. "The Lost Dream of Sex and Children in 'The Chrysanthemums.'" *Modern Fiction Studies* 11.1 (Spring 1965): 54-58.
McMahan, Elizabeth. " 'The Chrysanthemums': Study of a Woman's Sexuality." *Modern Fiction Studies* 14.4 (Winter 1968-69): 453-58.
Miller, William V. "Sexual and Spiritual Ambiguity in 'The Chrysanthemums.'" *Steinbeck Quarterly* 5 (1972): 68-75.
Renner, Stanley. "The Real Woman Behind the Fence in 'The Chrysanthemums.'" *Modern Fiction Studies* 31 (1985): 305-17.
Sweet, Charles A. "Ms. Eliza Allen and Steinbeck's 'The Chrysanthemums.'" *Modern Fiction Studies* 11.1 (1965): 54-58.
Timmerman, John H. *John Steinbeck's Fiction: The Aesthetics of the Road Not Taken.* Norman: U of Oklahoma P, 1986. 63-68, 169-77.

MY OEDIPUS COMPLEX by Frank O'Connor   [pp. 346-53]

"My Oedipus Complex" derives its humor partly from the accurate capture of the five-year-old's point of view and partly from its cheerful reworking of the Freudian theory.
According to Freud, at three or four the male child goes through a critical period in which he wants to have sex with his mother and to have his father conveniently

disappear—for example, by dying. The child feels affection for the mother and hostility toward the father as a competitor for her regard. The Oedipal complex is resolved when the child, by the age of six usually, learns to identify with the male parent as a model rather than a competitor. This identification proceeds due to the child's fear of castration if he continues his incestuous desires. O'Connor's version follows Freud in several respects, except that it rejects the dark sexual urges in favor of—literally—sleeping with the mother. And the resolution comes about through identification with the father due to shared jealousy rather than a horror of castration. Furthermore, in the story the father reciprocally learns to identify with the child. In brief, O'Connor accepts the basic Oedipal dynamic but gives the process more commonsensical causes and effects. (Notice, though, humorous touches such as the phallic nature of the knives, button-sticks, and smoking pipes over which Larry and Daddy scrap.)

The child's point of view in "My Oedipus Complex" is psychologically apt. Small children are egocentric: they believe that the world revolves around them, as Larry does. For example, he believes that he brought about both his father's return from the war and the birth of the new baby through his own prayers. He also assumes that he is the primary person in his mother's life. His lack of awareness about the sexual part of the parents' relationship is charming and slyly counter-Freudian. O'Connor suggests that sometimes jealousy is just jealousy, although any student of Freud would make something of the model railway in the end, given the locomotives and tunnels involved.

Questions for Discussion and Writing
1. In the opening paragraph, the child narrator says that he rarely saw his father, "and what I saw did not worry me." Why would it worry him? What would be the expected reaction of a child to his father's rare appearances?
2. "My Oedipus Complex" is told completely from the child's point of view. How reliable is Larry as the narrator of events? How does this point of view provide humor? How is sexuality involved in the story's humor?
3. Why does Larry call it an "irony" that his prayers were answered?
4. What is Larry's concept of God—for example, when he says, "I began to think that God wasn't quite what he was cracked up to be"?
5. What is Freud's theory of the Oedipus complex? How does the theory fit the story? In what ways does the theory *not* fit the story?

Suggested Reading
Hildbidle, John. *Five Irish Writers: The Errand of Keeping Alive.* Cambridge: Harvard UP, 1989.
Neary, Michael. "The Inside-Out World in Frank O'Connor's Stories." *Studies in Short Fiction* 30 (1993): 327-36.
Prosky, Murray. "The Pattern of Diminishing Certitude in the Stories of Frank O'Connor." *Colby Library Quarterly* 9 (1971): 311-21.
Steinman, Michael. *Frank O'Connor at Work.* Syracuse: Syracuse UP, 1990.
Tomory, William M. *Frank O'Connor.* Boston: Twayne, 1980. 130-31.

THE MAN WHO WAS ALMOST A MAN by Richard Wright [pp. 354-62]

This story concerns a poor black youth, Dave, whose need for acceptance and respect as a man is identified in the opening paragraph with possession of a gun: "One of these days he was going to get a gun and practice shooting, and they [the older fieldhands] couldn't talk to him as though he were a little boy." Almost seventeen, Dave's feelings of inferiority are clear reflections of the attitudes of those around him: he is referred to as a "boy" at least five times in the story, his mother compares him to hogs, and he feels exploited like an animal ("They treat me like a mule"). Wrapped up in his longing to assert his manhood is Dave's anger at being thought of as a "nigger." His mother calls him a "nigger" and he himself regards the other field workers as "niggers"—examples of the way that Dave and his family have internalized the demeaning image that the white majority has created for blacks.

Although readers will be generally sympathetic to Dave's situation and understand the source of his low self-esteem, Wright makes it clear that Dave is unprepared for the responsibilities of manhood and that his decision to gain respect and maturity by owning a gun is naive and misguided. Dave lies to his mother, pays too much money for an old gun that he has only the slightest idea of how to use, and is "helpless" to deal with the violent consequences that the gun causes. Instead of giving him the respect he craves, the gun brings more humiliation and increases Dave's subservience to the white landowner. In the end, when Dave jumps a train, naively believing it will take him "somewhere where he could be a man," the reader knows that the journey to manhood will be much longer and more difficult than Dave suspects.

Questions for Discussion and Writing
1. What needs does Dave hope to satisfy by owning a gun? What are the sources of Dave's needs?
2. What does the accidental shooting of Jenny reveal about Dave? In what ways could this "accident" be seen as a subconscious act of rebellion against exploitation and shame? Is there any other evidence of Dave's rebelliousness or hostility?
3. What does the description of the field, the store, and the house suggest about Dave's environment? How much do these living and working conditions affect Dave's attitudes and behavior?
4. What do you think of the story's ending?
5. Compare Dave's decision to leave town to Sammy's decision to quit his job (in the story "A & P").

Video: "Almos' a Man." 39 min., color, 1977. Film adaptation of "The Man Who Was Almost a Man." With LaVar Burton; directed by Stan Lathan. Available from Filmic Archives, Perspective Films, and Michigan Media.

Suggested Readings
Burgum, Edwin Berry. "The Art of Richard Wright's Short Stories." *Five Black Writers*. Ed. Donald B. Gibson. New York: New York UP, 1970.
Felger, Robert. *Richard Wright*. Boston: Twayne, 1980.
Hakutani, Yoshinobu, ed. *Critical Essays on Richard Wright*. Boston: G. K. Hall, 1982.
Loftis, John E. "Prey: Richard Wright's Parody of the Hunt Tradition in 'The Man Who Was Almost a Man.'" *Studies in Short Fiction* 23 (1986): 437-42.
Margolies, Edward. *The Art of Richard Wright*. Carbondale: Southern Illinois UP, 1969. 75-76.

A WORN PATH by Eudora Welty [pp. 363-68]

This is the story of a day's journey made by an old woman on foot into town to the doctor's office. The story is told through Phoenix's mind, and the single-mindedness of her trip tells us she is a survivor. The journey itself is the story: the obstacles and delays that Phoenix encounters represent life's uncertainties and difficulties. Although the path is worn, it is still dangerous to an old woman. But Phoenix meets each test and, like the mythical bird that rises from its ashes, she endures.

    The title suggests that this journey has been and will be repeated. Phoenix will survive in a society that discriminates against her and her race. Her determination and patience make it possible for her to complete this journey, which could symbolize life itself. Her journey is a labor of love, and the enduring value that the story endorses is the enabling power of love. She transcends the mythological significance of her name, just as she transcends the stereotype of the old black mammy, which is hinted at in the way the other characters talk to her. The absence of any note of complaint from Phoenix is eloquent testimony to her dignity and worth.

Questions for Discussion and Writing
1. Discuss the mythic and religious parallels in the story, including the title, Phoenix's name, and references to the Christmas season in which the story takes place.
2. What is the story really about? Write an essay in which you argue for the story's "most important theme" (in your opinion).
3. Compare Phoenix to Granny Weatherall [pp. 309-14 in the Anthology of Short Fiction].
4. Why do some readers think Phoenix's grandson is already dead? Is the story altered in a major way if this is true?
5. Write about the scene between Phoenix and the hunter: how does this encounter relate to the story as a whole?

Audio: "Eudora Welty." The author reads six stories, including "A Worn Path." 1956. Available from Caedmon Records and Poets' Audio Center.
    "On Story Telling." 53 min., 1961. Available from American Audio Prose Library.

Suggested Readings
Ardelino, Frank. "Life Out of Death. Ancient Myth and Ritual in Welty's 'A Worn Path.'" *Notes on Mississippi Writers* 9 (1976): 1-9.
Isaacs, Neil D. "Life for Phoenix." *Sewanee Review* 71 (1963): 75-81.
Keys, Marilyn. "'A Worn Path': The Way of Dispossession." *Studies in Short Fiction* 16 (1979): 354-56.
Orr, Elaine. "'Unsettling Every Definition of Otherness': Another Reading of Eudora Welty's 'A Worn Path.'" *South Atlantic Review* 57 (1992): 57-72.
Schmidt, Peter. *The Heart of the Story: Eudora Welty's Short Fiction.* Jackson: UP of Mississippi, 1983.
Welty, Eudora. "Is Phoenix Jackson's Grandson Really Dead?" *The Eye of the Storm: Selected Essays and Reviews.* New York: Random House, 1975.

THE SWIMMER by John Cheever [pp. 369-76]

This story presents one of Cheever's most scathing indictments of the shallow values of wealthy suburbanites, about whom he typically wrote. Neddy at the beginning of the story is a handsome, popular, successful man "who might have been compared to a summer's day," but by the end of the story he is a lonely, exhausted, ruined man who faces the winter of his discontent.

The time sequence may trouble students until they realize that time becomes telescoped following the turning point of the story—the storm which overtakes Neddy at the Levys' deserted home. After that, all the details of his swim down "the Lucinda River" on a glorious summer afternoon become increasingly grim. The startling images of autumn and blight suggest aging and impending death. This is no longer the robust, youthful Neddy but a much older man who has suffered some financial disaster and thus has lost the status he formerly enjoyed. At the public pool, where he is not insulated by wealth and privilege, he has no "identity tag" and is told to leave. Even the social-climbing Biswangers now shun him, as he formerly shunned them. He has lost his mistress, his fortune, his family, his home—his very identity. At the end when he finally reaches his empty, abandoned house, we see him—cold, weak, and uncomprehending—pounding on the door, trying "to force it with his shoulder," as he begins to cry "for the first time in his adult life."

One critic sees Neddy as "an epic hero of a sort," because he was betrayed by the values of his society and did struggle to complete his journey to the headwaters of the "Lucinda River." But most readers see Neddy as a literally disillusioned man, cut off from all human contact in an anguished state of existential despair.

Questions for Discussion and Writing
1. What can you say about the lives of the people in Neddy Merrill's social set? What is important to them?
2. What kind of person is Neddy? Why do you think he is called Neddy rather than Ned?
3. What is the turning point in his journey, which is also the turning point of the story?
4. Can you explain the shifting time sequence in Neddy's adventure? How does the experience change for him after he crosses the highway?
5. What seems to have caused Neddy's life to go from being, in effect, a carefree summer afternoon to being a lonely wintry night?
6. Write an essay relating the significance of the images of autumn, blight, and coldness to the changes in Neddy's life.

Film: The Swimmer. Directed by Frank Perry; with Burt Lancaster, Janet Landgard. 94 min., color, 1968.

Suggested Readings
Blythe, Hal, and Charlie Sweet. "Cheever's Dark Knight of the Soul: The Failed Quest of Neddy Merrill." *Studies in Short Fiction* 29.2 (1992): 347-52.
Coale, Samuel. *John Cheever.* New York: Ungar, 1977. 43-47.
Donaldson, Scott. *John Cheever: A Biography.* New York: Random House, 1988. 210-12.
Kozikowski, Stanley J. "Damned in a Fair Life: Cheever's 'The Swimmer.'" *Studies in Short Fiction* 30.3 (1993): 367-75.
O'Hara, James E. *John Cheever: A Study of the Short Fiction.* Boston: Twayne, 1989. 67-70.

Slabey, Robert M. "John Cheever; The 'Swimming' of America." *Critical Essays on John Cheever.* Ed. Robert G. Collins. Boston: Hall, 1982. 180-91.

I STAND HERE IRONING by Tillie Olsen [pp. 377-82]

This story is an often bitter and despondent recounting of the trials of being poor and having children. Olsen's monologue hammers home emotionally wrenching scenes and makes the needs and wants of both mother and child painful to the reader. When the mother refuses to give a conventional "love overcomes adversity" story, the reader must life in poverty with the single mother, rather than gloss over the difficulties. Here is a long tale of missed opportunities, intimidating professionals, and the grievous insufficiency of life at the edge of poverty. It is clear that the living conditions have created spiritual and emotional deprivation as well. The mother gives up much of her life and aspirations in order to care for her children. It is no mystery to her. She tries to suppress her own feelings as she recounts the upbringing of her talented daughter, Emily, to the imaginary audience of a school counselor. The self-control is admirable, if incomplete. Olsen reflects the common experiences of millions of people, and the reverberations strengthen the tone and impact of the story.

Questions for Writing and Discussion
1. The story is a monologue. What is the speaker's situation? Where is she and to whom is she talking? How does the device of having a specific listener in the story affect your role as reader?
2. Make a list of the major events of Emily's life. How would *you* sum up this life?
3. Ironing is emphasized in the title and mentioned several times in the story. Why?
4. Identify some of the conflicts in the story. Are any of them resolved?
5. Summarize the message of the story. Why is it worth reading?
6. Compare the narrator to Phoenix Jackson in "A Worn Path" [pp. 363-68 in the Anthology of Short Fiction].

Audio: "I Stand Here Ironing." 77 min., 1 cassette. Includes several selections. Available from American Audio Prose Library.

Suggested Readings
Bauer, Helen Pike. "'A Child of Anxious, Not Proud, Love': Mother and Daughter in Tillie Olsen's 'I Stand Here Ironing.'" *Mother Puzzles: Daughters and Mothers in Contemporary American Literature.* Westport: Greenwood, 1989. 35-39.
Faulkner, Mara. *Protest and Possibility in the Writing of Tillie Olsen.* Charlottesville: U of Virginia P, 1993. 104-05, 117-20.
Frye, Joanne S. "'I Stand Here Ironing': Motherhood as Experience and Metaphor." *Studies in Short Fiction* 18 (1981): 287-92.
Nelson, Kay Hoyle, and Nancy Huse, eds. *The Critical Response to Tillie Olsen.* Westport: Greenwood, 1994.
O'Connor, William Van. "The Short Stories of Tillie Olsen." *Studies in Short Fiction* 1 (1963): 21-25.

SEVENTEEN SYLLABLES by Hisaye Yamamoto   [pp. 383-91]

From the beginning of "Seventeen Syllables," we are aware of a cultural conflict between Tome Hayashi and her teenaged daughter (who has such an American name) Rosie. Rosie pretends to admire her mother's haiku because she doesn't want to admit that she has not mastered Japanese while "English lay ready on the tongue." She also does not admit that the haiku she likes is a humorous, colloquial one. In the end, Tome realizes that Rosie's promise never to marry is just a dodge like these.

Parallel plots concern the two females moving steadily away from the father's control. Ume Hanazono creates a strong intellectual life and companions, excluding the conventional, unartistic husband. Rosie discovers her sexuality and thinks much more of Jesus Carrasco than her father. Both women are veering toward danger.

Ume Hanazono's life ends when her husband destroys her haiku prize. In her unhappiness, Tome tells Rosie about her sad past and how her hormones landed her in America indebted to a slow-witted husband. Rosie, enrapt with sexual feelings herself, is not ready to learn from her mother's example. Her mother, no doubt envisioning her daughter's dreadful future, finds it difficult to comfort her.

Questions for Discussion and Writing
1. What conflicts between the mother and teenaged daughter are set up in the opening section of the story? Why are these conflicts and Rosie's way of dealing with them important to the story as a whole?
2. What does Rosie mean when she says that she "lived for awhile with two women"? Have you ever felt like this about a parent or relative? Might anyone see *you* as two people at some point in your life?
3. How does Ume's talent affect her husband? How does he express his feelings about it? How does he finally end her career as a poet?
4. What does Rosie feel for Jesus? List the various feelings she has and how she deals with them. Why are these feelings important when Tome finally tells Rosie the story of her marriage?
5. What does the visit to the Hayanos contribute to your understanding of Rosie, her mother, and her father?
6. Why does Rosie find that "the embrace and consoling hand came much later than she expected" in the end of the story?

Suggested Readings

Cheung, King-Kok. *Articulate Silences: Hisaye Yamamoto, Maxine Hong Kingston, Joy Kogawa*. Ithaca: Cornell UP, 1993.
Goellnicht, Donald C. "Transplanted Discourse in Yamamoto's 'Seventeen Syllables.'" *Seventeen Syllables* by Hisaye Yamamoto. Ed. King-Kok Cheung. New Brunswick: Rutgers UP, 1994. 181-93.
Mistri, Zenobia B. "'Seventeen Syllables': A Symbolic Haiku." *Studies in Short Fiction* 27 (1990): 197-202.
Yogi, Stan. "Legacies Revealed: Uncovering Buried Plots in the Stories of Hisaye Yamamoto." *Studies in American Fiction* 17 (1989): 170-74.

A GOOD MAN IS HARD TO FIND by Flannery O'Connor [pp. 392-402]

This is a difficult story for most students, partly because it has such realistic details combined with a fantastic plot and partly because it eludes any conception of "theme" or "moral" within normal reading experience. One cannot say that the family gets shot due to their unrelieved horribleness, because their encounter with the escaped prisoners is such a coincidence. And the Misfit, Bobby Lee, and Hiram are hardly embodiments of moral enforcement.

Perhaps the best way to approach the story is through the responses it elicits. Most readers will respond with a mixture of humor and horror, and a discussion of where these reactions originate is fruitful. We can see that phrases like "a lady," "nice people," "a good man," and "a gentleman" are used in bizarre contexts, and in general what people say is not in direct relation to reality. For example, the waitress responds to June Star's rudeness by saying, "Ain't she cute?" and the children's response to the car accident is "a frenzy of delight." The Misfit is the most polite character, and only the monkey and the cat behave reasonably.

Questions for Discussion and Writing
1. What is disturbing about "A Good Man Is Hard to Find"? What is funny? How is it different from other stories you have read?
2. Consider the grandmother, the mother, and June Star as three different types of women. How is each type truly awful in her own way? Why is Grandmother the main character of the story, do you think?
3. What would a person ordinarily mean when using the phrases, "a lady," "nice people," "a good man," and "a gentleman"? What do these phrases mean in the story? How do the portrayals of June Star and John Wesley relate to conventional ideas of childhood?
4. How are the grandmother and the Misfit alike? What is each one's view of the past? What does the Misfit mean by "She would of been a good woman, . . . if it had been somebody there to shoot her every minute of her life." Can you find any grain of truth in that statement?
5. What line of reasoning does the Misfit follow to justify his behavior?
6. List details that foreshadow the violent ending. Nonetheless, were you surprised by the closing? What other endings are conceivable once all the characters are gathered?

Suggested Readings
Asals, Frederick. *Flannery O'Connor: The Imagination of Extremity.* Athens: U of Georgia P, 1982. 142-54.
Browning, Preston M., Jr. "'A Good Man Is Hard to Find.'" *Flannery O'Connor.* Carbondale: Southern Illinois UP, 1974. 40-71.
Doxey, William S. "A Dissenting Opinion of Flannery O'Connor's 'A Good Man Is Hard to Find.'" *Studies in Short Fiction* 10.2 (1973): 199-204.
Hendin, Josephine. *The World of Flannery O'Connor.* Bloomington: Indiana UP, 1970. 148-51.
McFarland, Dorothy Tuck. *Flannery O'Connor.* New York: Ungar, 1976. 17-22.
Ochshorn, Kathleen G. "A Cloak of Grace: Contradictions in 'A Good Man Is Hard to Find.'" *Studies in American Fiction* 18.1 (Spring 1990): 113-17.
Renner, Stanley. "Secular Meaning in 'A Good Man Is Hard to Find.'" *College Literature* 9 (1982): 123-32.

DEAD MEN'S PATH by Chinua Achebe [pp. 403-05]

This story dramatizes the collision between progress and tradition. Achebe has said that Africans live at "the crossroads of cultures," and this story presents some of his "fascination for the ritual and the life on the other arm of the crossroads."

At first reading this brief tale seems to be a straightforward   account of the failure of a young, progressive schoolteacher to change the superstitious ways of an African village. But a closer look reveals the ironies in Achebe's presentation. The arrogance of the young headmaster, Michael Obi, is hinted at in the description of his wife, who has been "completely infected by his passion for 'modern methods,'" and in his own comment on the "grand opportunity we've got at last to show people how a school should be run." The climax occurs in the meeting between the headmaster and the village priest. Although Obi has been "outspoken in his condemnation of the narrow views" of others, he is revealed in this scene as the one with narrow views. He listens "with a satisfied smile on his face" and refuses to bend "regulations." Ironically, the more experienced priest is willing to compromise: "let the hawk perch and let the eagle perch." The outcome is inevitable, and Achebe drives home the irony in the last line of the state supervisor's unfavorable report, which criticizes "the misguided zeal of the new headmaster."

Questions for Discussion and Writing
1. Reread the last sentence of the opening paragraph. What is ironic about that statement? Did you notice the irony the first time you read it?
2. What do you think of Obi's wife? What is the significance of her "imitating the woman's magazine she read"? Why does the author include several paragraphs about her?
3. Why is Michael Obi unable to bring progress to Ndume School? Do you think he understands why he failed?
4. What is the central conflict in the story? How is it resolved?
5. Write an essay in which you explain what the headmaster might have done differently to achieve his goals.

Suggested Readings

Bagolin, F. Odun. *"Girls at War and Other Stories:* A Study of the Failure of the Elites in Moral Leadership." *Tradition and Modernity in the African Short Story: An Introduction to a Literature in Search of Critics.* New York: Greenwood, 1991. 65-80.

Carroll, David. "Short Stories and Poetry." *Chinua Achebe: Novelist, Poet, Critic.* London: Macmillan, 1990. 146-66.

Innes, C. L. *"Marginal Lives: Girls at War and Other Stories." Chinua Achebe.* Cambridge: Cambridge UP, 1990. 121-33.

Ohaeto, Ezenwa. *Chinua Achebe: A Biography.* Bloomington: Indiana UP, 1997.

Petersen, Kirsten, ed. *Chinua Achebe: A Celebration.* Portsmouth: Heinemann, 1990.

ROYAL BEATINGS by Alice Munro [pp. 406-20]

"Royal Beatings," overall, can be seen as a study of fragmentation: the prices the father charges do not match the work done, the past and the present seem unrelated, people's selves are divided among roles they play, true and false stories are mixed up, offenses are divorced from their punishments, people leave old homes behind.

The motif holding the story together is that of beatings: Becky Tyde's father is said to have beaten his family; he is beaten by the drunken young men (at more respectable men's instigation); Rose is beaten by her father (at Flo's instigation). The motivations of the batterers are blurry and not directly related to the crimes of the victims, and the outcomes are strangely peaceful. Acting out an unwritten drama seems to take precedence over rational behavior in the case of Rose's beating. The chronic dullness in ordinary Hanratty life seems broken only by overstimulating scandal or violence.

Rose's father is so removed in his workshop that perhaps the way Flo tries to draw him into the family is through involving him in the conflict between her and Rose, making him an actor in the play of the Royal Beating. The images of roles, acting, script, and dramatic structure are frequently invoked in the story of the beating, giving it some mythic strength as reflected in the title. By the end of the story, the characters are divorced from the events: Flo has "removed herself," Rose lives alone in Toronto, and Hat Nettleton, the dubious "living link with our past," is dead.

Questions for Discussion and Writing

1. Analyze the main characters in "Royal Beatings." In what ways is Rose like her father? How is she like Flo? What does it mean that the father quotes Spinoza and Flo doesn't know who that is? (Look up Spinoza for a deeper understanding of the father.) What is Flo's relation to the rest of humanity?
2. Consider the motif of beatings in the story: Becky Tyde's father beating his family, the horsewhippers beating Mr. Tyde, and Rose's father beating her. What similarities can you perceive? For example, do the people beaten seem to deserve the punishment? What are the outcomes?
3. List some different ways in which the past is broken off from the present in the story. For example, Rose loses her birth mother and fails to inherit her father's talents. Several characters disrupt their lives through moving.
4. Who is the main character, Rose or Flo? Defend your position.
5. How do the characters express intimacy? How do they avoid intimacy? Does Rose's family strike you as typical in any way?
6. List the images relating to theater in the telling of Rose's beating. What do these images imply about the beating? Look up the drama term *catharsis* and see whether it relates to the story.

Audio: "Interview." 72 min. Available from American Audio Prose Library.

Suggested Readings

Blodgett, E. D. *Alice Munro.* Boston: Twayne, 1988.

Carrington, Ildiló de Papp. *Controlling the Uncontrollable: The Fiction of Alice Munro.* DeKalb: Northern Illinois UP, 1989. 43-48.

Carscallen, James. *The Other Country: Patterns in the Writing of Alice Munro.* Toronto: ECW Press, 1993. 189, 190, 332-33.

Fowler, Rowena. "The Art of Alice Munro: *The Beggar Maid* and *Lives of Girls and Women.*" *Critique* 25.4 (1984): 189-98.

MacKendrick, Louis K., ed. *Probable Fictions: Alice Munro's Narrative Acts.* Downsview: ECW Press, 1983.

Murphy, Georgeann. "The Art of Alice Munro: Memory, Identity, and the Aesthetics of Connection." *Canadian Women Writing Fiction.* Ed. Mickey Pearlman. Jackson: UP of Mississippi, 1993. 12-27.

Rasporich, Beverly J. *Dance of the Sexes: Art and Gender in the Fiction of Alice Munro.* Edmonton: U of Alberta P, 1990.

A & P by John Updike [pp. 421-25]

"A & P" is a frequently anthologized story, perhaps because of the strong first person point of view. The narrator, a nineteen-year-old male, lets us in on his stream of thoughts unabashedly. Students may see how this point of view is different from an objective one. The mixed tenses (past and present) reflect the way someone might really tell a story out loud.

The narrator is certainly a disaffected youth, with something negative to say about everything from pineapple juice to Tony Martin. He obviously thinks his job, the people he works with, and the shoppers are beneath him. Thus, when he quits, he is not leaving behind a beloved career.

Women in particular come under Sammy's critical scrutiny, and the only female that seems to pass is Queenie (though parts of the other girls with her are magnanimously okayed). The fact that she ignores his dubious heroism, perhaps, is what pushes him to insist on quitting. It is interesting to ponder whether Updike was creating a chauvinist monster on purpose or whether he thought Sammy really was a small-town hero. Your students may be divided on the issue.

Adventurous students might also be interested in reading "A & P Revisited" by Greg Johnson, a contemporary retelling of Updike's story that hilariously transforms Queenie and her companions into UZI-toting, leather-jacketed terrorists. It's included in a collection of Johnson's stories *A Friendly Deceit* (John Hopkins UP, 1992).

Questions for Discussion and Writing
1. What is Sammy's attitude? List some of his remarks that show his attitudes.
2. Why do you think the story is written in mixed past and present tense?
3. Why does Sammy quit his job? Does he have more than one reason? Why does he see it as an act of heroism? Is it?
4. As the story closes, Sammy thinks "how hard the world was going to be to me hereafter." Will it? Why or why not?
5. Why do some readers find the story offensively sexist?
6. Rewrite a section of the story from a different point of view: Queenie's, Lengel's, the other shoppers', or an objective position. Show how point of view makes a difference in the story's interpretation.

Audio: "John Updike." The author reads six stories. 169 min. Available from American Audio Prose Library.

Suggested Readings
Bloom, Harold, ed. *John Updike.* Modern Critical Views. New York: Chelsea, 1987.
Luscher, Robert M. *John Updike: A Study of the Short Fiction.* New York: Twayne, 1993.

McFarland, Ronald E. "Updike and the Critics: Reflections on 'A & P.'" *Studies in Short Fiction* 20 (1983): 95-100.
Shaw, Patrick W. "Checking Out Faith and Lust: Hawthorne's 'Young Goodman Brown' and Updike's 'A & P.'" *Studies in Short Fiction* 23 (1986): 321-23.
Wells, Walter. "John Updike's 'A & P': A Return Visit to Araby." *Studies in Short Fiction* 30.2 (1993): 127-33.

KEEPING COMPANY by Claire Kemp   [pp. 426-29]

"Keeping Company" deals poignantly with contemporary and age-old issues. The problem of AIDS, which we quickly realize has reached James and Dennis, complicates further the friendship that springs up between a straight woman and gay men, to the disapproval of a straight husband. However, this is not the only conflict between Mary and William: they seem to disagree on many things, and William clearly believes that he is the one who should control the marriage. His building of the strong wall between the two houses is a childish effort, one that Mary never agreed to. It also is fruitless: she goes "over the wall" with a vengeance, and even takes pleasure in secretly feeding James's cooking to her husband. She hides other things from William, not wanting to face his anger and disapproval.

In marked contrast, James and Dennis share the closeness one associates with good marriages. They are sensitive to each other, talk constantly, complement each other's strengths, and generally live lives much more intertwined than Mary and William's. As often happens, William and Mary have very little idea of each other's everyday life. Ironically, James and Dennis are facing a death while Mary and William are facing a birth. The closing, in which Mary temporarily rebels openly but is quickly brought to heel, is sad and defeated.

Questions for Discussion and Writing
1. Reread the short opening section. Which parts set up the main conflicts of the story?
2. Why do Mary and William have such different attitudes toward James and Dennis? How would you describe Mary's personality? William's? What does Mary hide from William, and why? What does Mary look forward to about having a baby?
3. Compare the relationship between James and Dennis to Mary and William's relationship. Which is more like a desirable marriage? Why?
4. This story is laced with nature, clothing, food, and domestic details. Why do you think this is so? Did you notice these details as you read?
5. Does Mary finally assert her selfhood at the end of the story? What is the final mood?
6. Explain several different ways the title applies to the story.
7. Compare the way this story deals with AIDS—and people's reaction to the disease— with the way similar themes are handled in Harvey Fierstein's play *On Tidy Endings*.

LIFE by Bessie Head   [pp. 430-36]

The invasion of the cash economy into Botswana's village life has seriously interrupted its customary style, and "Life" could be seen as an allegory of this process. The flow of goods and services, including sex, in Life's village has traditionally had more to do with needs, family ties, social custom, and friendship than it has to do with cash. Life changes all that.

On another level, the story is also one of the oldest ever told, one of a lively woman or man brought low by marriage to a strict person who intends to change the other person. Lesego is compared to death, a judge, a banker, a gangster, and later, a king: none of these comparisons suggests that Life's warmth and humor will find the same in him. Lesego's rationality and coolness are repeatedly emphasized, while Life is repeatedly described as hysterical. Notice that upon marriage Lesego takes away Life's pleasures— money, music, and men. She is left without the inner resources that village culture has developed among the other women, and she languishes.

Head emphasizes that Lesego's murder of Life is not the ordinary, approved method of dealing with a straying wife. The villagers are amazed that he does not just leave her. However, his black-and-white thinking doesn't accommodate such a solution, and we gather that five years in jail won't change him.

Questions for Discussion and Writing
1. Why was Life treated so well on her arrival at the village? Have you ever known anyone like Life, who has an attractive "undertone of hysteria"? Why is Life repeatedly called hysterical? What does that word mean?
2. Why does Life fall in with the beer brewing women? What is the difference between them?
3. What is your first impression of Lesego? To what is he likened in Head's descriptions?
4. What did Lesego take away from Life when married? What is the significance of what he took away?
5. Though dull on the surface, village life created "people whose sympathetic and emotional responses were always fully awakened." Why couldn't Life fit into this mode?
6. The beer brewing women liken the story of Lesego and Life to the song "That's What Happens When Two Worlds Collide." Do you agree? What two worlds collided in this case?

Suggested Readings
Abrahams, Cecil, ed. *The Tragic Life: Bessie Head and Literature in Southern Africa.* Trenton: Africa World P, 1990.

Driver, Dorothy. "Reconstructing the Past, Shaping the Future: Bessie Head and the Question of Feminism in a New South Africa." *Black Women's Writing.* Ed. Gina Wisher. New York: St. Martin's, 1993. 162-64.

Eilersen, Gillian Stead. *Bessie Head 'Thunder Behind Her Ears': Her Life & Writing.* New York: Oxford, 1995.

Ibrahim, Huma. *Bessie Head: Subversive Identities in Exile.* Charlottesville: U of Virginia P, 1996.

Sample, Maxine. "Landscape and Spatial Metaphor in Bessie Head's *The Collector of Treasures.*" *Studies in Short Fiction* 28 (1991): 311-19.

WHAT WE TALK ABOUT WHEN WE TALK ABOUT LOVE by Raymond Carver [pp. 437-44]

Though some readers find no fascination in listening to rich people get drunk and babble, Carver must be admired for reproducing so accurately the timbre of the event (or non-event). As promised in the opening sentence, Mel does most of the talking in the story. Though he first asserts that spiritual love is the only real love (having been in the seminary but quit for medical school), he very soon abandons that stance. The violence and suicide of Ed, Terri's old boyfriend, provoke Mel, and he says that those acts were not driven by love. Terri uselessly insists, with Mel calling her "a romantic," further confusing the scene, while Laura and the narrator are so relativistic that they won't even condemn abusive relationships.

The narrator has some kind of definition of love, made obvious when he says of Laura, "In addition to being in love, we like each other and enjoy one another's company," as though the last two items were not included in the definition of love. The idea that love does not last tangles the issue further, with Terri claiming that Laura and the narrator are too newly wed to be experts and Mel being amazed that he used to love his first wife and now does not but loves Terri instead. The ideal of courtly love is suggested by Mel's ramble about knights—but so is the idea of not being injured. The tale of the old people who remain in love floats in and out.

As the story progresses, the effects of drunkenness come more and more into play, with the structure of the conversation becoming ever looser. At signs of sadness or conflict, the characters claim their love for each other, confounding the definition yet again. Toward the end, Mel segues into paternal love and is derailed by hatred for his ex-wife. Finally, the conversation, like the evening, fades into silence and darkness. The story delivers exactly what the title promises.

Questions for Discussion and Writing
1. What different definitions and descriptions of love come up during the conversation? Do the characters ever get anywhere with the subject? Why or why not?
2. What distinguishes this story from other stories you have read in this course? Do you think you could recognize another Raymond Carver story? How?
3. When the narrator says of himself and Laura, "In addition to being in love, we like each other and enjoy one another's company," what is he saying about his definition of love?
4. Reread the first two paragraphs of the story. What expository information do you get in these few sentences?
5. Carver captures the style and content of a certain kind of conversation with great accuracy. In writing, see whether you can capture the flavor of a kind of conversation that you frequently have or observe. First, look closely at the types of information Carver includes.

Audio: "Readings and Interview." 120 min., 2 cassettes. Available from American Audio Prose Library.

Suggested Readings
Campbell, Ewing. *Raymond Carver: A Study of the Short Fiction.* New York: Twayne, 1992.
Runyan, Randolph. *Reading Raymond Carver.* Syracuse: Syracuse UP, 1992. 131-35.
Saltzman, Arthur. *Understanding Raymond Carver.* Columbia: U of South Carolina P, 1988.

Simpson, M. "Art of Fiction: Raymond Carver." *Paris Review* 25 (1983): 193-221.
Stull, W. L. "Beyond Hopelessville: Another Side of Raymond Carver." *Philological Quarterly* 64 (1985): 1-15.

WHERE ARE YOU GOING, WHERE HAVE YOU BEEN? by Joyce Carol Oates [pp. 445-56]

Like "The Ransom of Red Chief" by O. Henry, this kidnap story has a disturbing twist: in this case, the victim halfway (or three quarters?) wants to go. Connie's life at home is a fairly normal, middle class white one. However, in her view it is insufferably boring and the people in it dullsville. Fueled by the pop music that infuses the story and her life, Connie has vague dreams of escape to a more exciting world. She escapes to tawdry teenaged hangouts and liaisons and invests them with romance through a transformation assisted by song lyrics. The thin line between reality and fantasy supports the motif of deceptions and illusions in the story.

After refusing to go to a terminally dull family picnic, Connie sits in the heat in a stupefied daydream and then listens for a hypnotic hour and a half to the Bobby King XYZ Sunday Jamboree. Then the bizarrely named Arnold Friend and Ellie Oscar fatefully drive up the lane. Connie's interaction with Friend is a drama of lies, hints, deceptions, suspicions, and finally threats. It has a shimmering air of unreality most of the time, with a repeated image of distracting reflections that fool the eye. Connie's state of mind is such that even though by the end of the story she knows that Friend is not one, that he has planned her abduction and will likely carry out his threats upon her family if she does not cooperate, the unknown looks better than the known. She voluntarily walks out to him.

In one sense, Connie acts heroically, saving her family by sacrificing herself. The heroism is tainted by the fact that she wants to leave her family anyway, and her future looks bleak anyway. At least, with Arnold she is going to "so much land that [she] had never seen before." He confuses her and seduces her with images from the popular songs that seem to be her sole connection to a better life, and she succumbs.

Questions for Discussion and Writing
1. How is this story different from what you'd expect from a kidnap story? What is the victim's attitude toward being abducted?
2. What role does popular teen music play in the story? Go back through the story and make a list of the places it comes up. How does it affect Connie?
3. What kind of life does Connie have at the beginning of the story? What makes her happy and unhappy? Would you call her a normal middle-class teenager? Why or why not?
4. Could you interpret one theme of this story to be reality versus illusion? What different parts of the story fit the theme?

Video: "Smooth Talk." A dramatization of the story; with Treat Williams and Laura Dern. 92 min., color, 1985. Available from Vestron Video, P. O. Box 4000, Stamford CT 06907.
"Joyce Carol Oates: American Appetites." 30 minutes, color, 1990. Available from Filmic Archives.

Audio: "Joyce Carol Oates." The author reads "Marya" and "Where Are You Going, Where Have You Been?" Available from American Audio Prose Library.

Suggested Readings

Coulthard, A. R. "Joyce Carol Oates's 'Where Are You Going, Where Have You Been' as Pure Realism." *Studies in Short Fiction* 26.4 (Fall 1989): 505-10.

Hurley, C. Harold. "Cracking the Secret Code in Oates' 'Where Are You Going, Where Have You Been?'" *Studies in Short Fiction* 24 (1987): 62-66.

Johnson, Greg. *Joyce Carol Oates: A Study of the Short Fiction*. New York: Twayne, 1994. 44-45, 148-51, 203-04.

---. *Understanding Joyce Carol Oates*. Columbia: U of South Carolina P, 1987. 98-103.

Schulz, Gretchen, and R. J. R. Rockwood. "In Fairyland Without a Map: Connie's Exploration Inward in Joyce Carol Oates's 'Where Are You Going, Where Have You Been?'" *Literature and Psychology* 30 (1980): 155-67.

Tierce, Mike, and John Michael Crafton. "Connie's Tambourine Man: A New Reading of Arnold Friend." *Studies in Short Fiction* 22.2 (Spring 1985): 219-24.

Urbanski, Marie. "Existential Allegory: Joyce Carol Oates's 'Where Are You Going, Where Have You Been?'" *Studies in Short Fiction* 15.2 (1978): 200-03.

Wegs, Joyce M. "'Don't You Know Who I Am?': The Grotesque in Oates's 'Where Are You Going, Where Have You Been?'" *Journal of Narrative Technique* 4 (1975): 66-72.

THE LESSON by Toni Cade Bambara [pp 457-61]

Bambara's "The Lesson" aptly teaches a lesson of its own: the unfairness of the distribution of wealth in a rich capitalist society—a society "in which some people can spend on a toy what it would cost to feed a family of six or seven" for a year. Sylvia, the feisty, street-smart narrator, knows all the rules of survival in her impoverished environment, but she doesn't quite grasp the lesson in socialist economics that Miss Moore is trying to teach the children by showing them the sailboat in F.A.O. Schwartz. The academically gifted Sugar gets the point at once, but Sylvia at the end of the story is only on the verge of understanding. Intuitively, she's angry; she just hasn't figured out yet who or what is making her furious. Her final line, "Ain't nobody gonna beat me at nuthin," suggests that she soon will get the message and direct her energy and ingenuity toward beating the system.

The story is saved from being overtly didactic by the colorful language and the astute portrayals of the youngsters, with their humorous nicknames and raucous banter. Sylvia, a smart kid with attitude, is the leader of the pack. Yet bright though she is, she misses the point of the lesson because her perceptions are colored by her antagonism toward all authority figures—especially the well-meaning Miss Moore, who represents the establishment only in Sylvia's mind. This antagonism makes Sylvia a somewhat unreliable narrator, especially concerning the right-minded Miss Moore and the other adults. Since the lesson Miss Moore is teaching is the lesson Bambara wants the readers to learn, Miss Moore is surely a more admirable person than Sylvia makes her out to be.

Questions for Discussion and Writing
1. How would you characterize Sylvia? What makes her first-person point of view effective? Is she a reliable narrator?

2. How would you characterize Miss Moore? Why doesn't Sylvia admire her, as the adults do? Why does Sugar not feel hostile toward Miss Moore, as Sylvia does?
3. Briefly describe each of Sylvia's friends. How do nicknames help characterize the ones who have them?
4. Why doesn't Sylvia get the point of the lesson being taught by the visit to the expensive toy store? But why is she so angry that she wants "to punch somebody in the mouth"?
5. What is the significance of the last line of the story? How does it relate to the lesson Sylvia was supposed to learn?
6. Write an essay discussing how Bambara manages to convey her revolutionary "lesson" without seeming didactic or preachy.

Audio: "An Interview with Toni Cade Bambara and Kay Bonetti." 90 min. The author discusses her writing style. Available from Audio Prose Library.

Suggested Readings

Burks, Ruth E. "From Baptism to Resurrection: Toni Cade Bambara and the Incongruity of Language." *Black Women Writers (1950-1980): A Critical Evaluation.* Ed. Mari Evans. Garden City: Doubleday, 1984. 48-57.

Cartwright, Jerome. "Bambara's 'The Lesson.'" *Explicator* 47.3 (Spring 1989): 61-63.

Hargrove, Nancy D. "Youth in Toni Cade Bambara's *Gorilla, My Love.*" *Women Writers of the Contemporary South.* Ed. Peggy Prenshaw. Jackson: UP of Mississippi, 1984. 214-32.

Tate, Claudia, ed. *Black Women Writers at Work.* New York: Continuum, 1983. 174-87.

Vertreace, Martha M. "Toni Cade Bambara: The Dance of Character and Community." *American Women Writing Fiction: Memory, Identity, Family, Space.* Ed. Mickey Pearlman. Lexington: UP of Kentucky, 1989. 154-71.

THE HOUSE ON MANGO STREET by Sandra Cisneros   [p. 462]

Sandra Cisneros writes that when she was a child, her family moved so often she thought her grandparents' house was home. "It was the only constant in our nomadic ramblings from one Chicago flat to another."

This story opens with a brief fictional review of those Chicago flats and within a space of a few paragraphs recounts the grinding hardship of being poor in a city. Even though the house on Mango Street is not the house of the family's dreams, with "a great big yard and grass growing without a fence," it is their own. No longer will the young narrator face humiliation by thoughtless people, like the supposedly good-hearted nun who blurts out, "You live *there?* The way she said it made me feel like nothing. *There.* I lived *there.* I nodded."

In the space of a page, Cisneros makes us realize that decent living space is a basic human need. But for marginalized people this need is often out of reach, even in this enormously wealthy society. Although she doesn't openly espouse Toni Cade Bambara's socialist ideology, Cisneros shares with her fellow writer the conviction that the United States has an unjust distribution of resources. She touches our hearts and lets us see that every family should have a house of its own.

Questions for Writing and Discussion

1. What do we learn about the narrator and her family from the details related in the first three paragraphs of the story?
2. How does the house on Mango Street differ from the places the family has lived before?
3. Why is the narrator so glad to be living in a house now that belongs to her own family?
4. Write as full a description as you can of the narrator, drawing on the details she reveals about herself and about her present and former environment.

Suggested Reading

McCracken, Ellen. "Sandra Cisneros' *The House on Mango Street*: Community-Oriented Introspection and the Demystification of Patriarchal Violence." *Breaking Boundaries: Latina Writings and Critical Readings.* Ed. Asuncion Horno-Delgado et al. Amherst: U of Massachusetts P, 1989. 62-71.

Olivares, Julian. "*The House on Mango Street* and the Poetics of Space." *Chicana Creativity and Criticism: Charting New Frontiers in American Literature.* Ed. Maria Herrera-Sobek and H. M. Viramontes. Albuquerque: U of New Mexico P, 1996.

Rodriguez Aranda, Pilar E. "On the Solitary of Being Mexican, Female, Wicked, and Thirty-Three: An Interview with Writer Sandra Cisneros." *The Americas Review* 18 (1990): 64-80.

THE RED CONVERTIBLE by Louise Erdrich   [pp. 463-69]

This story is one of fourteen related stories that make up Erdrich's first novel *Love Medicine* (1984), which chronicles the lives of two families on a North Dakota reservation between 1934 and 1984. "The Red Convertible" takes place in 1974, when Henry Junior comes back to the Chippewa Indian reservation after more than three years in Vietnam. The first-person narrator—Henry's youngest brother, Lyman—uses past tense to describe the finality of what happened to his brother and the red Oldsmobile convertible they once shared.

After an opening frame of four paragraphs, the story is told as a flashback, beginning with background on the two brothers and their pleasure in the car and then moving to Henry's return from Vietnam and his disorientation. When Henry fixes the convertible, he momentarily regains some of his former spirit, and the brothers get behind the wheel again, trying to recapture the carefree innocence of their youth. But Henry's inner turmoil, like that of the flooded river they park alongside, drives him to self-destruction. In the last paragraph, Lyman describes how he drove the car into the river after he couldn't rescue Henry, and the terrible irony of his opening remarks—"Now Henry owns the whole car, and . . . Lyman walks everywhere he goes"—is finally made clear.

Erdrich's use of symbolism (the convertible, the open highway, the river) is natural and unobtrusive. The story's episodic structure is loose and comfortable, like the relationship between the brothers; and the laconic, understated presentation of the narrator makes his emotional loss even more poignant and credible.

Questions for Writing and Discussion
1. How does the red Oldsmobile function as the story's central symbol? What changes does the car go through? How do these changes stand for what Lyman and Henry are going through?
2. Why is Lyman upset by the picture of himself and his brother? When does the picture begin to bother Lyman—before or after Henry's death? Do we know for sure? Does it make any difference?
3. Why does Lyman send the car into the river? Why are the car's lights left on?
4. Write an essay about the brothers' relationship.
5. Analyze a single episode in the story (such as the visit to Alaska or Henry's watching TV), and discuss its relation to the story as a whole.
6. Analyze the narrator of this story. Compare him to other first-person narrators (e.g., Sammy in "A & P" or Whitey in "Haircut").

Audio: Interview with Erdrich and her husband, Michael Dorris, about the centrality of a Native American identity to their work. 1 cassette, 50 min. Available from American Audio Prose Library.

Suggested Readings

Downes, Margaret J. "Narrativity, Myth, and Metaphor: Louise Erdrich and Raymond Carver Talk about Love." *Melus: The Journal of the Society for the Study of Multi-Ethnic Literature* 21.2 (1996): 49-61.

Flavin, Louise. "Louise Erdrich's *Love Medicine*: Loving over Time and Distance." *Critique* 31.1 (1989): 55-64.

Magalaner, Marvin. "Louise Erdrich: Of Cars, Time, and the River." *American Women Writing Fiction: Memory, Identity, Family, Space.* Ed. Mickey Pearlman. Lexington: UP of Kentucky, 1989. 95-108.

Slack, John S. "The Comic Savior: The Dominance of the Trickster in Louise Erdrich's *Love Medicine*." *North Dakota Quarterly* 61.3 (1993): 118-29.

Wong, Hertha D. "Louise Erdrich's *Love Medicine*: Narrative Communities and the Short Story Sequence." *Modern American Short Story Sequences: Composite Fictions and Fictive Communities.* Ed. J. Gerald Kennedy. Cambridge: Cambridge UP, 1995. 170-93.

VIDEO RESOURCES: GENERAL FICTION

The American Short Story Series I. 45 min., color, 1978. Nine film adaptations of short stories that appeared on PBS, including "Almos' a Man." Available from Coronet/MTI Film & Video.

The American Short Story Series II. 50 min., color, 1980. Eight programs, including adaptations of "Paul's Case," and "The Jilting of Granny Weatherall." Available from Coronet/MTI Film & Video.

PART III WRITING ABOUT POETRY

Chapter 10   How Do I Read Poetry? [pp. 473-76]

This brief chapter is a general presentation, an overview of terminology so that your students will have a base to work from. These concepts will all be more fully explained in the chapters following. Be sure to call to the attention of your students the useful list of "Critical Questions for Reading Poetry" at the end of this chapter.

One excellent way to introduce your students to the study of poetry is to dazzle them with its sound. If you read poetry well (or if you know someone who does), a prepared reading can help students hear the pleasures of the form. Another excellent choice is to play recorded poetry for the same purpose. Or, if you write poetry or have colleagues who do, you can arrange for a live poetry reading and, possibly, a discussion of why people write poetry and why it's important and valuable in our technological world.

Chapter 11   Writing About Persona and Tone   [pp. 477-93]

Encourage students to use the term *persona* or *the speaker* (instead of "the poet says") for the sake of accuracy. Sometimes poets do speak in their own voices, but often they do not. And when they do not, the persona frequently is voicing ideas and attitudes that are the opposite of those espoused by the poet. Tone is sometimes of little importance in a poem, but when tone is important, it can be crucial. To miss an ironic tone is to miss the meaning of the poem.

Who Is Speaking?   [p. 477]

As an introductory writing experiment, ask students to adopt a persona and write in the "voice" of that persona. For instance, have them write as a parent to a son or daughter at college who keeps asking for more money (or wants to drop out of school or has gotten in trouble with campus security). You can make the writing prompt as detailed or as general as you think it needs to be. You can also direct the writers not to identify their personas explicitly in the text and then have other students (in small groups or pairs) try to figure out who is writing. Ask them how they determined the identity of the writer (persona)—i.e., what clues were provided in the text?

What Is Tone?   [p. 478]

In this chapter we focus on verbal irony, since it's the main form of irony appearing in poetry. Because students frequently fail to pick up on irony, you may want to direct their attention to the other kinds discussed in the Glossary on page 1140—situational irony and dramatic irony.

To get at tone in written discourse, you can vary the above writing activity and direct your students to write more than one version of the same text—i.e., a letter from an angry, frustrated parent and one from an easy-going or permissive parent. Ask your students to discuss what changes in word choice and sentence structure occur as the tone changes.

A brief experiment involves asking your students to rewrite just a few lines of a poem to alter the tone. How many words have to be changed? Can one alteration change the tone? Insist that students find precise adjectives to describe the different tones they have created. Or ask your students to rewrite the titles of poems to suggest a different tone. What happens when we change "My Papa's Waltz" to "My Daddy's Dance" or "The Old Man's Rock 'n' Roll"? Can "The Ruined Maid" be retitled "The Fallen Woman"? Why didn't Hardy call his poem that?

Asking Questions About the Speaker in "My Papa's Waltz" [pp. 482-83]

There is a good deal of disagreement about the tone of this poem. Individual responses to these questions will vary a lot, depending on personal experience and taste. Encourage students to be honest, and allow for a variety of opinions.

Describing Tone [pp. 484-86]

Responses to these questions will vary, of course.

"The Ruined Maid"

1. An innocent young woman from rural England (probably Hardy's home of Dorset) encounters a friend ('Melia) who has run away to London. The unnamed young woman questions 'Melia about her fancy clothes and citified ways.
2. "Maid" means an unmarried young woman, a virgin. This last meaning is crucial to the ironic tone and the idea of lost innocence. Hardy does not mean a female servant.
3. One definition for the noun *ruin* is "physical, moral, economic, or social collapse." The poet's almost cynical point turns on the fact that 'Melia's supposed moral collapse is accompanied by physical, economic, and social improvement.
4. 'Melia is probably a well-paid prostitute or a "kept woman." The bracelets, feathers, gown, and painted face (lines 13-14) suggest her occupation, as does her "lively" lifestyle (line 20) and her tendency to "strut" (line 22). In current American slang we might call her a "party girl" or a "call girl."
5. The opening tone of the questioner's lines is one of amazement and disbelief; by the end of the poem she is speaking with admiration and envy.
6. 'Melia seems proud, proper, cool, and even condescending. One critic has said she speaks with "cheerful irony" about her "ruin." Certainly she does not act ashamed.
7. The use of "ain't" in the final line might be taken as a slip into her former vernacular speech, suggesting that her urban polish does not run deep. But it is also possible to see 'Melia reverting to the ungrammatical language intentionally, with obvious relish, to emphasize the difference between herself and her former friend. This interpretation reads the last line as a final mocking jab at her friend's excessive naiveté.
8. Hardy's tone is ironic, mocking, even sarcastic and cynical. The still innocent maid is poor, gullible, and confused; the ruined maid is self-possessed, attractive, and well fixed. This ironic reversal denies the traditional wisdom about the "wages of sin."

Stanley Renner provides some interesting social background and commentary on this poem in his article "William Acton, the Truth about Prostitution, and Hardy's Not-So-Ruined Maid," *Victorian Poetry* 30.1 (Spring 1992): 19-28.

"The Unknown Citizen"

1. He is identified by number—no name is given.
2. The speaker (persona) is a representative of the State, some bureaucrat who helps to keep track of the masses. The persona uses the plural to identify with the State that he or she works for, and to cover any personal responsibility for the opinions and conditions expressed or implied.
3. The name is comical, as is the rhyme.

4. The capitalization suggests that these concepts have become personified and are paramount in the society portrayed in the poem; they are impersonal entities that have become much more important than individual persons, who remain numbers.
5. The persona praises the Unknown Citizen for his conformity. Auden himself is critical of the Unknown Citizen and would surely deplore the ideas expressed by the speaker in the poem.
6. The poem is satirical. The tone of the satire is sometimes humorous, but overall, Auden takes a relentlessly critical approach in exposing the conformist, dehumanized society that the speaker represents and supports.

"Go, Lovely Rose"

1. It appears that the woman has rebuffed the speaker in some way, refuses to see him or receive his attention.
2. The rose is a traditional symbol of romantic love as well as of beauty that does not last long.
3. "Uncommended" means literally, unsung; thus she is unnoticed and hence unpraised.
4. "Wastes" in line 2 strikes a slightly harsh note, with overtones of pining away in love sickness. Both lines have an edge to them. Is it too much reality to suggest that she is wasting her life while her body is wasting away, anticipating the "die" of line 16? The "shuns" in line 7 suggests a deliberate, almost obstinate avoiding of life's pleasures.
5. The last imperative in the sequence of polite commands—go, tell, bid, *die*—startles us a little. But in the time period when the poem was written, the word *die* carried a double entendre: it meant also to experience sexual orgasm.
6. No, poems at this time were usually sung.
7. Cajoling, charming, graceful but quietly insistent, perhaps. There also seems to be just a touch of hostility or resentment lurking beneath the effortless charm of the speaker's words. The "then die" shocks us into focusing on the specter of age and death that *carpe diem* (seize the day) poems usually raise in their arguments for sexual pleasure.
   Contrast the tone of the speaker of this "invitation to love" lyric with that of the speaker of Andrew Marvell's "To His Coy Mistress" (p. 537) who seems more passionate and urgent in his entreaties.

"One Perfect Rose"

1. They both use the rose as a symbol of love, and they both employ a twist or turn in tone to make their points.
2. Parker's poem exploits the tonal shift to create a humorous, down-to-earth comment on romantic love (and romantic love poems).
3. The apostrophe changes the 2-syllable word to a one-syllable word that fits the iambic meter of the line. But the poet may also be mocking the artificial language of many love lyrics, which seem to resort frequently to this linguistic device—thus giving her own poem a quaint, old-fashioned touch.
4. An amulet is a magical charm, ornament, or signifier.
5. It changes from traditionally romantic to openly materialistic. The single word, "limousine" upsets all our expectations—in both rhythm and diction—and throws the whole stanza into another gear.
6. The total effect is parody. The tone is humorous and iconoclastic, as the writer slyly undercuts the established tradition of romantic idealism in poetry.

Analyzing the Student Essay [p. 493]

We have deliberately included a sample student paper that is flawed in order to allow your students to exercise their revising skills.

1. The student states what he takes to be Housman's theme in the final paragraph of the essay. But surely Housman intended the poem to convey a broader meaning than the student settles for.
2. The student identifies Housman as the speaker in the poem in the fourth paragraph ("Housman tries to convince us . . ."). The speaker seems to be a detached (but not necessarily impartial) observer who could indeed be the poet.
3. The student fails to identify tone in the poem, which makes the analysis go off the track. Surely, the speaker's tone is ironic. Who in his or her right mind would want to die young just in order to avoid seeing sports records broken? Although the student's opening sentence seems to use the same irony, he somehow misses seeing the irony in the poem itself.
4. The student says that Housman "tries to convince us that it is best to die young," but he has missed the gentle irony of the line, "Smart lad to slip betimes away." Yes, those "Eyes the shady night has shut / Cannot see the record cut," but who would willingly choose to have that happen? To say, as the student does, that the poet thus "applauds the athlete's death" is to take seriously a message that—at best—might be intended to offer some comfort, to find some positive note in the tragedy.
5. The student allows his own experience as an athlete to interfere with his understanding of the poem. He clearly agrees with the poet that sports records are not worth dying for, but he fails to see that Housman was being ironic. In the last paragraph, the student says that the poet "seems to think that setting records and living in the limelight are all that athletes are looking for in their lives." Not so. The poet, if able to respond, would probably say that the student makes some perceptive comments about the poem but unfortunately misses the point.

Certainly cultivating in your students a sensitivity to the literal and connotative meanings of words is crucial to their understanding and appreciation of poetry. We believe that the best way to go about making them responsive to the language of poetry is through close examination of numerous poems in class. Requiring students to learn definitions of the standard terms that are used in discussing poetry (metaphor, personification, paradox, etc.) may be counterproductive if your students already harbor negative feelings toward poetry. The important thing is for them to be able to *recognize* a metaphor and to grasp its meaning, not necessarily to be able to *define* one.

Examining Poetic Language [p. 500]

1. The poem establishes its comparison by contrasting the temperate loveliness of the beloved with the "rough winds," the too-hot sun, the fading sun, and the shadow of death. The poem is a tribute which immortalizes "the eternal summer," i.e., the unfading loveliness of the beloved.
2. Students should have fun with this assignment as they learn from it a great deal about the importance of rhyme and meter, as well as word choice. If any group feels intimidated by trying to write a serious poem as good as Shakespeare's, allow them to write a humorous version. Read the completed poems aloud to the class and ask them to discuss the effectiveness of the word choice and imagery. If some have attempted parodies, you might want to ask them to read Shakespeare's own parody, "My Mistress' Eyes Are Nothing Like the Sun" (p. 532 in the anthology).
3. The poem compares the questing of one's soul for meaning to the patient construction of a spider's web. The soul is personified. When your students substitute synonyms, they will become aware of the perfection of Whitman's word choice. You may want to put them in groups after they have written their versions in order to discuss how changing the words distorts the meaning, alters the images, and destroys the meter. Encourage them especially to see that "ductile" ("till the ductile anchor hold") is a key word in understanding Whitman's search for a belief that is flexible, not a rule-bound creed.
4. Wind is the element which could "cut" or "rend open" the heat. In the last sentence the wind is identified with a plough. The heat, then, is associated with the air, the element to be ploughed: "Cut the heat— / Plough through it. . . ."
5. In a general sense, the extended metaphor compares life to weaving a tapestry. A more particular meaning comes to light when students consider the nature of a tapestry, which frequently has a detailed, coherent pattern and may also tell a story. The persona in the poem tries to weave lasting meaning and pattern into his life span, only to find this task impossible. He takes several tactics, such as not looking behind him and tying new knots as they unravel, unsuccessfully. These tactics represent different ways of living—being future oriented and present oriented, respectively. His efforts to make a sensible narrative of both the past and the future are futile and, as we see in the last lines, these efforts also ruin present experience. The extended metaphor

suggests that trying to control our lives so that they acquire lasting meaningfulness is ill fated.

6. The central paradox in "My Son My Executioner" was nicely stated in a popular Bob Dylan song: "Everything not busy being born is busy dying." The new child promises an immortality of sorts (since he will probably live longer than his parents and hold them in his memory) while at the same time reminding his parents that they are themselves getting older, moving toward death.

Finding Lively Words and *Exercise on Diction* [p.502]

After your students complete the exercise on improving sentences from their earlier papers, you might put them in groups to discuss each other's word changes. Ask them to consider whether the changed or added words constitute an improvement or not. If not, ask them to think of another wording that would be better.

Sample Student Paper [pp. 502-09]

The second draft of the sample student paper was marked (as shown in the text) by the instructor. The final draft includes the changes the student, Sonya Weaver, made in response to those comments, plus some of her own revisions and editorial corrections.

After spending a few minutes reading and discussing Donne's poem (p 533 in the anthology), you might want to read Sonya's second draft aloud (as the class follows in their books). Ask them how they would have revised the marked passages. Then let them compare their changes with those Sonya made in the final draft. Discuss which revisions are better and why. Be sure that your students have pen and paper when they work on their suggested revisions. And try to allow time for them to devise good sentences.

Exercise on Poetic Form [p. 512]

In this exercise, students are asked to arrange the lyrics of a song in lines on a page. If you use this as an individual exercise, you may ask students to write answers to the questions in the assignment. As a small group activity, the exercise could be completed by four or five students listening to a cassette tape and deciding on the arrangement together. In this way, the questions will be answered in the course of the group's discussion. If more than one group works on the same song, it would be profitable to compare the two arrangements and ask each group to justify its decisions.

Experimenting with Poetic Forms [pp. 518-20]

1. *Sleep*—In the context of the poem, a sleeping/waking image is set up. Also, in the poem's imagery the small gunner's pit suggests the womb.

    Hunched—The connotations of *hunched* are more humble than those of *crouched*. *Crouched* can suggest a powerful animal waiting to spring, definitely not the appropriate image for the gunner.

    Fur—In context, the gunner is seen as a helpless animal. Literally, too, the fur on his flight jacket could freeze.

    Loosed—The connotations of the alternative, *freed*, are too positive.

    Nightmare—*Nightmare* creates an iambic rhythm with *fighters*, a rhythm which follows impressively the spondee of *black flack*.

    Washed—Although *flushed* is a more vivid verb, *washed* picks up the alliteration with *when* (the first word in the line) and carries a connotation of cleansing. Also, *flushed* may have too many associations with plumbing. *Washed* seems a surprising understatement.

    Hose—The meaning of *hose* is more accurate, both literally and imagistically. The brutal force of a hose's stream is more appropriate than the sloshing of a mop.

2. "We Real Cool" has a jazzy, syncopated rhythm created by the placement of the subject "We" at the end of the lines and by the shortness of the sentences. These two factors encourage a reading with unusual pauses, as in musical syncopation. The placement of "We" also functions to emphasize the word, perhaps stressing the egotism of the persona.

3. The alliteration of "s" sounds in "Eight O'Clock" suggests the evil hiss of a snake or the discouraging hiss of air going out of a balloon or tire, both negative in effect. The variety of "o" and "ou" sounds produces an ominous resonance, like the tolling of the bell which will mean the prisoner's doom. The repeated "k" sound in the second stanza is sharp and harsh, like the prisoner's fate and the sound of the gallows as the trap falls. Objectively, the poem tells the brief story of a prisoner who is listening to the town's church clock strike the hours until eight, which will be the time of his hanging. An objective account, of course, leaves out the subjective elements—the poetic effects and appeals created by alliteration, personification (the steeple in stanza 1 and the clock in stanza 2), and other devices.

4. This is a very demanding exercise, and some students will not see the differences in stanza use. In general the quatrains are coterminous with sentence units; the stanzas point out these syntactic structures. Some authors, like Donne and Cummings, play against the traditional expectations in surprising, even devilish ways.

5. First quatrain: "To do celestial chores." (This quatrain is the complete poem "For a Lady I Know" by Countee Cullen.)

   Second quatrain: "And see the men at play." (This quatrain is the complete poem "The Golf Links" by Sarah N. Cleghorn.)

   Third quatrain: "Were fields of harvest wheat." (from a poem by W. H. Auden)

   Fourth quatrain: "To watch his woods fill up with snow." (from "Stopping by Woods on a Snowy Evening" by Robert Frost)

6. Tell your students that they may add words as they rewrite the lines. There are no exact right answers, but here are our rewrites:
   a. Because he served the greater community in everything he did.
   b. He worked in a factory until the day he retired, except when he was in the war.
   c. How pretty a town anyone lived in, with the sound of bells floating up and down.
   d. The little men and small women didn't care for anyone at all.

7. If your students have difficulty writing couplets at first, let them use one of these first lines, providing a second line and a title themselves.

   a. They try to tell me writing's fun

   _____

   b. I sometimes wonder where I'd be

   _____

   c. An ocean breeze and a loving friend

   _____

Be sure that students get to see one another's efforts: have them pass their papers around or duplicate them or put a few on the board.

Ideas for Writing [pp. 521-23]

The Ideas for Expressive Writing involve creative composition. They can replace or supplement a critical paper on poetic form.

Topics 1 and 5 under Ideas for Critical Writing combine analytical writing with a comparison and contrast format, while topics 2 and 3 are straight analyses, requiring the writer to separate the elements of the poem and, ideally, to show how they work together to support or create the poem's meaning. Topic 4 calls for analyzing figurative language and commenting on the poet's viewpoint about closed form.

Exercise: Distinguishing among synonyms [p. 524]

a.   *Renowned* and *famous* both mean widely known and honored; *famous* is used in reference to all pursuits, while *renowned* usually refers to intellectual or artistic fame. *Notorious* also means widely known, but the reputation is likely to be a negative one.
b.   An *indifferent* parent is neither especially good nor especially bad; a *detached* parent is objective, not ruled by emotions; and an *unconcerned* parent is free of worry.
c.   To *condone* an action is to overlook the degree of wrongness or inappropriateness. *Excuse* is most often used to mean pardon for social errors, like sneezing or being late. To *forgive* involves letting go any bad feelings or resentment one may have about a wrong action.
d.   *Steal* is the most general word, meaning to take someone else's property without permission. *Pilfer* means to steal in small quantities and repeatedly, as, for example, your roommate might pilfer your beer supply. In the context of stealing, *robbery* usually means directly stealing from a person by using threats of violence or actual violence, whereas *burglary* involves breaking into a place intending to take something unlawfully, and *ransacking* involves a search for things to steal. *Looting* is stealing on a bigger scale, like the plunder that takes place in war or a riot.
e.   An *apparent* error seems to be real, but may or may not be. A *visible* error may be perceived by the eye. An *egregious* error is obviously bad.
f.   All three words, in the context of describing personality, imply high self-esteem. *Proud* is the most positive, suggesting that the high self-esteem is deserved, though it often also suggests unwarranted attempts at self-sufficiency. Both *pompous* and *arrogant* describe one with an exaggerated sense of self-importance; *pompous* also carries a meaning of stuffy and boring.

Exercise: homophones [p. 524]

a.   apprise—to inform; appraise—to evaluate
b.   anecdote—a little story; antidote—a remedy
c.   chord—musical note; cord—string or small rope
d.   elicit—bring out; illicit—not legitimate
e.   martial—pertaining to war; marital—pertaining to marriage
f.   statue—sculpture; statute—rule or law
g.   human—a person; humane—kind, merciful, compassionate
h.   lose—misplace, fail to win (verb); loose—not tight or dense (adjective)

i. idol—a worshipped symbol; idle—inactive, without a job
j. accept—approve, receive, take in; except—exclude, omit
k. simple—easy, uncomplicated; simplistic—ignoring complications or complexities, over-simplified
l. beside—next to; besides—in addition to, except
m. isle—small island; aisle—path or passageway
n. weather—atmospheric conditions; whether—if
o. incidence—rate of occurrence; incident—event or happening

Exercise: precise adjective forms [pp. 524-25]

a. An intelligible essay is merely understandable; an intelligent one is logical and thoughtful.
b. A hateful sibling is malicious; a hated sibling is intensely disliked, deserving or not.
c. A likely roommate is probable or promising; a likable roommate is pleasant.
d. An informed speaker knows the subject well; an informative speaker is enlightening.
e. A workable thesis is practical; a working thesis is temporarily adopted until it proves practical or impractical.
f. A liberal man is generally broadminded and generous; a liberated man is not guided by traditional sex roles.

Exercise: malapropisms [p. 525]

a. superficial
b. pinnacle
c. refuse
d. examinations
e. rude

Exercise: words that fit context [p. 525]

a. tenacity or steadfastness
b. obviously, support
c. rage

Sample Published Essay on Poetic Form [pp. 526-27]

Both you and your students should enjoy this well-written and insightful critical article by David Huddle explaining how the sound fits the sense of Robert Hayden's "Those Winter Sundays." The essay is remarkable in being free from jargon and addressed directly to its readers. It can serve as a model for student writing and teaches a great deal about the functions of poetic form in the bargain. Don't skip it.

71

WITH HIS VENOM by Sappho [p. 528]

Sappho, whose religion involved praising Aphrodite, the Greek goddess of love, wrote frequently of the effects of love, both delicious and devastating, "irresistible and bittersweet," on Aphrodite's human followers. In this poem she employs a controlling image (perhaps surprising to students who may not be familiar with the snake as an archetypal phallic image) to present love as an almost destructive force.

Questions for Discussion and Writing
1. Why do you suppose we still today speak of people "falling" in love? What does the expression have in common with the poet's presentation of love as a snakebite?
2. In what way can love be both bitter and sweet?
3. In a brief paper, compare the use of imagery in this poem with William Blake's imagery in "The Sick Rose" (p. 539).

WESTERN WIND (Anonymous) [p. 528]

This lament of a lover separated from his/her beloved gains poignancy from its simple language. Wind, rain, and aching desire are presented as equally natural, almost archetypal sources of sorrow. The assonance (*o* and *a* sounds) and alliteration and consonance (*w* and *r*) weave through the poem and help give it its lyrical quality. It may help to know that the moist, warm west wind of England brings rain and is a sign of spring.

Questions for Discussion and Writing
1. How does this poem make you feel? What pictures or images does it put in your mind?
2. What do the first pair of lines have to do with the second pair?
3. One critic (F.W. Bateson) has suggested that the speaker is invoking Christ (line 3), asking for help in obtaining sex. Another critic (Arthur Lewis) says the unhappy speaker is expressing a longing to go to bed with the loved one, so the word "Christ" is an exclamation. Which view do you prefer? Do you have a different interpretation?
4. Why do you think this very brief and very old poem has retained its universal appeal over so many years?

THEY FLEE FROM ME by Sir Thomas Wyatt [p. 529]

This is another lover's complaint, but it is a sophisticated and highly individual variation. The speaker laments that his former success with women has declined. He speaks of these women as if they had been tame animals which used to eat from his hand. But they are no longer tame; they fly at his approach. The metaphor of the hunt becomes clear when we know that hunting dogs "range" as they search for game, that "seek" is a command given to such dogs, and that "change" refers to an animal met by chance (which the dogs pursue instead of the quarry). Thus, the women have altered from tame animals to hunters themselves. In the second stanza the speaker erotically evokes a woman he particularly remembers, one who makes the advances and "catches" him in her arms. The speaker insists, in the last stanza, that this delightful occurrence was not a dream. He was presumably prepared to surrender—and be faithful to her—but the woman was not. She tames him and then forsakes him. He is free to do likewise, but his final question reveals that he is peeved and slightly confused by the role reversal: since she treats me in this fickle fashion, how should I treat her?

Questions for Discussion and Writing
1. What is the speaker's attitude toward the special woman of stanzas 2 and 3? Why does she stand out from the others?
2. How do the old loves (stanza 1) relate to the attitudes expressed in the rest of the poem?
3. What does the speaker suggest is the cause of his abandonment?
4. How is the speaker of this poem different from the one in "There Is a Lady Sweet and Kind"?
5. Write a character sketch of the speaker, paying particular attention to his views about love and women.

THE PASSIONATE SHEPHERD TO HIS LOVE by Christopher Marlowe [pp. 529-30]

Using the conventions of the pastoral (the speaker assumes the pose of a shepherd) the speaker-poet invites his loved one to join him in a carefree love. Students may not find the invitation convincing; it is too artificial and the enticements (which carefully avoid the mention of any sexual pleasures) are charming but modest. But what do contemporary swains promise their loved ones? Are the modern conventions any more persuasive? Certainly, the innocent tone will appeal to some students' romantic impulses. This poem should be studied in conjunction with Raleigh's reply.

Questions for Discussion and Writing
1. How does the young lover vary his appeals? Is there an implication that the object of his invitation is rejecting him?
2. Does the speaker go too far ("buckets of the purest gold") and lose credibility? Or is credibility even an issue in this kind of poem?
3. By the end of the poem, how convincing do you find the Shepherd's appeal? Just how "passionate" is he?

THE NYMPH'S REPLY TO THE SHEPHERD by Sir Walter Raleigh [pp. 530-31]

This is the famous critical response to Marlowe's poem. In it the speaker (the "nymph") systematically points out the illusory nature of the world offered to her by Marlowe's shepherd: men lie, weather turns bad, flowers and young women fade and wither as do gowns, skirts, and posies. In short, the poem offers a wry comment on love and the passage of time. The speaker implies that the shepherd's carefree love could not survive the passing youthful joys and her loss of beauty. The allusion in line 7 to Philomel is heavily charged with the tragic consequences of untrammeled lust. Philomel was raped by her brother-in-law, who tore out her tongue so she couldn't accuse him; the gods later turned her into a nightingale.

Questions for Discussion and Writing
1. How does the nymph counter the shepherd's pleasant pastoral images?
2. Note how the nymph mentions all of the images drawn from nature that were used in the Marlowe poem. But what does she do with them?
3. Notice the use of balance in lines 11, 12, 16. What do these lines mean? How do they epitomize the nymph's strategy in answering the shepherd?
4. Write your own response to the shepherd. Or write a counter-response to the nymph's reply. If you don't want to try verse, write a prose response.
5. Which of the two lovers, the shepherd or the nymph, do you like better? Which approach to love do you find more attractive? Write a comparison essay in which you defend your choice.

WHEN IN DISGRACE WITH FORTUNE AND MEN'S EYES (Sonnet 29) by William Shakespeare [p. 531]

This sonnet departs from the usual Shakespearean structure of three quatrains and a couplet: the last 6 lines form a unit (a sestet). In the first 8 lines the speaker cites circumstances when self-doubts overwhelm him; in the next 4 lines the speaker observes that the remembrance of the loved one ("thee"), which seems to occur at random ("haply" means "by chance"), lifts the speaker's spirits. The famous simile that ends the poem indicates that the speaker's joy is like the return of the lark's song at the beginning of the day. The lark's burst of joy suggests that heaven—called "deaf" in line 3—has suddenly become keener of hearing. The last two lines, comprising a separate sentence, sum up the ideas expressed in the lark simile (ll. 9-12), suggesting that the speaker's spirit is genuinely restored by the memory of "thy love."

Students might profit from paraphrasing the poem, as several words that sound familiar had different meanings than they have today. "Featured," for instance, meaning "alike in features," would paraphrase as "looking like." And "scope" could mean either accomplishments or breadth of understanding or knowledge.

Questions for Discussion and Writing
1. Is it believable that the mere thought of his beloved could change the speaker's whole outlook on life?
2. Summarize the speaker's state of mind before the turn or shift which occurs in line 9.
3. How does the meaning of the poem change if the reader interprets "thee" (line 10) and "thy" (line 13) to refer to God instead of a romantic lover?

4. Define the word *state* as it is used in this poem.
5. Write a brief essay in which you use this sonnet to develop a discussion of the effects of love on the human spirit.

LET ME NOT TO THE MARRIAGE OF TRUE MINDS (Sonnet 116) by William Shakespeare [p. 531]

This sonnet deals with the theme of love's stability and permanence. It treats its subject in a formal, rhetorical fashion. After the opening exhortation, which echoes the traditional marriage ceremony, the speaker goes on to explain his position by defining love, first negatively (ll. 2-4), then positively (ll. 5-8), and then negatively again (ll. 9-12). The poem's argument is wholly contained in the three quatrains, and the final couplet is more like a challenge to the reader to deny the consequences of the airtight logic of the preceding lines. But the final comment is personal ("upon me") just as the opening exhortation is personal ("Let me"), providing a subjective frame for the rather academic or universal definition of love that comes between.

The abstract concepts of time and space are applied to the investigation of love, but the language moves from the abstract ("alteration") to a concrete image based on navigation. This complex metaphor compares love to a kind of sea-mark (like the North Star), which is proof against storms (l. 6). The image of the third quatrain represents "rosy lips and cheeks" as coming within the "compass" (restricted space or area) of Time's bending sickle. "Bending" of line 10 and "alters" of line 11 tie up the last negative definition with the first one by recalling the "alters" of line 3 and the "bends" of line 4.

Questions for Discussion and Writing
1. What familiar part of the traditional Christian marriage service is echoed in the first line?
2. Notice that the poem celebrates "the marriage of true minds," not of bodies. In a brief paragraph, summarize in your own words the nature of this kind of love.
3. What are the two negative definitions that Shakespeare uses to describe true love?
4. What two comparisons does Shakespeare make in lines 5-8? What is the connection between "an ever-fixed mark" and "the star"?
5. What conflict between love and time is established in lines 8-12?
6. Compare the qualities of love expressed in this sonnet with those that John Donne evokes in "A Valediction: Forbidding Mourning" (p. 533).

THAT TIME OF YEAR THOU MAYST IN ME BEHOLD (Sonnet 73) by William Shakespeare [p. 532]

This sonnet explores the connections between mortality, death, and love. The time frame becomes increasingly shorter, moving (in the three quatrains) from a season to a part of one day to a moment of recognition. The bold and complicated metaphors picture the aging speaker as a winter-ravaged tree, the twilight moving into night, and a feeble fire choking on the ashes of its own expended fuel. The common link to the three quatrains (autumn, sunset, a dying fire) is diminution or dying. The couplet may need explication.

Questions for Discussion and Writing
1. How does the speaker portray himself in this sonnet?
2. What are the controlling metaphors in each of the quatrains? How are they related?
3. How is a body like boughs, and how are bare boughs like a ruined choir loft?
4. What happens to a fire when the fuel (wood, coal, etc.) becomes ashes?
5. How do you explain the idea expressed in the last two lines? Why would the loved one's love grow stronger when he/she sees that the speaker is getting older?
6. Does love always grow stronger between people as they get older? Write a brief response to this sonnet in which you explore the relationship between love and aging.

My Mistress' Eyes Are Nothing Like the Sun (Sonnet 130) by William Shakespeare [p. 532]

In Shakespeare's day it was fashionable for poets to imitate the sonnets of Petrarch, the Italian poet whose praise of his beloved Laura started the rage for sonnet writing. The result of all the imitation was a surplus of Petrarchan conceits (or elaborate comparisons). In Sonnet 130, Shakespeare, who often drew on Petrarchan conventions himself, pokes fun at poets who thoughtlessly use the exaggerated figures of speech. Shakespeare is confident that his readers have read numerous imitations of Petrarch, and he turns their clichés to his own uses. The last line is a bit difficult because the words *she* and *compare* are both nominals. It might be paraphrased this way: I think my love is as rare as any woman ("she") who is misrepresented ("belied") through false comparisons ("false compare").

Questions for Discussion and Writing
1. The comparisons that Shakespeare uses negatively in this sonnet were familiar enough in his time to be considered clichés even then. What is the poet's point in cataloging these overused images?
2. What is the speaker's attitude toward his mistress? Is he making fun of her? Do the "if . . . then" constructions help you to figure out the distinction the speaker is making between the artificial comparisons and his real-live girlfriend?
3. How do the negative connotations of the words *false* and *belied* help you to figure out that the last two lines contain a true appraisal of the speaker's mistress?
4. How does the poem's argument divide up among the three quatrains and the couplet?
5. Write your own parody of some form of writing that you think is sometimes overdone (such as advice columns, sports articles, celebrity profiles, articles in sensational tabloids like the *National Enquirer*, horoscopes).

The Flea by John Donne [pp. 532-33]

If you want to give your students an example of a startling metaphysical conceit, this *carpe diem* poem will serve nicely. The poem presents a playful plea to a lady to surrender her virtue because in the swollen flea that has bitten them both, their blood is already mingled (as he hopes their bodily fluids will soon be mingled in sexual intercourse). Their union, argues the lover, would be no more shameful than the bite of the flea. In stanza two, he pleads that she spare the flea since they are united in a blood marriage within it (even though her parents might not agree). If, from force of habit, she crushes the flea, she will be killing all mingled within it—self, lover, and flea, "three sins in killing three." In the last stanza, "cruel and sudden," the lady crunches with her fingernail the jet-hard shell of innocent flea, who did nothing sinful beyond taking a drop of her blood. But, since she feels no weaker from the loss of blood, he pleads that she need not fear a loss of virtue: it will diminish her honor no more than the trifling death of a flea. The lover's argument is clearly longer on wit than it is on logic, but the poem nonetheless is considered exemplary in its genre.

Questions for Discussion and Argument

1. What is the "little" thing the lover says the lady is denying him in line 2? Is it really a small matter? Be sure to put the poem in the context of Elizabethan times when you answer.
2. What action is the woman about to take at the beginning of stanza two? Whose are the "three lives" he wants spared?
3. In lines 12-15, what is the argument that her parents might not believe but he hopes the lady will? What are "the living walls of jet" in line 15?
4. In what sense will the lady be guilty of killing both the lover and herself if she kills the flea (lines 16-18)?
5. What has happened at the beginning of stanza three? Why is the lady's nail purple?
6. Write a careful paraphrase of the poem in which you state the lover's purpose and detail his argument. Conclude by speculating on what you think the lady's response might be.

A VALEDICTION: FORBIDDING MOURNING by John Donne [pp. 533-34]

In his biography of Donne, Izak Walton claims that the poet wrote this poem for his wife in 1611, when he was about to depart on a diplomatic mission to France. In the course of the poem, the speaker uses five conceits or metaphors to define the calm and quiet that he thinks should characterize his departure: 1) the death of virtuous men, 2) movement of the celestial spheres, 3) the assurance of spiritual love (as opposed to physical love), 4) the expansion of gold beaten into foil, 5) the conjoined legs of a drawing compass.

The simile of the first two stanzas must be linked to the title. The point is that the parting lovers should be like virtuous people who accept death easily because they are assured of being in paradise. The contrast between earthquakes (which can be accounted for) and the "trepidation of the spheres" (which is more significant but less destructive) sets up the contrast between the love of earthbound ("sublunary") lovers and the spiritual love of the speaker and his beloved. Their love does not depend on physical contact; it is as refined as gold, which can be expanded into gold foil without any break or separation. The final three stanzas develop the famous conceit in which the souls of the lovers are compared to a drawing compass (some students may visualize a directional compass). The best way to illustrate this famous conceit is to bring in a draftsman's compass (even a dime store variety) to demonstrate the movements described in the poem.

The student paper, "Images of Love," which is at the end of Chapter 12, analyzes these metaphors and their progression through the poem.

Questions for Discussion and Writing
1. What is a "valediction"?
2. Why does the speaker forbid mourning?
3. Explain the metaphor about the passing away of virtuous men (lines 1-4).
4. Explain the reference to astronomy in stanza three. (In the medieval cosmos, the heavenly bodies were thought to be fixed, while everything under the moon was subject to change.)
5. What distinction does the speaker make between "dull sublunary lovers" and the love that he and his loved one share?
6. What qualities of beaten gold make it an appropriate metaphor for the love that the speaker is describing? (Gold is refined, precious, durable, capable of being expanded greatly without breaking apart.)
7. Paraphrase the last stanza.
8. Compare the vision of idealized love that Donne projects in this poem to the one presented in Shakespeare's Sonnet 116 ("Let Me Not to the Marriage of True Minds," p. 531)

DEATH BE NOT PROUD by John Donne   [p. 534]

This sonnet is an intense and mocking (though not humorous) apostrophe (or address) to Death. Its central theme is based on the Christian belief in resurrection. The expression is paradoxical throughout. The speaker says Death should not be arrogant: Death is not final; neither is it "mighty" or "dreadful"; it's not even competent. Actually, Death is pitiful ("poor Death"); far from being terrifying, it really should be welcomed like "rest" and "sleep." And there are other reasons to deprecate Death: it's a slave to human will and depends on poison, war, and sickness. Sedatives are even more effective in producing sleep, so why is Death so swelled with pride? As the final couplet makes clear, we can transcend Death by robbing it of its dominion.

Questions for Discussion and Writing
1. What is the speaker's attitude toward Death in this poem?
2. How are paradox and personification used in this sonnet to signify a victory over Death?
3. Summarize each step in the argument which "proves" Death not to be very powerful.
4. How many times are death and sleep compared? What is the point of each comparison?
5. Upon what beliefs does the success of the argument depend?
6. In what senses are the speaker's final claims about Death not justified?
7. Write about your own view of death. Where do you agree and disagree with the view expressed in this poem?

BATTER MY HEART by John Donne   [p. 535]

Students well be interested to know that in early Christian mysticism the soul was often portrayed as a maiden with Christ as her bridegroom. And in the Petrarchan love sonnets,

78

the "reluctant woman" was often envisioned as a castle, her suitor presented as an "invading army." The sinner's heart is like a walled city, fallen to Satan (ll. 1-4); God, the rightful king, approaches and knocks, then breaks open the gates with a battering ram. The paradox of destroying in order to revive is the poem's unifying concept. It is based on the central paradox of Christianity—that one must die in order to gain new life.

Since contemporary readers are more likely to see the action in the poem as rape, it may help them appreciate the poem if they know that Donne intended romantic conquest. The speaker in the poem wants "Reason" (line 7) defeated in order to allow faith to hold sway. The "enemy" (line 10) is usually understood to be Satan.

Questions for Discussion and Writing
1. Paraphrase the poem, explaining as you do so, who is speaking and to whom.
2. What is meant by "three-personed God"?
3. Explain the paradoxes (apparent contradictions) in lines 1, 3, 13, and 14.
4. Explain the conflict in the poem. Who is "Your enemy" (line 10)? Why does the speaker want "Reason" overcome?
5. Write a paper explaining the use of woman as metaphor in this poem.

EASTER WINGS by George Herbert   [p. 535]

Some might call this a "picture poem" (or a "concrete" or "graphic" poem) since the words (turned sideways, as printed in *Literature and the Writing Process*) look like wings. Turned the other way (as poems are usually printed), it resembles the font containing holy water in some churches. But the arrangement of words on the page also reinforces the sense, emphasizing short lines, "Most poor" and "Most thin," in the same way that a very short paragraph stands out in prose, through contrast. One commentator points out that the lines are shortest when the speaker has become separated from God and grow longer as the speaker moves closer in praise of God. The poem suggests both verbally and visually the idea of resurrection and renewal of life. In line 19, the term "imp" in Herbert's day meant "to graft." Falconers would graft feathers to repair the damaged wing of a hawk.

Questions for Discussion and Writing
1. The lines of the poem appear to ebb and flow when turned sideways in reading position. How does the visual image relate to the meaning of the poem?
2. How does the repetition of the form in stanza two serve to reinforce the sense of the poem?
3. Write a paper comparing the image of the lark in this poem with the image of the lark in Shakespeare's "When in Disgrace with Fortune and Men's Eyes" (p. 531).

THE PULLEY by George Herbert   [pp. 536]

This poem provides a fairly typical metaphysical conceit, but the key to understanding the image presented (not visually but through the meaning of the lines) lies in the title. The human need for rest (which, in Christian belief, leads finally to eternal rest in God's breast) is conceived of as a vertical pulley, the kind that might be used to hoist a piano into a second-story window. A modern reader may find humor in this conceit—as well as in the puns and in the image of God pouring blessings like liquid from a glass—but Herbert's tone is, of course, quite serious and devout.

In line 2, "span" means the distance between thumb and little finger in an extended hand, so it could be paraphrased as "a short space." Lines 8 through 10 shift the image of God as "pouring" blessings to that of God as removing treasures, one by one, from a chest.

Questions for Discussion and Writing
1. Paraphrase the poem to show how the action of the pulley in the title underlies the meaning of the whole.
2. If God is bestowing on mankind the "jewel" of earthly rest, what other meaning of "rest" can be inferred from the last line?
3. Write a paper comparing the metaphorical conceits in this poem with those employed by John Donne in "A Valediction Forbidding Mourning" (pp. 533-34).

TO LUCASTA, ON GOING TO THE WARS by Richard Lovelace [p. 536]

This poem may refer to an actual parting: Lovelace fought in the service of Charles I during the Puritan Revolution (1642-45). The theme, which seems to be a serious one, is that Honor (duty to country and king) takes priority over duty to Lucasta. Lucasta is "chaste" and "quiet"; war is personified as a "new mistress" with greater vitality, and the speaker calls his departure an instance of "inconstancy." This comparison is in keeping with the light and witty tone (which may confuse some readers because of the seriousness of the message). The closing line makes a serious affirmation: the speaker's love for Lucasta is based on a greater love of honor, which is a driving force in the speaker's life.

Questions for Discussion and Writing
1. What is the tone of the poem?
2. What seems to be the speaker's attitude toward war? How old do you imagine the speaker to be?
3. What is the meaning of "nunnery" to the speaker?
4. Who is the speaker's "new mistress"?
5. Analyze the poem's contrast between the speaker's two mistresses.
6. What values or virtues are contrasted in the poem?
7. Compare this poem about war to Wilfred Owen's "Dulce Et Decorum Est" (pp. 582-83).

TO HIS COY MISTRESS by Andrew Marvell [pp. 537-38]

This is one of the most famous *carpe diem*, persuasion-to-love poems ever written. It incorporates a distinct syllogistic form (an if-but-therefore argument) that distinguishes it from other *carpe diem* poems. The title identifies the characters: the speaker is a would-be lover; he is addressing his "coy" (reluctant) lady. His argument is: if there were time, I'd woo you properly, but life is short and we'll be dead soon; therefore we'd better become lovers now.

The first section sets up a hypothetical situation in which there is vast space and time. The Ganges and Humber rivers are approximately on opposite sides of the globe. The allusions to Noah's flood and the conversion of the Jews evoke a span from Genesis to the Last Judgment. The speaker's "vegetable" (as opposed to rational) love will grow "vaster than empires but more slow."

The next section, beginning with "but," refutes the hypothesis of the first section. There is a note of urgency in the image of time's chariot pursuing them like an enemy, and the vastness of time is changed to deserts of eternity. The lines are full of images of death, dust, dryness, isolation. The speaker also bawdily sketches the consequences of too much coyness: no one makes love in the grave. In the last section, the speaker's logic (or pseudo-logic) requires that the lovers behave differently. The images change from slowness, distance, and great size to excitement and vitality: "fire," "sport," "devour," "roll," "tear," "rough strife," "run." Time becomes a slow-jawed, devouring beast that will itself be devoured by the vigorous lovers.

Questions for Discussion and Writing

1. What is the tone of the assertion in the first 20 lines? Are they sufficiently hyperbolic to be ironic or even playful?
2. How does the speaker's tone change after line 20?
3. In the second section (lines 21-32), why is time behind the speaker and eternity in front of him?
4. What words contribute to a third change in tone (after line 32)? Find verbs, nouns, and adjectives that connote urgency and vigor.
5. Why does the speaker use "am'rous birds of prey" instead of more conventional love birds (like doves or larks)?
6. In the 17th century, a cannonball was simply called a "ball." Do lines 42-44 describe a cannonball ripping through the gates of a fortified city?
7. What words and phrases have sexual connotations?
8. What universal human concern does this poem reflect? What basic human urges might be said to motivate the speaker? Is he interested only in seducing the woman?
9. As Raleigh did for Marlowe's "The Passionate Shepherd to His Love," write the coy mistress's reply to Marvell's speaker.

THE LAMB by William Blake [p. 538]

The childlike purity and pastoral bliss of this song arise from the abundant, positive depictions of a beneficent Lamb (Christ), who is nourishing, comforting, and joyful. The first stanza poses a question; the second supplies the answer with naive enthusiasm and assurance. The speaker unites himself, the lamb, and the infant Jesus in a pastoral vision of innocence and bliss. This a Romantic portrait of a benevolent world envisioned by the uncorrupted, natural child.

Questions for Discussion and Writing

1. What symbolic meanings are conveyed by the image of the lamb?
2. What feelings does this poem evoke in you?
3. What view of God and creation does this poem present?

81

4. How does Blake establish the Lamb as a symbol of creation?
5. Is the view of the world in this poem too good to be believable?

THE TYGER by William Blake [pp. 583-39]

Most interpreters of this poem see it as a treatment of the age-old question: how can we explain evil in a world created by an all-knowing, beneficent God? The fearful, ominous tiger burns brightly in the dark forests of primeval creation. The lamb is contrasted with the tiger in stanza 5, which apparently alludes to the expulsion of Lucifer from heaven (as described in Milton's *Paradise Lost*). The angels weep not only over Lucifer's rebellion but also over the introduction of evil into the world.

Questions for Discussion and Writing
1. What side of creation is presented in this poem? Is the creator of the tiger the same as the creator of the lamb?
2. What Christian metaphors do you find in this poem?
3. What mythological allusions are contained in lines 7 and 8?
4. Explain why "The Tyger" and "The Lamb" should be considered as a pair, one the reverse of the other.
5. Give your answer to this question: why does an allegedly all-powerful and beneficent creator permit evil at all?
6. Writing topic: Why does Blake answer his question in "The Lamb" but not in "The Tyger"?

THE SICK ROSE by William Blake [p. 539]

Students usually enjoy figuring out what the rose and the worm signify—and then deciding what the sickness might be. Since the rose is an archetypal symbol of sexual love, the meaning should be easily identified. But the worm, "That flies in the night [and thus is hidden] / In the howling storm" (a hint of catastrophe to come) lends itself to speculation. Critics have suggested syphilis, which in Blake's time did destroy life literally, or adultery, which (if discovered) could destroy the love existing in marriage. Today, the threat of AIDS comes to mind.

Questions for Discussion and Writing
1. Are there sexual implications in the poem?
2. How does personification expand the scope of this lament?
3. What do you think the rose and the worm might represent?
4. How does the description of the worm help to explain the rose?
5. What causes the rose to be sick?
6. Write an allegorical interpretation of the poem, explaining its hidden meaning.

LONDON by William Blake   [pp. 539-40]

This poem reflects Blake's distress with the suppression of human spirit, which he blamed on custom and politics. His idea was that humanity could flower if institutions could be eliminated or at least redirected. London represents a fallen world: everyone is blighted or plagued, and the midnight streets are filled with danger and misery. By contrast, the reader is reminded of privilege, soldiers, and palaces, all of which are aspects of oppressive authority.

Questions for Discussion and Writing
1. How does Blake convey the impression of pain and suffering?
2. Why does the speaker use the word *chartered* twice? What are its different meanings? (The streets are mapped; the privileged can hire the river for their use—in contrast to the misery of the poor.)
3. "The youthful Harlot's curse" is usually interpreted to mean venereal disease, which blinds the infant after birth. How does this information help you to understand Blake's metaphor in the final stanza? Why is this curse so important to the speaker?
4. What is the significance of the mention of a Church, a Soldier, and a Palace?

COMPOSED UPON WESTMINSTER BRIDGE, SEPTEMBER 3, 1802 by William Wordsworth   [p. 540]

Wordsworth defines poetry as "the spontaneous overflow of powerful feelings," which takes "its origin from emotion recollected in tranquillity." This sonnet presents an embodiment of his feelings of admiration for the serene, slumbering city. The poem is admired for the effectiveness of its personification and for the skillful melding of subjective response with objective observation (as in "felt, a calm so deep" followed by the calm glide of the river [lines 11-12]). Beneath the quiet serenity of the scene lies the powerful energy of the city, evoked in the final line by "that mighty heart," presently "lying still."

Questions for Discussion and Writing
1. What is the city compared to throughout the poem?
2. Discuss the features contributing to the personification.
3. Compare the description of Wordsworth's beautiful and tranquil city with Blake's description in "London" (p. 539)

THE WORLD IS TOO MUCH WITH US by William Wordsworth   [pp. 540-41]

This sonnet almost perfectly embodies the love of nature that lies at the heart of English romanticism. When the speaker announces that he would "rather be / A Pagan suckled in a creed outworn" (lines 9-10), he probably is thinking of the Greek culture in which nature had its own gods and goddesses. Still, the statement would have bordered on blasphemy in Wordsworth's 19th-century Christian England, thus lending considerable power to the closing sestet. The message is one that remains relevant today—"Getting and spending, we lay waste our powers" (line 2), thus losing the spiritual connection with nature that could enrich our lives.

Questions for Discussion
1. In what way, according to the speaker in the poem, have we "given our hearts away" (line 4)?
2. Why would the speaker be comforted by the sight of Proteus and Triton?
3. Why is Triton's horn described as "wreathed" (line 12)?
4. The poem is a sonnet divided into an octave and a sestet. Where does the sestet begin?
5. How is the poem unified?

KUBLA KHAN by Samuel Taylor Coleridge [pp. 541-42]

The circumstances of this poem's composition are almost as famous as the poem itself. According to Coleridge, "Kubla Khan" was a fragment preserved from a vision the poet had while under the influence of opium, taken for medicinal purposes. But its deeply affecting symbolism makes the poem more than just a drug-induced creation. Most critics think the "pleasure dome" is poetry itself, and the "sacred river" is the poet's flow of inspiration. There is less agreement about the "ancestral voices" and the "caves of ice."

Questions for Discussion and Writing
1. Coleridge called this poem a "fragment," but many readers consider it a complete work. What do you think?
2. Compare the first 36 lines to the rest of the poem. What does the "damsel with a dulcimer" represent?
3. The poem's final stanza switches from third-person to first-person. Why?
4. Write an analysis of this poem as a statement about the pleasures of art and the sinister forces that threaten it.

SHE WALKS IN BEAUTY by George Gordon, Lord Byron [p. 542]

This evocation of feminine beauty works from physical properties to an ethereal state, with the final emphasis on spirit and mind: the last stanza speaks of goodness, peace of mind, and innocent love. The opening simile may be accounted for by the fact that Byron was writing for his cousin, Lady Wilmot Horton, who was wearing a black dress with spangles when he first met her (because she was in mourning). Byron's description is rich in an abstract, allusive way, but it has no specificity to it.

Questions for Discussion and Writing
1. What mood does this poem create?
2. The light image introduced in the first stanza is the foundation of the poem, but just which image of light is dominate?

84

3. What does the word "eloquent" refer to? In those same lines, are the smiles on the cheek and the glow on the brow? How does that description work?
4. What are the speaker's attitudes toward women and beauty?

OZYMANDIAS by Percy Bysshe Shelley [p. 543]

The name "Ozymandias" is the Greek rendering of Ramses II, who was pharaoh of Egypt in the 13th century BC The sonnet's ironic comment on his pride suggests the futility of all pride based on great work. Line 8 may present a problem: the passions of Ozymandias were well read by the sculptor who mocked them (imitated them on the face of the statue and derided them as well). But the passions, explicit in the ruined visage of the statue, survive the sculptor who created the statue and the Pharaoh's heart that produced them.

Questions for Discussion and Writing
1. The statue which this poem is written about has been described as one of the largest in Egypt. It has this inscription: "I am Ozymandias, king of kings; if anyone wishes to know what I am and where I lie, let him surpass me in some of my exploits." Does having this information help your understanding of the poem?
2. Why did Shelley choose this decrepit statue of a great king as a subject for a poem?
3. What contrast is there between what the king said and how the statue now looks?
4. Do the words "that colossal wreck" refer to something more than the statue?
5. How does the final image (the lone, level sand stretching far away) work to reinforce the tone and theme of the poem?

ODE TO THE WEST WIND by Percy Bysshe Shelley [pp. 543-45]

In England the west wind brings spring and the accompanying regeneration of the earth. Spring causes in most people a lifting of spirits—and in poets a resurgence of creativity. The wind sweeps away the debris of winter and scatters the seeds that bring new life. In the first three sections, the speaker depicts the role of the wind through three seasons: first, on land during autumn; next, in the clouds during winter; and then, on a bay (which includes both land and sea) during summer. In sections four and five, the focus changes as the poet asks the wind to lift his sagging spirits and serve as inspiration ("Be thou me"). The final line succinctly reinforces the images of death and regeneration that are woven throughout the poem.

Questions for Discussion and Writing
1. Explain the paradox of the West Wind as "Destroyer and Preserver" (line 14).
2. What is the speaker's situation? What is his "sore need"? What does the speaker ask of the wind in lines 57-70?
3. In what ways does the complex rhyme scheme reinforce the meaning of the poem? [The couplets concluding each of the first three sections have a breezy sound conveyed by the repeated *e*'s.]
4. Write an analysis of the symbolic implications of the west wind.

85

ON FIRST LOOKING INTO CHAPMAN'S HOMER by John Keats   [pp. 546]

The controlling metaphor of this sonnet is the equation of reading with travel and exploration. In the octave the speaker reveals that he has read widely (traveled much) in great literature ("realms of gold") of western civilization ("western islands"). The travel and movement end with the speaker's triumphant discovery of the George Chapman translation of Homer. In the sestet, the basic metaphor is viewed from a different perspective: the speaker, comparing his feelings to those of explorers who find themselves gazing on something never seen before, is awed into stillness and silence.

That the first European to see the Pacific was neither Cortez nor Balboa makes no difference to the poem. Students might be interested to know that Keats wrote this poem immediately after he and a friend spent an entire night excitedly reading through Chapman's translation.

Questions for Discussion and Writing
1. What mood is this poem trying to convey?
2. What is the sonnet's central metaphor?
3. How does the progression of the thought follow the basic two-part division of the sonnet (into octave and sestet)?
4. What did reading Chapman's translation of Homer mean to the speaker? What is it that the speaker discovers?
5. Write a brief essay about an exciting discovery or event in your life. Be sure to explain what this highlight has meant to you.

ODE ON A GRECIAN URN by John Keats   [pp.546-47]

This poem is structured as a reading of the urn. It also brings up the contrast between timeless art and human mortality. The speaker muses on the unchanging beauty of the urn and his own suffering mortality. Grecian urns were vessels for the ashes of the dead; their carved or painted figures depicted a joyous afterlife in the Elysian fields. The design on the circular urn appears to continue forever (an image of eternity or the seamless perfection of art).

In the first stanza, the urn is addressed as a "bride," a "foster child," a "sylvan historian," and the poet sketches a montage of the pictures that cover it. In stanza 2, he moves closer and considers a piper and a lover, figures which animate the poem's central idea: some ideal, unheard music is more beautiful than that which can be heard. This idea is further illustrated in stanza 3 by a series of poetic observations. In stanza 4, the speaker imagines what is not represented on the urn and, in the final stanza, reflects on the conclusions to be drawn from the graceful ancient shape.

Questions for Discussion and Writing
1. The urn is called "sylvan" probably because it displays woodland scenes, but in what sense is it an "historian"?
2. How can unheard melodies be sweeter than heard ones?
3. Why are the figures so lucky to exist on the urn (ll. 15-27)?
4. What disadvantages do living lovers experience (ll. 28-30)?
5. What additional insight occurs to the speaker in stanza 4? (That the urn, whose world seemed perfect, is in some ways limited and desolate.)

6. How is the urn a "Cold Pastoral"? (It is lifeless clay and stands aloof from human change and suffering.)
7. How is it a "friend to man"? (It provides a resting place for human ashes; it teaches us through its beauty/truth.)
8. Compare the depictions of nature and art in this poem with the depictions in Coleridge's "Kubla Khan" (p.541).
9. Explain the closing line and give your reactions to this assertion about beauty and truth.

ULYSSES by Alfred, Lord Tennyson [pp. 547-49]

This is one of the great dramatic monologues of English poetry. Readers are usually divided in their opinions of Ulysses. To some he is a grand, noble man who refuses to give in to old age and death. To others he is a bombastic and haughty old man. Ulysses finds the meaning of life in action; and his past actions are a prologue and guide to the future, not merely dead memories (ll. 19-21). He is aware of his physical mortality, but he's determined to struggle against the spiritual death of surrendering action to memory and satisfaction to yearning. These inspiring ideas are undercut to some extent by the arrogance Ulysses displays toward his subjects, his wife, and his son. His disdain and bombast reach their peak in the last three lines.

Questions for Discussion and Writing
1. The poem divides into three sections. Outline the main ideas of each section.
2. Who was Ulysses and what had he done before the time of the poem? (Ulysses is the Latin name for Odysseus, hero of Homer's *Odyssey*, who brought about the destruction of Troy by developing the strategy of the Trojan horse. He spent 10 years at Troy and 10 years coming home. On his return trip he had one perilous adventure after another, encountering ghosts, sirens, monsters, and gods, and had amorous interludes with Circe and Calypso.)
3. What does Ulysses want? What is his attitude toward life in Ithaca?
4. What do Ulysses' past actions mean to him?
5. How does Ulysses contrast himself with his son?
6. Write a character sketch of Ulysses. How do you react to him and his views on how life should be lived?

THE EAGLE by Alfred, Lord Tennyson [p. 549]

This poetic fragment is packed with striking figures of speech. It also demonstrates meticulous word selection, alliteration, and assonance. Tennyson figuratively describes the way an eagle clasps a crag (as human fingers grasp something) and the eagle's elevated view of the world, as well as the speed and power of its attack.

Questions for Discussion and Writing
1. Does an eagle have hands? What does the speaker mean?
2. Is an eagle really close to the sun? What's the point of this image?

3. What does the word *ringed* signify? (The earth's horizons look like a ring when viewed from far above.)
4. How is the sea personified?
5. What properties of a thunderbolt are meant to be attributed to the eagle?
6. What is the point or purpose of this brief description?
7. Write a literal version of this description (don't use any figures of speech). What is lost?

MY LAST DUCHESS by Robert Browning   [pp. 549-51]

This dramatic monologue seems to allude to the life of Alfonso II, Duke of Ferrara, in northern Italy, whose first wife died three years after she was married to him. She was rumored to be a victim of poisoning. Through the offices of an agent (to whom the duke may be speaking in the poem), Alfonso married the sister of the Count of Tyrol four years later.
        The Duke's cold arrogance emerges from the outset of the poem. Selfish pride controls all his relationships with people. The Duchess is not alive but the subject of a painting by a famous artist. (Wives and works of art seem identical to the Duke—both are collectibles.) In lines 21-31, the poet engages our sympathies for the Duchess, despite the Duke's contemptuous criticism of her failings. What were the commands that ended her smiles? Browning once explained: "That she should be put to death, or he might have had her shut up in a convent."
        Lines 47-53 make it clear that the Duke has been addressing the emissary of the Count whose daughter he hopes to marry. Has the Duke unwittingly revealed too much of his cruel nature, or was he just making it clear what he will expect from his new duchess? Critics have taken both sides of this question: some seeing him as calculating and in control; others suggesting that his arrogance is almost pathological and leads him to say too much (note the abrupt shift in the subject in line 47—has the Duke realized he should shut up about his last duchess?).

Questions for Discussion and Writing
1. Who is speaking to whom? What is the situation?
2. According to the Duke, what were the Duchess's faults? Do you trust the speaker's account of the Duchess and her "failings"?
3. How does Browning make us understand that the Duke's remarks are biased?
4. To what extent is the Duke's attitude about women typical of his society?
5. Does the Duke's carefully controlled composure slip as he relates his story about the last duchess? Or is he intentionally letting the emissary know his (the Duke's) feelings about women and wives?
6. What evidence is there that hypocrisy is another aspect of the Duke's character? Why does he three times deprecate his ability to relate precisely what he wishes?
7. What is the effect of mentioning another work of art at the end of the monologue? What does this remark show us about the Duke? Is there any significance to the statue of Neptune taming a seahorse?
8. Although the Duke is unsympathetic, are you still fascinated by him? If so, explain why.
9. How would the Duke's refusal "to stoop" and his insistence upon the importance of his "nine-hundred-years-old-name" (or comparable attitudes) be manifested today?

10. This poem is written in rhymed couplets. Why doesn't it seem like there is that much rhyme when you read it?
11. If you were the emissary for the Count whose daughter the Duke hopes to marry, what would you report to your master? How would you describe the Duke? What advice would you give to the Count concerning the marriage of his daughter?
12. One critic, Leonard Nathanson, comments that "the Duke performs the very act he asserts to be the most repugnant to his nature; after sacrificing his wife rather than his dignity, he sacrifices his dignity." Write any essay on this and the other ironies that you detect in the poem.

WHEN I HEARD THE LEARN'D ASTRONOMER by Walt Whitman [p. 551]

Whitman clearly would rather gaze at the beauty of the stars than hear a scientific description of them. He was much interested in science and paid tribute to discoveries in the new science of geology (of fossils, strata, and earth's age) in "Song of Myself." But he was also a transcendentalist who found God in nature, so reducing the stars to figures, charts, and diagrams would surely strike him as misguided.

Questions for Discussion and Writing
1. Why is the speaker in the poem unable to appreciate the astronomy lecture?
2. Whitman's lines neither rhyme nor scan, so what makes this a poem? [The arrangement of lines on the page, the deliberate repetition in the first four lines, and the cadence]
3. Do you think poetry and science are antithetical? Write an essay about the similarities and differences between the methods and purposes of science and poetry. Use specific poems to illustrate your points.
4. Write a paper comparing this poem with Dickinson's "There's a Certain Slant of Light" (p. 553).

ONE'S-SELF I SING by Walt Whitman [p. 551]

In these brief stanzas, which open *Leaves of Grass*, Whitman presents several major themes of that long poem. First, he "sings" of the need for each person to be recognized as an individual while belonging to the democratic masses. Then, he insists that the body is a suitable subject for the poetic muse, just as much as the brain is—an idea quite startling in his day—as was his next assertion that the female deserves equal praise with the male. Finally, he salutes the "Modern Man," who enjoys a vibrant life in a free nation whose laws stem not from a king, but from divine law.

Questions for Discussion and Writing
1. What does the persona mean by the word "sing"?
2. Explain what Whitman means by praising "physiognomy from top to toe." What would poets previously have praised? (The mind and soul, not the body itself, as Whitman does.)
3. What in the poem suggests Whitman's love for America?

DOVER BEACH by Matthew Arnold [p.552]

The persona in the poem is standing at a window with his beloved looking from the white cliffs of England across the moonlit channel toward France. (Since the poet is male, it seems reasonable to assume that the persona is also.) He calls his love to the window and muses on the beauty of the landscape and the "eternal note of sadness" in the sound of the sea. The tide is in, and he remarks that the "Sea of Faith" (religious belief) was once "at the full" but now has retreated (under the onslaught of scientific discoveries of Darwin and others that contradicted the biblical account of creation). The solution posed in the poem for the resulting uncertainty is to have faith in each other, because the poet envisions a world without religious faith as being a place of darkness and strife. ("Shingles" are gravel beaches.)

Questions for Discussion and Writing
1. Describe the setting of the poem.
2. To whom is the persona speaking?
3. What is the cause of the "sadness" in line 14? What is the speaker's response to the ebbing "Sea of Faith"?
4. What could have caused the "Sea of Faith" to be retreating like the tide? Note the date of the poem.
5. What solution does the persona pose as a solution to the loss of religious faith?
6. Write an essay in which you analyze how images of sound and sight—or lack of sight—contribute to the effectiveness of the poem.

SAFE IN THEIR ALABASTER CHAMBERS by Emily Dickinson [p. 553]

The first stanza of this poem describes the Christian dead quietly and meekly awaiting the resurrection. The images, although cold, suggest peace, calmness—security, even. Dickinson is envisioning these dead as inhabiting crypts of cool, white alabaster—hence the "Roof of Stone." The "Rafter of Satin" suggests the lining of the casket itself. In the second stanza the poet describes the passing of eternity in terms of arcs describing the swirling of the solar system. (Think of the sun god in his chariot sweeping a grand arc across the sky.) She concludes with a reminder that all are mortal, even those who wear crowns and enjoy power. The final line suggests, with its images of absolute soundlessness, the small impact such lives have in the cosmic scheme of things. The "dots" may be flakes of snow landing on "a Disc of Snow" (i.e., a snow-covered landscape viewed from a great height). Note how the snow image reinforces the cold, white images of the first stanza.

Questions for Discussion and Writing
1. What does alabaster look and feel like? Why is it the perfect word choice to the describe the chambers (crypts)?
2. Why are the dead described as "members of the Resurrection"?
3. What is the meaning of line 5?
4. Can you paraphrase the last stanza?
5. Write an essay discussing how the images of cold and white contribute to the effectiveness of the poem.

THERE'S A CERTAIN SLANT OF LIGHT by Emily Dickinson [p. 553]

The overall meaning of this poem is easy to grasp but individual lines pose difficulties. Dickinson is describing here the depression we sometimes feel on a dreary winter afternoon which brings thoughts of our own mortality (like Melville's Ishmael who felt a "damp November" in his soul and took to drifting along with funeral processions). The "Heft / Of Cathedral Tunes" suggests those weighty Bach pieces often performed in church. Since Dickinson was a transcendentalist, the "Heavenly Hurt" does not mean sent from God, but rather a cosmic lancing of the soul, "where the Meanings" of our metaphysical doubts are pondered. The "it" in line 9 probably refers to the same antecedent as the "it" in line 5—the "Heavenly Hurt," the sadness of which she speaks. Thus, "None may teach it—Any—" could mean that no one can alter this effect in any way. The last two lines describe the relief we feel when the depression lifts, putting "distance" between us and our contemplation of death.

Questions for Discussion and Writing
1. What is the "Heavenly Hurt" that Dickinson discusses in the poem? Why would it tend to strike on "Winter Afternoons"?
2. What does "the Heft / Of Cathedral Tunes" refer to?
3. Why does Dickinson describe the "Meanings" as "internal"?
4. How do you interpret the last two lines?
5. What does this poem say about faith and mortality? What concept of God is implied in the poem?

HE PUT THE BELT AROUND MY LIFE by Emily Dickinson [p. 554]

The persona in this poem is addressing her new husband (or perhaps her father). The capital letter on "He" does not mean that the man is Christ since E. D. was capricious in her capitalization. Notice the similarities to Browning's "My Last Duchess" in the general oppressiveness of the male, the reference to a duke, and the use of the word "stoop" in the second stanza. Since the ellipsis is easily filled in, the only difficulty in the first stanza occurs in the last line: the speaker envisions herself as hereafter "a member of the Cloud." This image could suggest the sort of "soft eclipse" (to use her phrase from a similar poem) that occurs when a woman surrenders her name and her individuality in marriage. Or it could be an allusion to Book III of *Gulliver's Travels* in which the society living on the cloud treats women as inferiors. Those "little toils that make a circuit of the rest" are all those small services that a genteel housewife would perform for her husband in order to make the household run smoothly. A circuit is one of her favorite images for wholeness. At the end of the poem, the persona envisions herself, like Browning's duchess, not allowed to smile or associate with anyone other than her husband, since he demands her entire attention. Thus, the theme of the poem concerns the restrictive nature of marriage for a woman in the nineteenth century.

Questions for Discussion and Writing
1. Who is the "He" in the poem?
2. How does the persona feel toward him?
3. What could it mean to be a "member of the Cloud"?
4. How would you describe the attitude of the persona? Polite? modest? submissive?

5. Write about an occasion when someone in authority (parent, teacher, law officer) put restrictions on your freedom. What was your response? Do you wish now that you had reacted differently?

MUCH MADNESS IS DIVINEST SENSE by Emily Dickinson [p. 554]

Dickinson states quite succinctly in this little poem one of the important truths of human survival: it's dangerous to be a nonconformist—even, or especially, if you're right. She begins by pointing out that many things condemned as crazy by society actually make good sense. We think at once of Galileo and Darwin and others who discovered truths that society didn't want to hear about. She then says that much of what people accept as sensible is patent madness. Consider the nuclear arms race, for example. Her final line, asserting that dissenters will be "handled with a Chain," probably reflects the treatment in her day of chaining asylum inmates to the wall. Today, students are more likely to think of handcuffed protesters.

Questions for Discussion and Writing
1. Can you think of an example, perhaps historical, of something that was considered madness that turned out to be the truth?
2. Can you think of something that is accepted by most people in society that you consider "madness"?
3. What does it mean that "the Majority / In this, as All, prevail"?
4. What does Dickinson mean by "handled with a Chain"?
5. Discuss the conflict between the individual and society expressed in this poem.
6. Do you think this poem is in any way autobiographical?

BECAUSE I COULD NOT STOP FOR DEATH by Emily Dickinson [p. 554-55]

This poem reveals Dickinson's calm acceptance of death. She presents the experience as being no more frightening than receiving an unexpected gentleman caller. Stanza three presents stages that the persona reviews during this journey to the grave—childhood (the recess scene), maturity (the ripe, hence, "gazing" grain), and death (the setting sun)—as she passes to the other side where she experiences a chill since she is not warmly dressed. In fact, her garments are more appropriate for a wedding—a new beginning—than for a funeral, which we tend to think of as an ending. Her description of the grave as her "House" indicates how naturally she depicts this new state. The eternity she spends there seems timeless to her. If the poem has a theme, it is a transcendental one—that death is not to be feared since it is a natural part of the endless cycle of nature.

Questions for Discussion and Writing
1. What is the action described in the poem?
2. Death is personified in the poem. What sort of person is he?
3. What do the images in stanza three suggest? What is the "House" in lines 17-20?
4. Do the clothes the speaker is wearing suggest typical burial garments? If not, what do they suggest?

5. What is the persona's attitude toward death?
6. Why couldn't the speaker stop for death?

I HEARD A FLY BUZZ—WHEN I DIED — by Emily Dickinson [p. 555]

In this remarkable poem the persona describes her own peaceful death as it occurs. Students who are unfamiliar with the 19th-century tradition of deathbed rituals will miss the light tone. Dickinson is poking gentle fun at the common practice of gathering the family at the bedside to wait for Christ, the King, to come and—figuratively, of course—take the departing soul to heaven. This tradition was so widely accepted that when *Uncle Tom's Cabin* was staged, the dying little Eva was taken by angels (lowered and raised on wires) straight up through the ceiling. Dickinson may also be playfully introducing a fly, a common symbol for Satan, instead of the expected Christ. But, remember, that in her belief, a fly was simply one of "Nature's people"—and this is a gorgeous bluebottle fly, not at all a loathsome creature to a nature-lover. In addition to satirizing the foolishness of the deathbed watch, Dickinson perfectly portrays the transcendental acceptance of death as a natural passage in the eternal cycle of life.

Questions for Discussion and Writing
1. What happens to the persona at the end of this poem?
2. Who is the "King" whose appearance is expected at the bedside?
3. How does it change the event to have a fly appear instead of the King? Does the speaker appear disappointed?
4. Does the speaker's dying seem traumatic or peaceful?
5. What do you call the figure of speech illustrated in this image: "Blue—uncertain stumbling Buzz —"? (Besides the onomatopoeia in *buzz*, the phrase provides a remarkable example of *synesthesia*, combining images of sight, motion, and sound.)
6. Write an essay comparing this poem to Katherine Anne Porter's "The Jilting of Granny Weatherall" (pp. 309-14).

THE DARKLING THRUSH by Thomas Hardy [p. 556]

This poem is remarkably optimistic to have been composed by Thomas Hardy. He fuses the old, worn-out year and the old, worn-out century and discovers "Some blessed Hope" in the song of the "aged thrush," who represents the dying year and the dying century. "Frail, gaunt, and small, / In blast-beruffled plume," the bird suggests the tribulations and scant accomplishments (in Hardy's usually pessimistic view) of the past century. But with his "carolings / Of such ecstatic sound" the thrush offers with his farewell song ("His happy good-night air") the promise of better things to come.

Questions for Discussion and Writing
1. Why does Hardy include the date as a kind of epigraph at the beginning of the poem?
2. Why is the thrush old and bedraggled?
3. Write a paper discussing the images of death, dreariness, and gloom in the poem. Conclude by showing how this imagery contributes to the effectiveness of the poem.

CHANNEL FIRING by Thomas Hardy [p. 557]

Written just prior to the outbreak of World War I, "Channel Firing" is much more than an anti-war poem. Hardy is also sharply criticizing religion for not preventing war, nationalism for causing war, and mankind for insanely participating in war. Hardy's skeptical concept of the deity is given voice in the poem, along with men who died (perhaps in some previous war) and are startled awake in their tombs by gunnery practice in the Channel. Nature, too, is disturbed by the thundering guns. God cynically assures all that the situation is normal: men are preparing for war, preparing to make the earth run red with blood, just as they have done again and again since the time of Stonehenge.

Far from being a loving God, Hardy's deity takes a perverse enjoyment in observing the disasters human beings bring on themselves; he never intervenes. "Ha, ha," laughs God, as if savoring the suffering to come after the day of judgment. "Mad as hatters," he jocularly calls warmongering mankind. Religion has been no help in stopping the madness. The dead Parson admits his preaching was wasted. The other dead have no hope that humanity will ever change. Neither has Hardy. For as the places mentioned in the last two lines suggest, mankind's "readiness to avenge" has been rampant since recorded memory and will continue till the end of time.

Questions for Discussions and Writing
1. Identify the speakers in the poem.
2. How would you describe the attitude of God toward the behavior of men preparing for war?
3. What do the awakened dead think about the firing?
4. What is the significance of the three places mentioned in the last two lines? How do they relate to the theme?
5. Write an essay focusing on Hardy's attitude toward religion in the poem.

THE WINDHOVER by Gerard Manley Hopkins [p. 558]

The ellipsis in the opening line may cause difficulty. Hopkins surely means that he caught sight of a windhover, a type of falcon that can hover on the wind. Probably the grandeur of the bird is being compared to the grandeur of Christ. "Rung upon the rein" refers to the long rein that trainers use to keep horses circling, and "wimpling" mean rippling. Critics disagree over the meaning of "Buckle!" Some read it as a buckling on (like armor) of all the qualities mentioned. Some read it as suggesting the breaking of Christ's body on the cross. Some read it as a cry asking the bird to come down to earth; others as an injunction to human beings to buckle down to their duties, to make fire flash from the plow through the "sheer plod" of their labors.

Questions for Discussion and Writing
1. What is a windhover? Does the one in the poem literally get caught or is it merely caught in the poet's sight?
2. What is the comparison being established by Hopkins here?
3. What words suggest the majesty of the bird?
4. What do you take to be the meaning of "Buckle!" in line 10?
5. Can you explain how the images in the final stanza relate to the meaning of the poem?
6. Write a paragraph in which you compare two unlike things by means of some traits

they have in common. Choose an abstraction that you will make clear in your comparison by selecting concrete things that share similarities with it (as Hopkins does by comparing the glorious majesty of Christ with the soaring bird).

PIED BEAUTY by Gerard Manley Hopkins [p. 558]

Students will probably need to look up the meaning of "pied," or they may be able to guess that it means essentially the same as "dappled." The poem praises the variety and contrasts found in nature and in the work of human hands, since all is (in the poet's view) God-given. The phrase "All things counter, original, spare, strange" suggests how interesting as well as beautiful this variety makes our lives. The beauty of the poem lies in its imagery and word choice.

Questions for Discussion and Writing
1. What words in the poem did Hopkins coin?
2. Can you describe what he means by "landscapes plotted and pieced"?
3. Why does the poet praise things made by human hands as well as things in nature?

SPRING AND FALL by Gerard Manley Hopkins [p. 559]

The poet here imagines Margaret grieving over the approaching death of nature in autumn (the grove "unleaving"—dropping its golden leaves). The syntax needs untangling in lines 3 and 4: Can you with your fresh (innocent) thoughts care for the things of man as you do for these (falling) leaves? Lines 11 through 13 are also in need of paraphrase: "Sorrow's springs are the same" suggests that even spring leads eventually to fall (death), and no mouth or mind has expressed what the heart, the spirit, can understand. "Fall" in the poem also has the meaning of humanity's fall from grace—the fall that brought death into the Garden of Eden. Thus, the "blight man was born for" is both death and original sin. So, Margaret, without knowing it, mourns her own death as well as that of the falling leaves.

Questions for Discussion and Writing
1. What does Hopkins mean in his unusual phrase "Goldengrove unleaving"? In other words, why is Margaret grieving?
2. Can you paraphrase lines 3 and 4, straightening out the syntax?
3. Does the fall of the leaves suggest any other kind of fall, perhaps a metaphorical one?
4. Can you explain why Margaret is, in effect, mourning for herself?
5. Why is the poem entitled "Spring and Fall" instead of simply "Fall"?

TO AN ATHLETE DYING YOUNG by A. E. Housman [pp. 559-60]

In this poem Housman appears to be congratulating a young athlete for having died in his prime, since his glory would have faded quickly as he aged. Presumably he is not serious in recommending early death as a remedy for loss of fame but is commenting on the way we tend to remember the best of those who die before their laurels (in the poem, wreaths of laurel bestowed on early gladiators to be worn as a crown of triumph) have faded. President Kennedy is one good example; Amelia Earhart is another; perhaps even Elvis Presley, although his laurels were beginning to go a trifle limp. You may need to explain the image in the first stanza of the athlete being carried in a chair through the town as a celebration of his prowess; he would, of course, be once more "carried shoulder-high" in his coffin. Note, too, the first stanza is in past tense, the rest of the poem in present.

See the student paper on this poem, which misses the irony. It is presented for analysis and discussion in Chapter 11 (pp. 490-92).

Questions for Discussion and Writing
1. What is "the road all runners come" in line 5? What is that "stiller town" the road leads to?
2. What is the significance of the laurel in line 11?
3. How valuable is the approbation the lad receives in the final stanza? Would it have been worth dying for?
4. What point do you think Housman is making here?
5. Write a paper comparing this poem with Emily Dickinson's "Because I could not stop for Death" (p. 568) or with John Updike's "Ex-Basketball Player" (pp. 632-33).

LOVELIEST OF TREES by A. E. Housman [p. 560]

If you ask your students to write on a slip of paper the age of the speaker in the poem, you'll probably be surprised by the variety of the responses. Perhaps they think it's a trick; perhaps they have no idea what "threescore" means; perhaps they don't know that 70 years is the expected human lifespan given in the Bible. In any event, you can use this opportunity to stress once more the need for close reading of poetry. You may also need to remind your class that cherry tree blossoms can be white, as well as pink. The poem is a lovely lyric using praise of nature's beauty to comment on the brevity of human life. Note also the suggestion of rebirth in the reference to "Eastertide" and also in the cyclical reference by which the white blooms of the first stanza become snow in the last.

Questions for Discussion and Writing
1. How old is the speaker in the poem?
2. What images connect the first and third stanzas?
3. What associations can you make with the white blossoms in the first stanza and with "snow," the last word in the poem?
4. Does the poem have a theme? If so, can you state it?

THE SECOND COMING by William Butler Yeats [pp. 560-61]

Yeats developed a complex personal mythology which sheds light on this poem, but it can be understood without special knowledge. He believed that civilizations moved in cycles of two thousand years; the passing of one and the rising of the next would be accomplished in great upheaval. Although the poem makes use of Christian imagery (appropriate to the ending of the era following the birth of Christ), the "Second Coming" anticipated in the poem sounds anything but Christ-like.

The first stanza depicts a world out of control, perfectly conveyed in the image of the falcon beyond hearing its handler. The "ceremony of innocence" (baptism) has been drowned in the "blood-dimmed tide." The lines, "The best lack all conviction, while the worst / Are full of passionate intensity," are prescient in their apt description of what happened in Nazi Germany as Hitler rose to power. The huge beast that "slouches toward Bethlehem" can be seen as fascism, which drenched much of the world in blood during World War II. Yeats, of course, in 1921, simply saw it as the coming civilization—as violent and pitiless as the one that is passing. The phrase "twenty centuries of stony sleep" refers to the pre-Christian era which was "vexed to nightmare by a rocking cradle"—by the birth of Christ, who did not, after all, prove to be the Prince of Peace.

Questions for Discussion and Writing
1. What is the state of the world being described by the speaker in the first stanza? What does "the ceremony of innocence" suggest?
2. What sort of Second Coming is being described here?
3. Why does Yeats envision the "rough beast" as coming from the desert? What associations can you make with a desert?
4. Can you explain lines 19 and 20? Whose rocking cradle is it?
5. What does the beast represent?
6. Write a paper discussing the bird imagery in the poem. Consider why the falcon/falconer image is particularly appropriate. Why is the beast accompanied by the reeling shadows of "indignant desert birds"?

SAILING TO BYZANTIUM by William Butler Yeats [pp. 561-62]

Considered one of the finest poems in the language, "Byzantium" presents an aging man's response to his loss of sexual vitality. The "country" in the first line may be Ireland, but it could also be the country in which we all must live—within our own bodies. The speaker in the poem seeks to be freed from his body, that "tattered coat upon a stick," and teach his soul to sing so that he can find satisfaction in "monuments of unaging intellect," instead of the sensual pleasures enjoyed by the young. As a metaphor to represent all artistic and intellectual accomplishment, he chooses "the holy city of Byzantium" with its gorgeous mosaics in St. Sophia's, depicting on the walls saints "standing in God's holy fire." He wants to be freed from sexual passion ("Consume my heart away; sick with desire / And fastened to a dying animal"—his body) so that he will be able to concentrate on less earthly matters. In the final stanza he asks to be reincarnated as a beautiful mechanical bird, such as an Emperor might own, to entertain the court with his song (poetry) about literally everything—past, present, or future.

Questions for Discussion and Writing
1. What does the imagery in the first stanza suggest? Why does Yeats describe the young as "those dying generations"? Do you know the Renaissance meaning for the word "die"?
2. What is that "country" referred to in the first line?

97

3. Why does the speaker want to sail to Byzantium? Can you explain what Byzantium symbolizes? Why is it a perfect choice?
4. What is the "dying animal" in line 22 that the speaker wants to be freed from?
5. Write a paper discussing how the images interrelate to give the poem an almost perfect unity.

RICHARD CORY by Edwin Arlington Robinson   [p. 562]

Part of the success of this poem lies in the way it builds to an unexpected climax. But certainly the simplicity of the speaker's diction contributes to its effectiveness, as does the spare imagery ("he glittered when he walked"), and the rhyme and rhythm. The theme addresses the problem of illusion versus reality. We are often deceived by the surface of things. Young people, for instance, often long for the life of a rock star—to be an Elvis Presley or a Janice Joplin—but when that idol dies of a drug overdose, the glittering life looks considerably tarnished. Students may state the theme as "It's better to be poor than to be rich and miserable," which is an acceptable response, but encourage them to learn to state themes in more sophisticated language. See Paul Simon's version of the Richard Cory story on p. 627.

Questions for Discussion and Writing
1. Who is the speaker in this poem?
2. What sort of person is Richard Cory? What does it mean to be "a gentleman from sole to crown"?
3. Trace the motif of images of royalty in the poem. What do they suggest about Richard Cory and those who admired him?
4. Can you state the theme of the poem?
5. Compose a poem or an essay in which you present some illusion that you accepted as truth until confronted by reality.

A MAN SAID TO THE UNIVERSE by Stephen Crane   [p. 563]

This poem puts into epigrammatic form the theme of Crane's short story, "The Open Boat": the "universe" (God) cares nothing for humanity.

WAR IS KIND by Stephen Crane   [p. 563]

By far Crane's finest and most widely reprinted poem, "War Is Kind" presents the same strongly antiwar theme as *The Red Badge of Courage*. Stanzas 1, 3, and 5 directly address those who survive war but lose those they love, whereas stanzas 2 and 4 seem to be spoken to the military (especially in lines 20-21). Notice that the meter changes in the indented stanzas, suggesting the cadence of marching men—until the final melodious line, "A field where a thousand corpses lie." The incongruity between the sound and the meaning reinforces the already acute irony of the line. Lines 25 and 26 are admired for the

98

moving simplicity of the image (the "bright splendid shroud" being the son's dress uniform) and the wonderfully effective use of alliteration. The short 3-word lines which serve as a refrain are most emphatic.

Questions for Discussion and Writing
1. Why do you think Crane indented stanzas 2 and 4?
2. In stanzas 1, 3, and 5, who is being addressed? Why did the poet write three long lines and two short ones in those stanzas instead of four long lines?
3. Why is the flag referred to as "the unexplained glory"?
4. What is the tone of the poem? And the theme?
5. Write a paragraph praising something that you detest. Remember: in writing ironically, you must exaggerate considerably to let your readers know that you couldn't possibly mean what you say.

WE WEAR THE MASK by Paul Laurence Dunbar [p. 564]

Dunbar's poem, written half a century before the civil rights movement in this country, is an anguished cry of suffering and protest. The mask worn by blacks in the poem is the pretense of happiness, which contributed to the stereotype of those happy slaves down on the plantation—an illusion accepted by some southerners to justify their racist position during the Civil War and for a long afterwards. The debt to be paid "to human guile" would be the price of using guile in order to deceive whites into thinking black people are happy. The word "subtleties" in line 5 surely means subterfuges or deviousness, as Milton used the word to depict the "subtle serpent" in the Garden.

Questions for Discussion and Writing
1. Who is speaking in the poem? Who are the "we"?
2. What does line 3 mean? What is the meaning of "subtleties" in line 5?
3. The poet doesn't say why the mask is necessary. Can you tell why?
4. How would you state the theme of this poem?
5. People often behave as if happy when secretly they are seething over some real or imagined wrong—especially people who have little power, like children, women, or the members of minority groups. If you have ever had such an experience, describe it in writing and try to explain just how the incident made you feel. How do your feelings match those expressed in Dunbar's poem?

MENDING WALL by Robert Frost [pp. 564-65]

This poem may or may not be about walls. Certainly the lines, "Before I built a wall I'd ask to know / What I was walling in or walling out / And to whom I was like to give offense," call to mind several famous walls, like the Iron Curtain, the Bamboo Wall, the Great Wall of China, and the Berlin Wall, not to mention metaphorical walls that separate people who fail to communicate or who hold opposing positions. Frost portrays the neighbor (who finds walls necessary for no good reason) in such an unflattering light that most readers fail to notice that the speaker (who wryly questions the need for walls) is not exactly rational about them himself and also that he is the one who lets the neighbor know when it's time to repair the wall in the poem. One critic has suggested that the poem is about two kinds of people: conservatives and liberals; in which case, we can perhaps safely say that the poet favors a liberal bent.

Questions for Discussion and Writing

1. Who is the speaker in the poem? What sort of person is he or she? What sort of person is the neighbor?
2. Why is the wall in the poem made of stones? [It's located in Frost's native, rocky New England.]
3. How does the speaker feel about walls? About hunters?
4. What makes this seemingly casually narrated anecdote a poem?
5. What do you think Frost's theme is?

BIRCHES by Robert Frost [pp. 565-66]

Many students will have no idea what the activity of swinging birches is, and some will not even know which kind of tree is a birch, so pictures may be useful in introducing the poem. The birch is a tall, straight, flexible tree, and it is possible to climb carefully to the thin top of the main trunk and then, flinging your body outward as a weight, make the whole tree bend down close to the ground and drop you off. In the poem, Frost uses this activity symbolically as a way of "getting away from it all" yet still feeling attached to the earth. The speaker does not wish for complete release from adult life but for a brief respite.

Questions for Discussion and Writing

1. Why does the speaker prefer to think that the birches have been bent by boys instead of by ice storms? Refer to lines 23 to 27 for his image of the boy.
2. Explain the extended comparison in lines 41 through 49.
3. Why does the speaker insist that he would want to return to earth? He says, "Earth's the right place for love." Do you agree? What does this statement imply about the speaker's philosophy of life? How do you interpret the last line in terms of how one should live?
4. What is the meter of the poem?
5. Write a short essay or long poem about some childhood pleasure you wish you could sometimes recapture.

FIRE AND ICE by Robert Frost [p. 567]

Frost here considers the two popular concepts concerning the end of the world—the Biblical apocalypse of fire and the scientific speculation during Frost's day of a gradually cooling earth ending in ice. The speaker associates the heat of passion with fire and the coldness of hate with ice. The key to the poem lies in the final coupling of "ice" with the ironic understatement of "suffice," to suggest that hate is ultimately stronger than desire.

1. Why does the persona associate "fire" with desire and "ice" with hate?
2. Why does he choose "fire" and "ice" as the two possible ways that the world might end?
3. How does the word "suffice" as a rhyme for "ice" affect the meaning of the poem?

THE ROAD NOT TAKEN by Robert Frost [p. 567]

A quick reading of the poem suggests that the persona is recommending nonconformity— take the road through life that is "less traveled by"—follow Thoreau and march to the beat of a different drum. But what, then, is the meaning of lines 9 and 10: "Though as for that, the passing there / Had worn them really about the same"? The next stanza reinforces the impression that the paths, in truth, look similar: "And both that morning equally lay / In leaves no step had trodden black." But the persona has just said he chose "the other . . . / Because it was grassy and wanted wear." Is this an unreliable narrator? Could this be a paradox? How does the persona know at the end of the poem that he "took the one less traveled by" if both paths appear the same? And why the "I— / I" near the end? Is that merely a contrivance to get the rhyme and meter right? This deceptively simple little poem can spur a stimulating discussion.

Questions for Discussion and Writing
1. What does the persona seem to be recommending in the poem?
2. Do lines 9 through 12 contradict that meaning?
3. What effect does the repetition of "I" produce in lines 18 and 19? Why do you think the poet chose the dash?
4. Write a poem of two stanzas on any subject using Frost's meter (iambic pentameter) and rhyme scheme.

DESIGN by Robert Frost [p. 568]

Frost's description of the spider in this sonnet presents the perfect image of innocence, being plump and dimpled, like a baby, and white besides. As critic Randall Jarrell notes, the spider holds the moth up, like a priest presenting a "sacrificial victim" at a Devil's Mass, and the moth is "full of the stilling rigor of death." The line, "Mixed ready to begin the morning right" makes this "witches' broth" sound like a nourishing breakfast cereal. And the flower that should have been blue has been turned to white—a white suggestive of Melville's whale. The speaker's questions in the sestet lead us to speculate on who or what controls the universe. The "design" of the death described seems so deliberate as to suggest some malevolent force "of darkness to appall" (the spider was "brought," the moth was "steered"). But perhaps even more chilling is the implication in the final line that nothing controls our fate, that there is no god, that all is pure chance.

Questions for Discussion and Writing
1. How does the title relate to the poem?

2. What associations do you get from the words used to describe the spider? How do you usually think of spiders?
3. What is the tone of "Mixed ready to begin the morning right"?
4. What do the speaker's questions lead you to consider? What answers does the poem suggest?
5. Write an essay focusing on Frost's ironic use of white in the poem.

PATTERNS by Amy Lowell [pp. 568-70]

This narrative poem, written near the beginning of the first World War, is set in an earlier period to remind us that war is a "pattern" of behavior deeply ingrained in supposedly civilized societies. Using gorgeous imagery, the poet presents a contrast between the freedom of nature and the constraints of social "patterns." Lowell chose an historical setting in England (perhaps the Renaissance or the 18th century) when women's attire was astonishingly constrictive with tight, whalebone-enforced corsets; towering powdered wigs; stiff brocaded gowns with trains; and pointed, high-heeled shoes. Men's clothing, too, at the time was cumbersome. The persona envisions her "heavy-booted lover" (line 49), with a sword, with buckles on his shoes (line 46) and buttons on his waistcoat (line 51) that bruise her tender flesh.
     Even nature has been imposed upon by humans; the garden is laid out in patterns (line 4). ("Thrift," by the way, in line 13 means a vigorous growth of vegetation.) The socially-enforced stiffness of the persona is best conveyed by her stoical response to the footman who brings news of her lover's death. She sheds no tears and has "no answer" (line 70)—just a polite, "See that the messenger takes some refreshment" (line 69). One does not weep in front of servants. "I stood upright too, / Held rigid to the pattern / By the stiffness of my gown" (lines 74-76), she explains. In contrast, earlier in the poem, the flowers in the garden are "blowing" (line 3) or they "flutter in the breeze / As they please" (lines 23-24). The water from the fountain is "plashing" (line 28) and "dripping" (line 31) and "sliding" (line 37). In her erotic fantasy, the persona becomes at one with nature and embraces with wild abandon her intended husband—who has, of course, just died "In a pattern called a war" (line 105). The persona's outburst—"Christ! What are patterns for?"—is heartfelt and invites us to question also. The poem presents a poignant protest against war—as well as against other social restrictions that limit human feeling and freedom.

Questions for Discussion and Writing
1. Can you describe the persona in the poem? Who is she? What is her social class? What news has she recently received?
2. Why is the persona's attire described at such length?
3. How many patterns can you detect in the poem?
4. Discuss the implications of line 40: "What is Summer in a fine brocaded gown?"
5. Why is war referred to as a "pattern" in line 105?
6. Consider some of the social restrictions or behavior patterns that have been relaxed in recent years. Write an essay arguing that we are better off as a result—or the reverse. Consider, for instance, social attitudes toward illegitimate children, divorce, cohabitation without marriage, being openly gay, acceptance of welfare, school dress codes.

FOG by Carl Sandburg [p. 570]

This famous poem conveys a single image without making a point or establishing a theme. In this respect, it is similar to haiku. Your students will find it instructive to compare this poem (which they probably read in high school) with the fog-as-cat image in lines 15 through 23 of Eliot's "The Love Song of J. Alfred Prufrock" (p. 578). They should easily see that Eliot presents a far better picture of the behavior of both cats and fog.

GRASS by Carl Sandburg [p. 571]

This poem can be interpreted in two ways. Some see the grass as the healer of wounds, as allowing conflicts to be forgotten so that peoples of nations formerly at war can get along with each other, even visiting as tourists. But considering that the poem was written at the end of World War I and makes reference to previous battles, that reading overlooks the obvious fact that the healing never lasts, the conflicts go on. Especially in light of all the wars fought since Sandburg wrote, the poem is more aptly read with the grass as a sinister persona—as the silent collaborator of those who wage war, enabling them to continue the ghastly carnage because people so quickly forget the bodies piled high once they are out of sight under the grass. The cool, almost smug tone of the poem supports this reading also.

Questions for Discussion and Writing
1. Who are the "passengers" who "ask the conductor: / What place is this? / Where are we now?"
2. Does the work of the grass ("I cover all") serve a useful purpose or a sinister one?
3. Can you describe the tone of the poem?
4. What is Sandburg's theme?
5. Write a paper discussing the ways in which the memorial in Washington to the Vietnam War dead differs from the usual monuments honoring dead soldiers. Consider why some patriotic groups at first were offended by the monument.
6. Compare this poem to "Facing It" by Yusef Komunyakaa (p. 629).

CHICAGO by Carl Sandburg [pp. 571-72]

Sandburg's debt to Walt Whitman is evident throughout this poem, beginning with his admiration for the subject (although it was New York, not Chicago, that Whitman loved). And Whitman loved city life for the same reasons Sandburg does: its vitality, its bustle, its excitement, its blatant maleness—"stormy, husky, brawling laughter of Youth, half-naked, sweating, proud. . ." The construction and poetic elements of the poem are also Whitmanesque: the catalogs; the balanced elements; the bold, hard images; the powerful rhythms; the deliberate repetition of words at the beginnings of lines (8-9, 26-27, 28-31). The poem seems to sprawl like the city but is really quite nicely unified by the balanced structure and by the repetition at the end of the catalog from the beginning (with slight variations) . The poem's enthusiastic embrace of the common man and admiration for masculine energy and accomplishments also capture the essence of Whitman's democratic spirit—and, one presumes, the essence of the city of Chicago not long after the turn of the century.

Questions for Discussion and Writing
1. What are the defining characteristics of Sandburg's Chicago?
2. How does he handle the city's obvious drawbacks—its violence and brutality?
3. What makes this piece a poem? That is, what elements of poetry are functioning in this unpoetic-sounding poem?
4. Write an essay discussing the effectiveness of Sandburg's personification of the city throughout the poem. Does it work throughout, or do you find it strained at times?

THE EMPEROR OF ICE CREAM by Wallace Stevens   [p. 572]

Although the poem deals with funeral proceedings, it celebrates life. Before dealing with the difficulties, you should establish clearly what's going on. The "roller of big cigars" is probably just that—a cigar maker, likely a neighbor of the dead woman, who will whip up the funeral meats, so to speak. Women will drop by the visitation (or perhaps it's a wake) in their everyday clothes, and boys will bring homegrown flowers wrapped in newspapers. The woman described in stanza two was poor, like her friends in the first stanza, to judge from the cheap, battered dresser and the home visitation. The "fantails" are pigeons she embroidered on the sheet that covers all but her "horny" feet, which bespeak age perhaps or maybe just a hard life without benefit of sufficient baths and softening creams. She is cold and dumb (mute), of course, because she is dead. Stevens explained the meaning of "Let be be the finale of seem" as ". . . let being become the conclusion or denouement of appearing to be: in short, ice cream is an absolute good," which isn't a great deal of help except that it keeps us from misreading the Emperor as death. "The poem," he goes on to say, "is obviously not about ice cream, but about being as opposed to seeming to be." The associations with ice cream are (except for its coldness) quite positive; it is delicious and always a treat. So, the Emperor of Ice Cream may represent the imperative need to get on with life's sensuous pleasures instead of dwelling morbidly on death. If anyone can figure out why those curds in the kitchen cups are "concupiscent," we would certainly be grateful to hear. Stevens said the curds merely express "the concupiscence of life," which fits our reading of the poem.

Questions for Discussion and Writing
1. What is going on in the poem? Can you explain where these people are gathering and why?
2. How much can you tell about the woman in the second stanza?
3. What kind of associations do you have with ice cream? What, then, do you suppose the Emperor of Ice Cream represents? Why is he an "emperor"? [Could it be that he knows how to move people via the pleasure principle?]
4. Can you describe the tone of the poem?
5. What might be its meaning?

ANECDOTE OF THE JAR by Wallace Stevens   [pp. 572-73]

Stevens wrote in a letter that he always felt two ways about Tennessee, and "Anecdote of a Jar" is easier to understand armed with this knowledge. The jar, a human-made object, gives order to the wilderness around it, just as artists create order from disorder, meaning from meaninglessness. It is round (the perfect shape), tall, and "of a port" (meaning "of import"). So far, so good. In the third stanza, though, the more negative side of the organizing jar comes through. It "took dominion," rather bossily, and "was gray and bare" in contrast to the fertile wilderness. The jar is utterly wrong for the setting: "like nothing else in Tennessee." Perhaps the artist violates the subject of art. The reader needs not decide between the two facets of the jar, since Stevens did not. Consider that an *anecdote* is usually a story with a humorous or unimportant meaning.

Questions for Discussion and Writing
1. What is an anecdote? How long is it, usually? What, in general, is the purpose of an anecdote? How seriously is it meant to be taken?
2. Give a description of the jar. Describe the wilderness around it. What are some differences between the jar and the wilderness? Which seems more powerful?
3. Wallace Stevens wrote in a letter that he always felt two ways about Tennessee. Do you think he feels two ways about the jar, too? What positive and negative effects does the jar have upon the wilderness?
4. Develop an explanation of the poem based on the jar as "art" and the wilderness of Tennessee as "nature."

DANSE RUSSE by William Carlos Williams   [p. 573]

Presumably the poem is called "Russian Dance" because the Russians dance with a wonderful abandon, as does the speaker in the poem. The time is early morning, with the sun just rising through the mist, as he revels in his total freedom of expression achieved by being alone. His dance, both sensuous and self-centered, expresses his happiness in simply being himself as well as in being by himself while living in a household peopled by a wife and children. By declaring himself the "happy genius of my household," he envisions himself as the lucky icon, a sort of god-figure, who in certain cultures is in charge of keeping everyone in the family contented. The space before the last two lines gives emphasis to the speaker's final statement as well as separating the description of his activities from his observation concerning them.

Questions for Discussion and Writing
1. What does the French phrase *Danse Russe* mean? Why do you think Williams chose that title for his poem?
2. Where is the speaker and what time is it?
3. Why is he dancing naked?
4. Why do you suppose Williams left the space before the last two lines?
5. Does the poem have a theme? State it.

THE RED WHEELBARROW by William Carlos Williams [p. 573]

This piece, which has both baffled and delighted many readers, belongs to the school of imagism discussed in the text in connection with H. D.'s poem "Heat." What makes Williams's poem more puzzling than most imagist poetry is the first two lines: "so much depends / upon," a statement that seems to demand an interpretation. *What* depends upon this wheelbarrow and these chickens, students will want to know. One writer suggests that it could be "the sheer joy of the poet at bringing the outside world into the poem and thus into relation with himself." Another finds the poem sentimental: "At its worst this is togetherness in a chickenyard." X. J. Kennedy reveals the circumstances under which the poem was written: Dr. Williams, he says, supposedly "was gazing from the window of the house, where one of his patients, a small girl, lay suspended between life and death." Knowing the occasion of the writing, observes Kennedy, allows us to read it as "a kind of prayer, a work of compassion." But since the poem itself provides no clue to the situation underlying its composition, you may want to consider whether it is successful or sentimental or simply incomprehensible.

Questions for Discussion and Writing
1. Does the poem need to be interpreted, or should readers just enjoy the sharply revealed images?
2. What makes this a poem? Do you consider it a successful one?
3. Write a paper in which you discuss the difference between the images in this poem and those in a poem where the images carry the meaning of the work, like Blake's "London" (p. 539), Whitman's "A Noiseless, Patient Spider" (p. 497), or Sandburg's "Grass" (p. 571).

PIANO by D. H. Lawrence [p. 574]

The persona, like the boy in Joyce's short story "Araby" (p. 295) recalls a childhood emotion from the vantage point of an adult's perspective. The poem hovers on the verge of sentimentality but is saved from it by the specific images that recreate for readers what he felt as a child—the joy and warmth and security associated with his loving mother. The woman singing in the first line triggers with her soft singing these memories of his mother. He manfully struggles to resist "the insidious mastery of song" but the sound "betrays me back." Eventually—despite the singer's change from a soft song to a loud lively one, played with feeling—the speaker can't keep from dissolving in tears. Even though he is aware that his recollections are nostalgic and heightened by memory ("the glamour of childish days is upon me"), he nonetheless cries "like a child for the past."

Questions for Discussion and Writing
1. Where is the speaker in the first line of the poem? In line 3?
2. Who is the woman in the first line? In line 4?
3. Why does the speaker say the music "betrays" him back to his childhood?
4. The speaker resists crying because in 1918 it was considered unmanly to weep. Does he try for any other reason to stem "the flood of remembrance"?
5. Is this poem sentimental? If not, why not?

SNAKE by D. H. Lawrence [pp. 574-76]

The realistic presentation of the snake's visit results from Lawrence's having experienced this brief episode while living near Mt. Etna in Sicily. Since snakes carry several archetypal meanings, the poem invites multiple interpretations. Because of the serpent in the garden, snakes are associated with evil, often with Satan (this one comes from "the burning bowels of the earth"). Snakes are also phallic symbols and, as such, associated with power, vitality, and the life force. Lawrence's snake also carries an air of mystery, a god-like majesty (until frightened, when he "convulsed in / undignified haste"), which may also be associated with the phallus. And primarily, Lawrence's snake is poisonous, hence dangerous. The speaker has good reason to be frightened of him, but the speaker's response is ambivalent. He says, "I liked him" but then confesses, "I was most afraid, / But even so, honoured still more"; he scares the snake away, then he wishes he were back. When the snake starts to depart, the speaker becomes agitated and feels, "A sort of horror, a sort of protest against his withdrawing into that horrid black hole." A psychoanalytic critic would surely see in that line the fear of the male of being engulfed by the female. But the speaker is sorry afterward and feels he has some "pettiness" to expiate for having frightened "one of the lords of life." The confusion of the speaker may reflect his own confusion concerning the nature of evil. If the snake represents Satan, the speaker's attraction to and at the same time repulsion by evil is a typical human reaction. Or his conflicting responses to the snake may mirror his ambivalent attitude toward his own sexuality.

Questions for Discussion and Writing
1. Carefully notice all of the associations that Lawrence attaches to the snake. What are the snake's main attributes?
2. What are the various responses of the speaker to the snake?
3. Can you account for the persona's fondness for the snake even though he knows it to be poisonous and dangerous?
4. What is the significance of the reference to the albatross in line 66? [Coleridge's Ancient Mariner was cursed for injuring an albatross, a creature embodied with the life force, like Lawrence's snake.]
5. Write a paper examining and explaining the symbolic significance of the snake in this poem.

IN A STATION OF THE METRO by Ezra Pound [p. 576]

Notice that this imagist poem, unlike Williams's "Red Wheelbarrow," asks for no interpretation. It simply records the poet's impression of an experience in Paris, one which he described this way: "I got out of a 'Metro' train at La Concorde, and saw suddenly a beautiful face, and then another and another, and then a beautiful woman, and I tried all that day to find words for what this had meant to me." He first produced a thirty-line poem, then reduced it to these two memorable juxtaposed images.

Questions for Discussion and Writing
1. What does the term "apparition" mean? Why is it a perfect word choice?
2. What are the two metaphors coupled in the poem?
3. What does the second line tell you about the faces in the first line?

4. Try to convey your own impression of a memorable moment in two brief lines using primarily imagery—no verbs and, if possible, no use of *like* or *as*.

THE RIVER-MERCHANT'S WIFE: A LETTER a translation by Ezra Pound [pp. 576-77]

Pound's poem, almost a paraphrase rather than a translation, reflects his poetic sensibilities as well as those of the original author. The poem is admired for its simplicity and total absence of sentimentality. The opening line refers to the traditional way in which little Chinese girls have their hair cut. So, we know that the persona played with her present husband when they were children, was married to him by family decree rather than by choice at fourteen, and at fifteen fell in love with him ("I desired my dust to be mingled with yours / Forever and forever and forever"). Now the speaker is sixteen, and her husband has gone on a business trip. We know she misses him because the cheerful chatter of monkeys overhead is to her a "sorrowful noise." Obviously she is lonely because the moss has grown under the unopened gate. But her desire to see him again is so strong that she will leave her cloistered home and come to meet him—undoubtedly a daring and brave act on her part. The details about her shyness in stanza two reinforce how eager she is now to be reunited with her "Lord" in order to go out of her sphere.

Questions for Discussion and Writing
1. Can you tell what the first line of the poem means?
2. What details let us know that at age fifteen the speaker fell in love with her husband to whom she was married at fourteen?
3. What sort of life does the persona lead? How can you tell? What kind of person is she?
4. What details indicate how much she misses her husband now? Why is her suggestion that she will come to meet him particularly touching?
5. What does the poem tell you about the position of women in Chinese culture at the time the poem was written?

THE LOVE SONG OF J. ALFRED PRUFROCK by T. S. Eliot [pp. 577-80]

The persona is walking through a rather rundown section of London to a highly fashionable, late afternoon tea at which he arrives just as the poem ends. Once students discover that the speaker is talking to himself, that he is both the "you" and the "I," the poem becomes manageable. They may also need help in seeing the "love song" of the title as ironic since it is clearly not a love song at all but a wimpy debate about whether he dares to ask the lady an "overwhelming question"—probably whether he might sit beside her or take her to dine or some such inconsequential thing. Since the whole comic but somehow touching scene depends upon Prufrock's self-centeredness, coupled with his exaggerated fears of inadequacy, you might start with a thorough discussion of his character, beginning with his name (a "prude" in a frock coat, which happens to be what he is wearing). The poem doesn't reveal much about the lady he wishes to approach, but the response expected from her (in lines 96-99) suggests she has a demeanor of bored sophistication (which is reinforced by the refrain, ". . . the women come and go / Talking of Michelangelo"). So, poor Prufrock talks himself out of even asking her and resigns himself to walking alone on the beach, convinced that he will never hear the mermaid's sexy song. The "human voices" of the last line are the voices he hears upon arriving at the party, waking him from his reverie to "drown" in the sea of people among whom he feels so inadequate. Despite the comic tone, Eliot is seriously criticizing the triviality and sterility of the society presented here.

Questions for Discussion and Writing
1. Who is speaking in the poem and to whom?
2. What is the situation depicted?
3. What sort of person is J. Alfred Prufrock? Why is he so wary about going to this party? Why does he consider parting his hair behind? What does it mean to measure out one's life with coffee spoons? Why do women make him so nervous? Why does he think he should have been a crab, "Scuttling across the floors of silent seas"? Why does he exaggerate so? Is he right in deciding that he's more like Polonius than Hamlet? Why does he wonder if he dares to eat a peach? Why does he decide the mermaids will not sing for him?
4. The poem at first seems disjointed. Can you see any way in which it is unified?
5. Can you explain the last three lines?
6. Write an essay discussing how the sea functions as a controlling image in the poem. Or write an essay showing how the epigraph provides a clue to the narrative technique.

AMERICA by Claude McKay [p. 581]

McKay is another black writer, like Paul Laurence Dunbar, who was expressing his resentment at the treatment of blacks in America long before the Civil Rights movement. In this sonnet the feelings of the persona are ambivalent: he loves the land that oppresses him and will not cry out against it. Instead, he delivers a warning: he sees the strength of America being undermined, worn down, by racial injustice (as a granite monument is eroded by the winds of time) and warns that the country cannot survive it. He predicts that her "granite wonders" (those splendid monuments, especially the Lincoln Memorial, which signify the ideals embraced by the country in theory but not in practice—liberty, equality, justice for all), those "priceless treasures," are crumbling and will end up "sinking in the sand." His tone is fervent but rational—and remarkably unresentful.

Questions for Discussion and Writing
1. Who is speaking in this poem?
2. Explain the metaphors in the first three lines.
3. What does the speaker love about America? What does he regard as a threat to her strength?
4. What are the "granite wonders" of line 10? What do they signify?
5. Can you describe the tone of this work?

WHAT LIPS MY LIPS HAVE KISSED by Edna St. Vincent Millay [p. 581]

Many poems lament a lost love, but this sonnet seems sadder than most because the persona laments the loss of love itself. The images perfectly reinforce her melancholy, her recognition that love may never return again: the rain, the ghosts, the tree—in winter silent of birds. This loss is more final, more irreparable, than the loss of a specific lover (whom she might hope to replace). She mourns "unremembered lads" who, like the birds, have "vanished one by one." The final image suggests Shakespeare's "thy eternal summer shall not fade," but Millay's summer (her delight in sexual love) has faded, and the poem offers little hope that the warmth of passion will return.

Suggestion for Discussion and Writing
1. Discuss imagery in the poem, especially the contrast between the winter images at the beginning and the "summer" of the last two lines.
2. How does sound reinforce the meaning and contribute to the tone of sadness?
3. Write a paper comparing this poem with "They Flee from Me" by Thomas Wyatt (p. 529).

OH, OH, YOU WILL BE SORRY FOR THAT WORD! by Edna St. Vincent Millay [pp. 581-82]

In this sonnet the speaker comes to the realization that her husband is perhaps more "enemy" than "friend" when he takes away her book and insults her intelligence (in line 5). Her strategy for dealing with him is to pretend for the present to be the pretty bubblehead that he apparently thinks he married. But she will also be "crafty, soft and sly," for she plans, on some otherwise ordinary day, to leave him flat. We may be quite sure that when he whistles, she will not come back. "Prink" (line 6) is an earlier form of "primp," a term applied only to females, meaning to fussily touch up makeup and hairdo.

Questions for Discussion and Writing
1. Why is the speaker in the poem angry?
2. What does she plan to do in response to the insult?
3. What is the speaker's tone in ll. 5 and 6? Read the lines aloud in the appropriate tone.
4. In 1923 when the poem was written, what qualities would have been expected of "a wife to pattern by" (line 11)?
5. In the final line, what does the speaker imply that her role as wife is similar to?

FIRST FIG by Edna St. Vincent Millay [p. 582]

This delightful little verse praises hedonism. One might call it a *carpe diem* poem with Millay seizing the night instead of the day, which is appropriate since we associate romance and revelry with night rather than day. She borrows Shakespeare's metaphor of life as a candle and adapts it to suit her meaning of getting as much pleasure as possible out of living, even if it means enjoying a briefer span. The "lovely light" makes the trade-off worth it.

Questions for Discussion and Writing
1. Explain the metaphor in this little poem.
2. What is the attitude of the speaker? How do you know?
3. Why is the poem called "First Fig"?

DULCE ET DECORUM EST by Wilfred Owen   [pp.582-83]

Owen died in the trenches near the end of World War I not long after writing this
powerful poem, which was published posthumously. The persona describes weary troops
slogging through the mire (which often literally sucked the boots off their feet) away from
the front, so exhausted that they fail to hear the "hoots" of the gas canisters dropping just
behind them. These canisters have spent their fuel; thus they, like the men, are exhausted
("tired") after their journey through the air. One soldier fails to struggle into his gas mask
in time, and his death throes—described in telling detail—haunt the persona. The last
lines condemn the ancient practice of glorifying war (in epic poems, in popular songs, in
heroic monuments, in John Wayne movies, in patriotic speeches) that for ages has served
to fire the ignorant enthusiasm of young men to seek the "desperate glory" mendaciously
associated with war. (Students may remember Crane's "unexplained glory" in "War Is
Kind" [p. 563] and Henry Fleming in *The Red Badge of Courage*, who at the beginning of
that novella was desperate for glory.)

Questions for Discussion and Writing
1. Can you explain what "Five-Nines" are? Why does the persona describe them as
   "tired"?
2. Why is the man in stanza two described as "drowning"? What is that "green sea"
   actually?
3. What is the "desperate glory" mentioned in line 26? Can you think of any examples of
   it in literature you have read?
4. Do people still tell "the old Lie" today? If not, can you figure out why?
5. Write an essay comparing this poem with Richard Lovelace's seventeenth-century
   work, "To Lucasta, on Going to the Wars" (p. 536).

IN JUST- by E. E. Cummings   [p. 583]

On first reading, the lively and energetic sounds of this poem suggest the celebration of
spring and the innocent fun for children that comes with this season. However, the
strange little balloonman holds a mysterious power over the children with his whistle "far
and wee," reminding some readers of the Pied Piper, who led all the children out of
Hamlin. Be sure that your students understand that in this context, the word *queer* meant
odd or strange, not homosexual, or they may come to some misguided conclusions about
the poem's meaning. Sexuality, for sure, is what must be associated with the balloonman
due to his identification with Pan. The separate, gendered activities that the children come
running from emphasize their separate realms of play, which they leave behind to heed the
balloonman's whistle. Spring, of course, is also associated with sexual activity, so it
seems clear that under the playful tone lies an end-of-innocence motif.

Questions for Discussion and Writing
1. Which children's names are run together? Which are separated? What activities are each pair engaged in when they heed the balloonman's whistle? Considering your answers to these questions, what does the poem emphasize about the children?
2. What do you know about the goat-footed god Pan? If you can't place him, look him up. Why is the balloonman described as Pan-like?
3. What is the powerful whistle that makes kids come running from their play? In other words, what is calling "far and wee" to the children? The change in the typography of balloonMan in line 21 may give you a clue.
4. What effect do the unusual line division and spacing have when you read the poem? For example, if you were reading the poem aloud, how would you intone and pace the last three words?

NEXT TO OF COURSE GOD AMERICA I by E. E. Cummings [p. 584]

By the end of the poem, we realize that it is a political speech, given perhaps at a campaign rally. The high-sounding illogic of it is simply an exaggeration of the empty and frequently contradictory rhetoric found in patriotic diatribes. The lack of punctuation and meaningless line breaks emphasize the smooth flow of nonsense pouring from the speaker's lips. The last line points up the speaker's blustery style and also his comfortable position (in contrast to the boys who died in the war).

Questions for Discussion and Writing
1. Point out several patriotic clichés in the long quotation from the political speech. Why are they jumbled together, without conventional punctuation? Which ones contradict each other?
2. What does the last line of the poem reveal to you?
3. This poem by Cummings is a parody of a patriotic speech. Try writing a similar parody of a speech or conversation you frequently hear—a phone call from your parents, a neighborhood gossip, a locker room chat.

SHE BEING BRAND by E. E. Cummings [pp. 584-85]

In this poem Cummings humorously describes a young man's experience of driving a new car in terms that suggest he is initiating sex with a woman (for the first time with her). Since cars (and ships and airplanes) are commonly referred to as "she," this risqué comparison works almost perfectly from foreplay to climax. (It seems unlikely, though, that he would have "felt of her radiator" with a car.) The poem is full of ribald innuendo and double entendre, some of which may be too bawdy to discuss in class ("oiled the universal joint," for instance, and "barely nudging my lever"). But students enjoy figuring out the comparison and are pleased by understanding the double meanings without help.

Questions for Discussion and Writing
1. What two activities are being compared in the poem?

2. Point out and explain (if not too embarrassing) several words or phrases that carry a double meaning.
3. Discuss how the punctuation and placement of lines on the page enhances the narrative.
4. Write a paper comparing this poem with Sharon Olds's "Sex Without Love" (p. 626).

PITY THIS BUSY MONSTER,MANUNKIND by E. E. Cummings [p. 585]

The enemy in this poem is "Progress," presented as a high-technology spiritual void, in which modern science performs miraculous feats that are ultimately meaningless. "Progress" is described as "a comfortable disease," but a fatal one. The poem suggests that humans have lost their place in the natural world by trying to control and analyze it. The clever wordplay emphasizes the negativity (un-ness) of science-mad humanity.

Questions for Discussion and Writing
1. How does the speaker define "Progress?" What extended metaphor is used?
2. What does the poem suggest about technological advancement? Write a short essay agreeing or disagreeing with the point of view.
3. List quirky words in the poem. Write an essay explaining how unusual words add to the meaning of the work.

REAPERS by Jean Toomer [p. 586]

"Reapers," with its steady rhythm and onomatopoetic *s* and *c* sounds, drives home the inexorable process of the world's work. Students may need to look up reapers, scythes, and hones to visualize the poem's images. The slaughter of the field-rat makes the work seem heartless, as do the silence and the color black. The fact that Death is called "The Grim Reaper" must come into play here. The poem is an excellent example of crystallized imagery.

Questions for Discussion and Writing
1. Read the poem aloud. Notice several patterns of sound. How do they relate to the picture described in the poem?
2. Does the speaker of the poem, the viewer of the scene, see life as a joyful romp, a dashing adventure, or a predetermined grind? How do you know?
3. Death is sometimes called "The Grim Reaper." Do you think Toomer had this in mind when he wrote "Reapers"? Why?

DAYBREAK IN ALABAMA by Langston Hughes [p. 586]

The power of this poem lies in its lovely imagery, which equates racial harmony, a beautiful dawn, and music. A certain pathos is created by our feeling that the speaker,

113

who speaks in a non-standard, childlike idiom, has hopes of "when I get to be a composer" which are just as unlikely to be fulfilled as a dream of amity among the races.

Questions for Discussion and Writing
1. In the speaker's view, what is "natural"?
2. What is the speaker of the poem like? How do you think he is different from the poet, Langston Hughes?
3. Write a poem or essay about something that you would like to capture in music if you were a composer.

MOTHER TO SON by Langston Hughes   [p. 587]

This poem is a fine example of an extended metaphor: the implied comparison between life's progress and climbing a stair carries through the entire poem. "Mother to Son" consists of one long stanza, but asking your students to divide it into stanzas will produce a discussion of the three basic parts of the poem. The first section describes the mother's hard life; the second section suggests the growth and discovery she has nonetheless experienced; and the third section attempts to persuade the son to persist toward his own goals. The image of the "crystal stair" standing for an easy life may be unfamiliar to your students, but visualizing it will convey the meaning clearly.

Questions for Discussion and Writing
1. What is the extended metaphor in this poem? Who is the speaker, and what has her life been like? What would a "crystal stair" life be like?
2. Break the poem into three stanzas. Explain why you divided the lines as you did.
3. How is the relationship between the mother and son here traditional? Is it unconventional in any sense? What does the mother want the son to do, and why?
4. What do you think of Hughes's use of dialect in the poem? Did you find it distracting? What function does the dialect serve?

HARLEM (A DREAM DEFERRED) by Langston Hughes   [p. 587]

The "dream deferred" in the poem is, of course, the same dream that the Rev. Martin Luther King later made the centerpiece of his famous "I Have a Dream" speech: the dream of equality in American society. The poem suggests through metaphor the psychological damage of unrealized hopes—of promises given to African Americans and not fulfilled, going all the way back to the forty acres and a mule promised to each black family following the Civil War. The simple structure, the spare diction, the scabrous similes, the stunning last line, all mesh perfectly to produce a poem of remarkable power and portent. Read it aloud for full effect.

Students may be interested to know that Lorraine Hansberry chose the second line from this poem as the title of her play, *A Raisin in the Sun,* in which she elaborates on the themes expressed in the poem. The play appears in the drama anthology on pages 1011-1066.

Questions for Discussion and Writing
1. What is the "dream deferred," mentioned in the opening line?
2. What effect do all the visual images describe?
3. How do these consequences culminate in the meaning of the final line?
4. Examine the similes Hughes employs to evoke the effects of the deferred dream, and write an essay discussing the social implications these images convey.

THEME FOR ENGLISH B by Langston Hughes [p. 588]

Students enjoy this poem because they've probably received an assignment like the English teacher gives here. The contrast between the English teacher's assumptions and the student writer's is clear. The belief that what comes out of you is by its nature true sounds strange to the student. In his theme, he experiments with different ways to describe himself: the details of his physical situation, his likes and dislikes, the difference in race between him and his classmates and teacher, his citizenship, and so on. It seems that he stops in relief when he reaches the bottom of the page.

Questions for Discussion and Writing
1. What would you write if you had the assignment that the speaker's teacher gives the class? How would you decide what to include?
2. What is the student's attitude toward the assignment? How can you tell?
3. The teacher says, "And let that page come out of you—then, it will be true." What do you think she means by this? What ideas about writing does she probably hold?
4. Do you think the racial difference is an important part of this poem? Or do you think the main point is about how the teacher and the student look at things differently?

THE NEGRO SPEAKS OF RIVERS by Langston Hughes [p. 589]

The key to this poem is understanding who the "I" is that is speaking. Because of the various time periods, we know that it cannot be one person, though the title says "The Negro." Therefore, "The Negro" must stand for the whole race. The traditional symbolic meanings of the river are those of rebirth (as in baptism) and of the journey of life. Perhaps in this case, Hughes was writing about the journey of a whole race. The poem embraces a sense of racial history as soul-deepening.

Questions for Discussion and Writing
1. Do some research on the proper names used in the poem. Who is W. E. B. Du Bois, and why is the poem dedicated to him? What do the place names have in common?
2. Look carefully at the experiences listed in stanza 2. Could they just as effectively be listed in another order? Why or why not? Why are these specific activities listed?
3. Compare and contrast "Harlem" (p. 587), "Theme for English B" (p. 588), and "The Negro Speaks of Rivers." What conclusions can you come to about the importance of a poem's narrator?
4. What is a soul that "has grown deep like the rivers"? What do you associate with rivers? What symbolic meaning do rivers frequently have?

NOT WAVING BUT DROWNING by Stevie Smith   [p. 589]

This poem concerns the difference between public image and inner reality. On a literal
level, the drowned man (who, given poetic license, may speak for himself), was
misinterpreted in his death throes; other people thought that he was cheerily waving.
Even when these people find that he's dead, they misinterpret the cause of death. The
dead man takes his insistence to a metaphorical level, saying that he was alienated and
misunderstood all his life.

Questions for Discussion and Writing
1. Who are the two speakers in the poem? How does one misunderstand the other?
2. The lines "I was much too far out all my life / And not waving but drowning" are
    obviously meant to carry more than a literal meaning. What does the dead man mean?
3. In what ways might your outward demeanor be contrary to the "inner you"? Write an
    essay about how you or someone you know might give a false impression to others.

INCIDENT by Countee Cullen   [p. 590]

This simple lilting poem conveys a grim experience: a young boy's introduction to
mindless racism. Although he is unfamiliar with the other boy's ugly reaction, somewhere
deep within he understands how devastating and pervasive it is. It blots out nine months
of experience in Baltimore. Of course, racist attitudes will shadow the speaker's life
forever.

Questions for Discussion and Writing
1. Though the main point of "Incident" is unstated, its theme is clear. How would you
    state it in a sentence?
2. "Incident" is very simple in form and language. Why do you think the author chose
    this simplicity?
3. Write an essay about your own introduction into a part of the adult world that you
    weren't aware of as a child or youth.

THE UNITED FRUIT CO. by Pablo Neruda   [pp. 590-91]

Students need some basic understanding of colonialism to grasp this poem. Many may not
understand how the move to a corporate-run cash economy affects a small country in
every way. Clearly, Neruda sees the effects as ugly. After Chile's heroic fight for
independence, he is aghast at its new enslavement to entities like the United Fruit
Company, which objectify the culture and people. The images of rotten fruit and
swarming flies reinforce the horror.

Questions for Discussion and Writing
1. What is surprising about the opening of the poem? What would you expect after
    reading the first three lines?

2. What has corporate colonialism done to Chile, in the speaker's view? What is associated with the flies and the fruit?
3. Who are Trujillo, Tacho, Carias, Martinez, and Ubico? Compare this list of specific names with the description in the last stanza.

MUSÉE DES BEAUX ARTS by W. H. Auden [pp. 592-93]

A reproduction of Brueghel's painting *The Fall of Icarus* appears above the poem on p. 592; many of the details mentioned in the poem are in the painting. Other paintings referred to are Brueghel's *Nativity* and *The Martyrdom of St. Stephen*. The poem takes up the "human position" of mythic events, saying that even as a miracle or tragedy is in progress, for most people everyday life is continuing as usual. The sense of historical relativity is reinforced by the mundane specific details, and whether so-called earthshaking events really are that momentous is called into question.

Questions for Discussion and Writing
1. What are the two kinds of events contrasted in this poem?
2. Compare the painting *The Fall of Icarus* (p. 592), the story of Icarus, and the poem. What are some similarities and some differences?
3. Find in a book or gallery a painting that appeals to you; write a poem or story about it.

STOP ALL THE CLOCKS by W. H. Auden [p. 593]

Auden's charming tribute to a dead (or perhaps only departed) lover gives modern voice to the traditional classical elegy in which a friend or admirer makes extravagant pleas that all of nature should mourn in respect for the departed—that stars no longer shine, rivers no longer flow, breezes no longer blow. Auden playfully requests signs of mourning both modern and distinctly urban: clocks, telephone, black-gloved traffic policemen, and (a witty touch) "crepe bows round the white necks of the public doves. Here instead of imploring the heavens to mourn, Auden would send airplanes to announce in skywriting his lover's death.
     The tone is light, almost humorous, yet somehow the poem is still touching, especially the last two stanzas. Anyone who has lost a lover has felt the same. (And line 12 does suggest that the lover has left rather than died: "I thought that love would last forever: I was wrong.") To some readers, the images may seem exaggerated even in these final stanzas—but not to those recently bereft of love. The poem has acquired some fame of late by its recitation in the popular film *Four Weddings and a Funeral*. And your students may be interested to know that the lover Auden mourns was surely not a woman, but a man.

Questions for Discussion and Writing
1. What is a poem called that mourns and honors someone who has died? Is this one typical of the genre?
2. Do you think the lost lover in this poem is dead or merely departed?
3. What is the tone of the poem? What are your clues?

117

4. Do you think that the poem is just a parody, or do you think that Auden truly cared for his lost love? What makes you think so?
5. Write an elegy of your own—serious or playful—about a person (or a pet) you loved and lost.

DOLOR by Theodore Roethke   [p. 593]

Roethke, who once was a lively and engaging teacher, is perhaps expressing his sadness about the deadening conformity and monotony of so many classrooms. One can also see the catalog of objects and the monotonous rhythm as conveying the "endless duplication of lives" (line 8) of office workers. Ironically, the only thing alive in the poem is the dust, "Dropping a fine film on . . . the duplicate grey standard faces" (lines 12-13).
    One critic notes that Roethke's lines 1 and 9 echo a couple of Eliot's memorable lines in "The Love Song of J. Alfred Prufrock" (p. 577):
        And I have known the eyes already, known them all—
        And I have known the arms already, known them all—
and
        I have seen the moment of my greatness flicker,
        And I have seen the eternal Footman hold my coat and snicker.
The dolorous tone is similar in both poems also.

Questions for Discussion
1. What is the setting of the poem?
2. How does the rhythm reinforce the meaning?
3. Do you see any irony in lines 9-13?
4. What word would you choose to describe tone in this poem?
5. What is the theme?

I KNEW A WOMAN by Theodore Roethke   [p. 594]

This poem draws its strength from its many evocative comparisons. The woman is compared to a goddess, a bird fancier, a dancing teacher, a sickle, a goose, and a musician, to name a few. The speaker is obviously obsessively in love with her, but at least sees the humor in his own obsession. Notice that we almost always see the woman in motion; thus Roethke avoids the traditional objectification of the beloved woman.

Questions for Discussion and Writing
1. List some of the things that the woman is compared to. What do they have in common? What comparisons strike you as unusual in a love poem?
2. Explain the image of the sickle and rake in stanza two.
3. Write an essay explaining how the speaker of the poem gently makes fun of himself for his obsession with the woman.

ONE ART by Elizabeth Bishop [pp. 594-95]

This poem is a tightly crafted villanelle. Bishop manages to say something worthwhile while adhering to the tricky rules of this form, which requires using only two rhymes and repeating two of the lines according to a set pattern. Line 1 is repeated as lines 6, 12, and 18; line 3 as lines 9, 15, and 19. The first and third lines return as a rhymed couplet at the end. The rhyme scheme is aba (abaa for the last stanza). Bishop varies line 3 as she repeats it; she also uses ingenious rhymes ("last, or" in l. 10) and off rhymes ("fluster" and "gesture") to meet the demands of the very limited rhyme scheme.
        The poem's meaning is also somewhat tricky. On the literal level the speaker seems to say that it's easy to lose things (it's something you can "master"—or learn to deal with) and that loss is not "disaster." But as the poem progresses and the losses move from the trivial (keys) to more significant things (time, beloved places, a loved one), we realize the speaker is being ironic, that losing is difficult and not something one can "master" (except to ignore or accept the losses). The parenthetical imperative in the last line suggests that the speaker is forcing herself to admit that some losses are indeed disastrous.
        The references to a lost "continent" and a lost love may be personal: Bishop lived for many years with a lover in Brazil and wrote this poem after she returned to America.

Questions for Discussion and Writing
1. What is the form of this poem? What effect does the repetition have on the tone and point of the poem?
2. What experiences does the poem relate?
3. What kinds of loss does the speaker mention?
4. Is losing an art? Is it really "easy"? How does one "master" it? Has the speaker mastered it?
5. What is the significance of the parenthetical command "(*Write* it!)" in the last line?
6. Compare this poem to Dylan Thomas's "Do Not Go Gentle into That Good Night" (p. 598), another villanelle.

AIDS by May Sarton [pp. 595-96]

Sarton explores the ways in which the unfailingly fatal disease of AIDS affects everyone. The "we" of the poem clearly includes AIDS victims and their friends and lovers; your students may also point out that the society in general has been challenged by the epidemic. The seeming oxymoron of "reckless design" is reflected in the subtle and irregular rhyme scheme of the poem. The speaker grapples with the strange mixture of "despair and hope" that the disease evokes and actually manages to end on a positive note, suggesting the renewal of love.

Questions for Discussion and Writing
1. Who is the "we" referred to in the poem?
2. When the friend in stanza 4 says, "I go where I have never been," what does he mean? How does his experience relate to the rest of the poem?
3. "AIDS" includes two unusual one-line stanzas. What is the effect of these stanzas? Why are they set off from the other lines?

4. What does the line "We are blest" mean? How does the speaker manage to pull a positive meaning out of the AIDS experience? Do you know of other, similar experiences which bring about "a new grace"?

THOSE WINTER SUNDAYS by Robert Hayden [p. 596]

This poem is about the expression of love, as is clear from the last line. The father's thankless and painful work to nurture his family is presented as a repeated ritual. The image is unusual, since it is conventionally mothers that do the unregarded labor which children grow up to recognize as valuable. On the other hand, the inability to communicate feelings verbally, which we see between men in this poem, is typically male. See the published critical article "The 'Banked Fire' of Robert Hayden's 'Those Winter Sundays'" by David Huddle in Chapter 13.

Questions for Discussion and Writing
1. The speaker is clearly looking back at a pattern of life he experienced as a child. What does he know now that he didn't know then?
2. What kind of home was the speaker's? How do you know?
3. What are the various expressions of love? Which ones are "lonely and austere"?
4. What is the religious meaning of the word "office"? How does that connotation fit the use of the word in this poem?

THE DEATH OF THE BALL TURRET GUNNER by Randall Jarrell [p. 596]

Your students will probably need an explanation of a ball turret gunner to visualize the action of this poem. The ball turret is a windowed machine gun nest hanging from a bomber plane. One small man and two machine guns squeezed inside. The turret could rotate to track attacking planes. The poem's image is of the gunner as an unborn animal in the womb. The first person point of view makes the closing especially unexpected. See the first exercise in "Experimenting with Poetic Forms," p. 518, which deals with the word choice in this poem.

Questions for Discussion and Writing
1. The concepts of sleep and waking, dreams and nightmares, and life and death are important in this poem. How are they interrelated?
2. What is the State in line one? Why is it capitalized?
3. What makes the closing line so disturbing?

TO THE MERCY KILLERS by Dudley Randall [p. 597]

This powerful rejection of euthanasia is a Shakespearean sonnet. The strong language, as well as the concise form, lends the poem its vigor. The speaker clearly feels that despite the outward appearance of suffering and the experience of pain, there is something still valuable in life, which should not be cut short.

Questions for Discussion and Writing
1. Point out the ironic word choice in the first two lines of the poem.
2. Why does the speaker want to be allowed to live even when enduring the horrors he describes? Do you agree with his position?
3. What is the implied comparison in the last line?
4. Write a short response in which you agree or disagree with the poem's main argument.

TRAVELING THROUGH THE DARK by William Stafford [p. 597]

The moral ambiguity behind our everyday decisions is exemplified in the speaker's encounter with the dead deer on the road. He needs to do a violent act in order to save drivers behind him who might cause more death by swerving to avoid the deer on the narrow road. These drivers are humans like whomever has shot or run into the deer in the first place. Human needs and goals, signified by the loving description of the car, take precedence over wilderness ways, signified by the doe's pregnancy. These are probably some of the hard thoughts the speaker refers to in the last stanza.

Questions for Discussion and Writing
1. Brainstorm about what interpretations of the poem's title are possible.
2. Why does he roll the dead deer into the canyon? Does the doe's pregnancy make any difference?
3. The poem includes vivid details about the speaker's car. How do they add to your understanding of the poem as a whole?
4. Look carefully at the last stanza. What do you think the speaker "thought hard" about? Who are "us all"? Why does he call his thought "my only swerving"? In the first stanza, he thinks about rolling the deer "into the canyon"; in the last stanza, he uses the words "into the river." Do you see a reason for the change in phrasing?

THE FORCE THAT THROUGH THE GREEN FUSE DRIVES THE FLOWER by Dylan Thomas [p. 598]

The first two stanzas of this poem set up the basic idea that all of nature, including humanity, is driven by the same powerful life force. Throughout, the poem refers to the speaker's inability to communicate with the other elements of nature, perhaps a frustration for a speaker invented by a poet, to whom communication is paramount. The third and fourth stanzas continue the life force idea but in images a bit more obscure and with more of an orientation toward death. The death images are repeated in the final two lines, which suggest a kinship that all mortals have with death.

Questions for Discussion and Writing
1. How would you define the force that the speaker insists runs throughout nature?

2. Divide the images in the poem into two groups, images of growth and life, and images of death and decay. Which receive more emphasis? Can you explain this in the context of the poem's meaning?
3. What is the meaning of the repeated words "I am dumb"? Why is it a key phrase in interpreting the poem?

DO NOT GO GENTLE INTO THAT GOOD NIGHT by Dylan Thomas [pp. 598-99]

This poem was addressed to Thomas's dying father. One interesting thing about it is its complex form; it's a villanelle, which you may want to define for your class. The poem basically exhorts the father not to accept death passively. Stanzas two through five give examples of people who admirably fight death: wise men (writers, philosophers), good men (philanthropists, social reformers), wild men (poets, artists), and grave men (scholars, perhaps religious philosophers).

Questions for Discussion and Writing
1. What do the repeated images, "That good night" and "Dying of the light" stand for.
2. What repeated pattern can you see in stanzas two through five? What kinds of people are described in these stanzas?
3. Explain the seeming contradiction in line seventeen.

FERN HILL by Dylan Thomas [pp. 599-600]

This poem, with its odd syntax and quirky use of language, is best grasped when heard. Then, the joyful rhythm and shower of imagery overtake the rational explication (which will often be foiled). The poem expresses the speaker's attitude toward his childhood on his aunt's farm, which was secure, joyous, close to nature, and, as suggested in stanza four, Edenic. In stanza five, a new undercurrent appears in phrases like "my heedless ways" and "so few and such morning songs," implying that childhood's end is coming. It does, in stanza six, and the closing is poignant but not bitter.

Questions for Discussion and Writing
1. What was the speaker's childhood like? What were some of his pleasures?
2. What comparison does the imagery in stanza four suggest?
3. What does the speaker feel about the end of childhood? How can you explain the seeming contradictions of "green and dying" and "sang in my chains"?

SADIE AND MAUD by Gwendolyn Brooks [pp. 600-01]

This poem is dated in an interesting way. Clearly, the speaker thinks Sadie, who "stayed at home" and bore two out-of-wedlock children, had a better life than Maud who "went to college." That "Ma and Papa / Nearly died of shame" seems quaint, even hard to believe today. But at the time Brooks wrote this poem, she felt the proprieties governing the lives of young women were too restrictive—as they were. Today, many people think we have moved too far in the other direction, since the cost of caring for literally thousands of out-of-wedlock children has become a heavy social burden.

Stanza four implies that Sadie's girls will follow their mother's lifestyle, not their aunt's, since Sadie "left as heritage / Her fine-tooth comb" (lines 15-16). That comb is the emblem of Sadie's irrepressible (irresponsible?) lifestyle, as "one of the livingest chits / In all the land" (lines 7-8). The word "chit" means an immature young girl.

Questions for Discussion and Writing
1. What is the attitude of the speaker toward each young woman, Sadie and Maud?
2. What was Sadie's heritage, symbolized by her "fine-tooth comb"?
3. What is the meaning of the poem?
4. Do you agree with Brooks's theme? Why or why not?
5. Write a poem about Sadie and Maud in which Maud, the one who goes to college, has the better life.

THE BEAN EATERS by Gwendolyn Brooks [p. 601]

Perhaps inspired by Picasso's "The Frugal Repast," this poem also paints a picture of a poverty-stricken couple who continue to live after life has lost its zest. Reminders of their past surround them in their "rented back room," but the overall tone remains grim.

Questions for Discussion and Writing
1. Why is the couple eating beans? How do you know?
2. What overall impression does the list at the end of the poem give you?
3. Why does the writer include the phrase "Mostly Good"? Why aren't the people described as "Good"?
4. Write an essay in which you relate the couple in this poem to the couple in the story "A Summer Tragedy" by Arna Bontemps (p. 333).

CONSTANTLY RISKING ABSURDITY by Lawrence Ferlinghetti [pp. 601-02]

"Constantly Risking Absurdity" is an extended metaphor comparing a poet to a circus performer who risks absurdity (such as a clumsy misstep) and death (such as a fatal one). These seem to represent the two kinds of error that a poet can commit—being unintentionally laughable or totally lifeless and unmoving. The comparison also suggests an element of exhibitionism and trickery in both pursuits. The poet seeks Beauty by taking the way of truth, perceiving truth accurately, presenting it in an entertaining and arresting way to the audience.

Questions for Discussion and Writing
1. How is writing poetry like being a circus performer, according to the poem? What are the dangers? How does the writer risk absurdity and death?

123

2. Explain the arrangement of lines. What element of the poem does it seek to emphasize?
3. What is a "charleychaplin man"? What does the description say about poets?
4. In the speaker's opinion, what is the purpose of poetry? Point out which lines provide evidence for your answer.
5. What kind of poem fails in its acrobatic performance? Can you find an example in this book or elsewhere?

THE GOOSE FISH by Howard Nemerov   [pp. 602-03]

This narrative poem has a formal rhyme scheme (aababccdd) and regular rhythm that are reminiscent of a ballad, as is the tale. The story is an example of dramatic irony, in which we, watching the scene, are led to understand quite a bit more than the lovers do about their situation. The lovers decide that the goose fish is a special optimistic sign, while the speaker leads us to believe that the situation is laughably common, sordid, and trivial in the big scheme of things.

Questions for Discussion and Writing
1. What happens in the poem? Tell it in story form.
2. What relationship are the lovers in? How do you know? Look at the author's word choices to help you decide.
3. Why does the appearance of the goose fish disconcert the lovers? How do they finally interpret the sudden turning up of the dead fish? How does the speaker lead us as readers to interpret it?
4. What is the "joke" in line 41? Do lines 43-45 help explain what it is?
5. What do the words "goose" and "fish" mean when they are applied to people? Do these meanings function in terms of the poem?

LOVE CALLS US TO THE THINGS OF THIS WORLD by Richard Wilbur   [pp. 603-04]

Your students will be lost if they have never seen the laundry hung out to dry between tall apartment buildings in the city. Because the dwellings are so high, the clotheslines are strung between buildings across the light courts, and the clothes are pinned, item by item, to the line out of an open window and then fed out into space by means of pulleys. When dry, they are taken in using the pulleys. The speaker of the poem describes waking to see the garments moving with the wind and the operation of the pulleys. Still half-asleep, he has a vision of heavenly purity and joy; as he awakens, he accepts the colorful, flawed real world.

Questions for Discussion and Writing
1. In what state of consciousness is the speaker when his eyes open at the beginning of the poem? How might this account for what he sees out the window? What meaning does he assign to what he sees?
2. How do you respond to the word *rape* in line 19? Can you speculate on why the writer chose such a strong word there?

3. Describe the shift between stanzas 4 and 5. What is happening to the speaker? What is the difference between "the soul" before and after this shift? Which relates to the title, the first or second state of consciousness?
4. What additional meanings can you ascribe to the "difficult balance" in the last line ?

HOME IS SO SAD by Philip Larkin [p. 604]

Several readings of this poem are possible, depending upon whose home this was. Of course, it is Everyperson's home (the universal idea of home), but whose point of view are we hearing? Is this the home of a mother whose children have grown and moved away, leaving her "bereft / of anyone to please" (lines 3-4)? Have the former inhabitants perhaps died, leaving the house "bereft" of their presence? The personification of the house serves to make the reader feel somehow that this family was valuable, that they are missed by the house itself is touching.

The "joyous shot at how things ought to be / Long fallen wide" (lines 7-8) suggests that the aim of the family to be happy went wide of the mark. Yet the images following—"the pictures and the cutlery. / The music in the piano stool. That vase"— seem deliberately ordinary and functional. The implication may be that no family achieves a bull's eye with that shot at complete harmony, making the family who once lived here not dysfunctional but simply a typical one.

Questions for Discussion and Writing
1. Whose home is being described in the poem?
2. What effect is gained by the personification of the house?
3. Do you think the family was happy or otherwise?
4. Write a poem about your home, personifying the house to show how it might respond to activities of your family.

THE LEAP by James Dickey [pp. 605-06]

The speaker of the poem has vivid memories of seventh grade when he reads in the newspaper that an old classmate has killed herself. The visual imagery stands out in this poem—the racing children, the clumsy dancers, the dusty playground, and both leaps. The speaker wants to remember Jane as a lively, spontaneous seventh grader and is sad to hear that the "eternal process / Most obsessively wrong with the world" dragged her down so. He clearly feels his own age and mortality when he finds out Jane's fate.

Questions for Discussion and Writing
1. What does the title of the poem mean?
2. What happens to boys and girls around seventh grade? What images show that the narrator here is aware of the significance of the time his memory reconstructs?
3. What is the "eternal process / Most obsessively wrong with the world"? What does the narrator think happened to Jane? What personal meaning does her suicide hold for him?
4. Why does the speaker examine his own hands at the end of the poem?

O TASTE AND SEE by Denise Levertov   [p. 606]

The persona muses on a subway Bible poster and transforms its meaning on her own terms, probably quite different from what the Bible promoters meant. She defines "Lord" as "all that lives to the imagination's tongue," taking off from the exhortation, "O taste and see." Her sensualist and transcendental interpretation culminates with an allusion to a Garden of Eden where plucking and eating the fruit is the right thing to do. Your students may find the poem easier to follow if they imagine that the words "if anything" in line 6 are punctuated on both sides by commas.

Questions for Discussion and Writing
1. The first line of the poem is an allusion to Wordsworth's "The World Is Too Much With Us" (p.540). Reread both poems. All in all, do you think that the speaker in Levertov's poem disagrees with the speaker of Wordsworth's? Why or why not?
2. What is the personification in lines 6 and 7? Can you develop its meaning in a sentence or two?
3. Explain the choice of details in lines 8 and 9. Is it a complete list?
4. To what Bible episode do lines 14 through 16 allude?
5. Is the speaker's point of view on the holy way to live in accordance with the agenda of the Bible poster? Explain your reasoning.

THINGS by Lisel Mueller   [pp. 606-07]

This poem ponders the human tendency to project familiar characteristics onto other things, even when it's a stretch to do so. Your students may be familiar with the psychological term *projection*, a defense mechanism in which we assign our own feelings and motivations to other people: for example, an angry person sees other people as angry, a victimized person sees others as victims, and so forth. In the poem, Mueller sees our projection of our own bodies onto objects as stemming from some of the same defensive functions—to escape loneliness and danger.

Questions for Discussion and Writing
1. What is the tone, or voice, of the poem? Look especially at the first line for information about how it is to be read. Also consider the level of the vocabulary used.
2. Why do we use human words to name the parts of objects, according to Mueller?
3. What are the examples in the last stanza of things that are "beyond us"? Why are these more beyond us than the examples in the other stanzas?
4. Give some other examples of how we humanize non-human objects. Do you agree with Mueller's explanation of why? What are some examples of how we project our own characteristics onto other people?

O BRAVE NEW WORLD, THAT HATH SUCH PEOPLE IN IT by Lisel Mueller   [p. 607]

The title is taken from Act 5, Scene 1 of Shakespeare's *The Tempest*. In this scene, the nubile Miranda first lays eyes on a group of men together. She has spent her life on an enchanted island with only her father, Prospero, the spirit Ariel, and the monstrous Caliban as examples of males. When she sees the shipwrecked newcomers, she exclaims, "How beauteous mankind is! Oh brave new world / That has such people in it!" She marries one of them and joins the world beyond the magical island. In this story, Mueller seems to see the story of every girl, who leaves an enchanted state of freedom to serve an ordinary man.

Questions for Discussion and Writing
1. Who is "you"? What is fated for her? What age and sex do you think is the speaker of the poem? Why?
2. Contrast the worlds presented in stanza 1 and stanza 2. What is the speaker's preference? What will be the girl's preference?
3. The title is a quotation from Shakespeare's *The Tempest*. Review Act 5, Scene 1 of the play to see why the author made this choice. How does it explain the world of stanza 1?
4. What analogy is developed in stanza two?
5. What is "the one flawless place," in the speaker's opinion?

WOODCHUCKS by Maxine Kumin   [pp. 607-08]

This poem has an easy conversational style and an unusual, inconspicuous rhyme scheme (abcacb). These fit with its offbeat subject—getting rid of the woodchucks who are eating the garden. The speaker first tries a cyanide bomb. When that doesn't work, she resorts to shooting the woodchucks one by one, which brings out a side of her that she didn't know about and is not very comfortable with. The effect of coming face to face with the prey instead of having them "die unseen" haunts her.

Questions for Discussion and Writing
1. What kind of person is the speaker of the poem before she starts shooting woodchucks? What details let you know?
2. What side of her does the killing bring out? How is the order of the killings significant?
3. Why does the speaker assert that it would be better if the woodchucks had "consented to die unseen"?

APRIL INVENTORY by W. D. Snodgrass   [pp. 608-09]

The title holds a key to this poem; the speaker is doing a kind of spring housecleaning of his life so far. In contrast with the recurrent spring and the continual youth of his students, he feels his own age progressing steadily. He has not been a big success in the academic world: he suggests that he has found scholarly pursuits dry and meaningless. However, on a note of hope, he feels that he has learned and taught some things of value in his life, mostly about people and nature. He even doubts whether he could see the loveliness and gentleness around him if he were a successful "specialist."

Questions for Discussion and Writing
1. What do the words in the title suggest? What is the speaker doing an inventory of?
2. What is contrasted with the students' youth? What is contrasted with scholarly knowledge? What is the speaker's attitude toward scholarly pursuits?
3. What does the speaker think is truly of value in life?

A SUPERMARKET IN CALIFORNIA by Allen Ginsberg [p. 610]

Walt Whitman (1819-1892), addressed in this poem, was the major poetic influence on Allen Ginsberg. Both American poets share a lively democratic sense, an exuberant celebration of nature, and a free verse rejection of poetic conventions (and most others). Both revel in sexuality and left-wing political ideas. Both write poetry marked by lists or catalogs of details piled enthusiastically upon each other. "A Supermarket in California" was written 100 years after Whitman published his famous and infamous *Leaves of Grass*. These facts explain much about the "Supermarket" poem.

Questions for Discussion and Writing
1. Look up short biographies of Whitman and Ginsberg. What similarities exist between the two poets? How much time elapsed between their works? What light does your reading throw on "A Supermarket in California"?
2. Look up Charon and Lethe, and explicate the last paragraph of the poem.
3. What does the speaker mean by "the lost America of love" (line 11)?
4. Imitating Ginsberg's freewheeling form, write a fantasy about you and one of your heroes in a supermarket.

AUTUMN BEGINS IN MARTINS FERRY, OHIO by James Wright [pp. 610-11]

This poem, which associates the coming of fall with the opening of football season, suggests a cause-and-effect relationship between the dreary realities of the parents' lives and the way their teenaged sons play football. The fathers, working their jobs or lingering over beers, dream of heroes, and the mothers long for love. The speaker believes that the sons see their only chance at heroism and love on the football field; they fling themselves wildly into the fray. The fact that in the midwest, October brings the last beautiful weather before winter sets in parallels the barely pre-adult age of the football players.

Questions for Discussion and Writing
1. Who is the "I" of the poem? What is he doing?
2. What do the men described in lines 2 through 4 have in common? What kind of lives do they have? What kind of heroes are they dreaming of?
3. Who are the women in the second stanza? What does the image of "starved pullets" mean to you?
4. The third stanza begins with the word "Therefore," stating a cause-and-effect relationship. What is the cause-and-effect relationship in the poem? What do you make of the phrase "suicidally beautiful"? What does the speaker believe about football?

YOU ALL KNOW THE STORY OF THE OTHER WOMAN by Anne Sexton [p. 611]

"She" in the poem is the other woman, the mistress of a married man. And the story, of course, is that she is a convenience, bound to ignominious secrecy and ultimate disappointment. "A little Walden" compares the love nest to Thoreau's idyllic retreat from civilization, but, as we find out in line 5, "it's a bad translation," not quite idyllic. All the comparisons emphasize the brevity and fleeting nature of the lovers' encounter, as well as the objectification of the woman, which is crystallized in the final simile.

Questions for Discussion and Writing
1. Concentrate on the title. Do you all know the story of the other woman? What is "the conventional wisdom" about what happens to the other woman?
2. This poem depends on metaphors and similes for its meaning. Identify and explain five of them. Why does the last simile make the point unmistakable?
3. How does the man behave after he has had sex with the woman? Write a paraphrase of lines 6 through 14.

CINDERELLA by Anne Sexton [pp. 611-14]

Your students will probably enjoy this revision of the Cinderella story. By the closing, they will perceive what the narrator really thinks about the story: that it is purely fictitious. Through the use of humorous comparisons and side remarks to the reader, the speaker makes it clear that she takes the whole thing with a grain of salt. The final line emphasizes the narrative as a *story*, not true to life. There is an underlying bitterness toward the story, as though it misleads young girls into believing such things really happen.

Questions for Discussion and Writing
1. What do the stories in the first four stanzas have in common? How are they related to the Cinderella tale?
2. How does "Cinderella" differ from the usual telling of the tale? Does it differ primarily in content or in style?
3. Most readers find this poem at least somewhat funny. What is the source of its humor?
4. What attitude toward the Cinderella story does the poem project? How can you tell? Is there a serious point as well as a humorous one?

LIVING IN SIN by Adrienne Rich [p. 614]

This poem vividly defines the contrasts between the woman's expectations of "living in sin" and the rather grim reality. Her romantic vision is supplanted by a scruffy everydayness, with cockroaches, squeaky stairs, loud plumbing, and a lackadaisical lover. The piano isn't the only thing that's out of tune. The woman's disappointment subsides in the evening, when she is "back in love again," but the closing image of the impending morning foretells another day of disappointment.

Questions for Discussion and Writing
1. What two things are being contrasted in this poem? Which part is emphasized? Why?
2. How does the final image unify the poem and reinforce its meaning?
3. Write about an experience in which you expected one thing and got quite a different one.

AUNT JENNIFER'S TIGERS by Adrienne Rich [p. 615]

The controlling image of the prancing tigers serves both to unify the poem and to amplify Aunt Jennifer's plight in her oppressive marriage. The gorgeous tigers, "proud and unafraid," provide a sharp contrast with the woman who created them with her "terrified hands." Unlike the tigers, who "pace in sleek chivalric certainty," Aunt Jennifer "flutters" under the domination of her husband. Although absent from the poem, the husband's domineering presence is felt in "The massive weight" of the wedding band that "sits heavily" on her hand. Unlike the tigers, who "do not fear the men beneath the tree," Aunt Jennifer was "terrified" into submission by unnamed "ordeals she was mastered by." In the last stanza we see that Aunt Jennifer will escape her confined, fearful existence only in death, but her spirited tigers "Will go on prancing, proud and unafraid."

Questions for Discussion and Writing
1. What human traits do the tigers possess? What kind of life do they lead? What does "prancing" suggest?
2. What kind of life does Aunt Jennifer lead? How do the tigers help you to understand her plight? Why might she have chosen them for her tapestry?
3. What does Aunt Jennifer's wedding band symbolize? What is a wedding ring supposed to symbolize?
4. Although her husband never appears in the poem, what can you tell about him from the poem?
5. Write a paper analyzing your response to the tigers in the last stanza, still "prancing, proud and unafraid." Are you comforted that Aunt Jennifer's artistic creation will live after her? Or are you sad that she was so unlike her tigers?

MIRROR by Sylvia Plath [p. 615]

The mirror in this poem is personified, given a human voice to express its point of view on its important role in the woman's life. In the first stanza, the mirror acts as a truthful "little god," and in the second stanza it acts as a reflecting lake which contains both the past and the future. Both the god and the lake images connote power, which mirrors certainly have over people, especially women. The poem is basically free verse, but all lines contain five stressed syllables in a kind of sprung rhythm.

Questions for Discussion and Writing
1. Consider the use of personification in this poem. What difference would it make if the mirror had no voice: for example, if the poem began, "The mirror is silver and exact. It has no preconceptions"?

2. What reason can you see for the stanza division? What two characters does the mirror choose to describe itself?
3. Why does the mirror call candles and the moon "those liars"?
4. Write a poem or essay from the point of view of some nonhuman object that has importance in your life. Use personification to give the object its own voice.

METAPHORS by Sylvia Plath [pp. 615-16]

"Metaphors" does have many qualities of the riddle—the pattern of suggestive comparisons leading to the answer, the reflexive form (nine lines of nine syllables, a line and syllable for each month of pregnancy). Though many people see the poem as a light hearted comment on the state of pregnancy, negative images dominate, and the last three lines seem quite resentful. The joke, it appears, is not funny.

Questions for Discussion and Writing
1. What *is* the answer to the "riddle in nine syllables"? How is the poem like other riddles?
2. How many nines can you find in the form of the poem? [The word "Metaphors" has nine letters; there are nine lines, each composed of nine syllables.]
3. The tone of this poem is a matter of debate. Some readers see it as a light-hearted acceptance of the awkward pregnant state, while others see it as grimly fatalistic. What do you think? Give support from the poem.

DADDY by Sylvia Plath [pp. 616-18]

The two main allusions in the poem are to Nazi authoritarianism and to vampire lore. The Nazi and the vampire, both victimizers, are associated with the speaker's father and, later, a husband who was like him. The speaker is the victim; thus, she identifies herself as a Jew. The tyrannical father continues to plague her long after he is dead, and the speaker has to kill off both her father and her husband in her own psyche to be free of them.

Questions for Discussion and Writing
1. What are the two main historical (or literary) phenomena that you need to know in order to understand the poem? What do they have in common?
2. What different things has the speaker done to try to free herself from her father's tyranny?
3. List some words which describe the tone of the poem.
4. Critic A. Alvarez describes "Daddy" as a love poem. How do you react to that designation?
5. Write an essay considering whether you will ever be free of your own parents.

131

EX-BASKETBALL PLAYER by John Updike   [p. 618]

Though aging ex-cheerleaders are a common target of sympathy, ex-basketball players rarely get much. This poem chronicles in rich detail the dead-end life of a man whose only golden moments were as a sports star—and that, only in a small-town high school. Your students may know such a person. The details, which give the poem its authentic flavor, also date the poem, and your students may need to see pictures of old-fashioned gas pumps to enjoy stanza two. A good companion poem is "To an Athlete Dying Young" by A. E. Housman (p. 559).

Questions for Discussion and Writing
1. What is the story of Flick Webb's life? How do both his first and last names fit his life story?
2. Who is the narrator of the poem? How old is he? Where does he live?
3. Though the poem has no regular rhyme, it follows patterns. Explain the logic of the stanza breaks and line breaks.
4. See whether you can write a description of some familiar part of your home town with as much detail as Updike gives in this poem. You might add a town character if you know one.
5. Compare this poem to A. E. Housman's "To an Athlete Dying Young" (p. 559).

ETHICS by Linda Pastan   [pp. 619]

"Ethics" looks back upon a classroom experience that the author has found memorable. She clearly brings forth the students' feelings of restlessness and half-heartedness. She remembers when she would imagine her grandmother as the old woman and a time when she devised a clever answer. When, many years later, the author finds herself in almost the same scene as the ethics question involved, she thinks about how the question missed the point. Everything is inexorably headed toward oblivion, beyond ethics.

Questions for Discussion and Writing
1. Who is the "I" in the poem? How can you tell that the narrator is most likely Linda Pastan?
2. How did the students respond to the teacher's ethical question? What details show how they felt? Did the teacher ask the same question every year? Did the narrator take the same ethics class every year?
3. The year that Linda asked her clever question, how did the teacher answer? Was it a good answer, do you think?
4. What does the narrator, as an adult, think about the teacher's question? Explain the last sentence.
5. Write a poem or essay about a classroom experience that stands out in your memory. Include at the end what you think of the experience now that you are older.

PREFACE TO A TWENTY VOLUME SUICIDE NOTE by Imamu Amiri Baraka [pp. 619-20]

The title provides an important key to this poem. The writer has obviously decided to put off committing suicide for quite a while, since twenty volumes take a long time to write. If we identify the speaker with the poet, we can see the poet's life work as a long suicide note. Lines one through eleven described the perceptions of a person having a breakdown. The rest of the poem seems to give a reason for not committing suicide: either the sweet vulnerability of his daughter or the fact that her perceptions, too, are offbeat. Both reasons may apply.

Questions for Discussion and Writing
1. What is peculiar about the title of the poem? When is the writer going to commit suicide?
2. What is the writer experiencing in the first eleven lines of the poem?
3. What effect does the vision of his daughter have on the writer?

BIOGRAPHY by Imamu Amiri Baraka [pp. 620-21]

This chilling poem attempts to capture the hanging death of the speaker's grandfather. The title implies that the victim's whole life is captured in the scene. The confused images reflect the nightmarish quality of the event, in the same way a filmmaker might use frantic splicing of shots. We can follow the focus from the hanging itself, to the Klansmen riding away laughing in the moonlight, back to the lonely figure as it "hangs / hangs." The shape of the poem on the page reproduces the image of something or someone hanging.

Questions for Discussion and Writing
1. How did the grandfather die? Who killed him? How do you know?
2. Point out places where the images do not fit together logically. How can you account for the author's use of confused images? Rewrite part of the poem in usual prose form (you will probably have to do some filling in).
3. What is the dictionary meaning of *biography*? What does the word suggest as a title for this poem?
4. Why are the words arranged on the page the way they are?
5. Write an account of how someone died or of some other intense experience, using a form and style like Baraka's in "Biography."

HANGING FIRE by Audre Lorde [pp. 621-22]

This poem is an insightful reproduction of the train of thought of a fourteen-year-old female. The mixture of everyday worries ("I have nothing to wear tomorrow") and deep anxieties ("will I live long enough / to grow up") as they run through her mind is humorous but true to life for adults as well as teenagers. The refrain emphasizes that she feels a lack of attention from her mother. However, given the rest of the evidence, we are not sure whether her mother is knowingly neglecting her (in the bedroom with a lover, some readers believe) or whether the speaker is momentarily frustrated with her mother's absence and responding in an exaggerated way. The title has to do with firearms that fail to go off—"hanging fire." These guns are dangerous because they might explode at any time.

Questions for Discussion and Writing
1. Do you think that the teenager's thoughts in this poem are true to life? Can you remember similar thoughts when you were around fourteen? What kinds of concerns does the speaker have?
2. Find out what the title means. How is it appropriate for the poem and the speaker?
3. What do you think of the refrain ("and momma's in the bedroom / with the door closed")? Is the speaker a victim of neglect?

BARBIE DOLL by Marge Piercy [p. 622]

Though this condemnation of sex role expectations may seem heavy-handed to older students, younger ones usually appreciate it. The Barbie Doll is a perfect symbol of utterly unobtainable female appearance: if you have such a doll, you might measure the body parts and note the odd proportions of torso to leg, leg to neck and head, waist to bust, and so on. The girlchild in the poem is well socialized into her role, and the discovery that intelligence, strength, personality, and charm-school self-improvement cannot redeem her "big nose and fat legs" drives her to suicide—or perhaps plastic surgery, a metaphoric death which "cuts off" the ugly parts and destroys her original looks (and her identity?). She looks perfect in her casket (her new self?), though, dressed in a nose and nightie like Barbie's.

Questions for Discussion and Writing
1. What led to the suicide in the poem? Is it an actual suicide? What else could it be?
2. Why is the poem titled "Barbie Doll"? What qualities do you associate with Barbie?
3. What does the poem say about the connection between looks and personal identity?
4. This poem was written in 1973. Could it have been written yesterday? In other words, do you think girls' socialization has changed very much since 1973?

THE WOMAN IN THE ORDINARY by Marge Piercy [pp. 622-23]

This poem contrasts the inner and the outer woman within one character. The theme is clear: a powerful person is hidden by an outer demeanor of self-effacement and conformity. The interesting element is the imagery associated with each side. The outward woman is called a "girl" and described as "ivory soap," "pebble smooth," and "a Christmas card virgin." The inner woman is described with noisy, strong images and complex ones like "acid and sweet like a pineapple." True to this complexity, the last two lines compare her to a bomb and a flower—but the flower is one that causes strong allergic reactions in many people.

Questions for Discussion and Writing
1. Who is "the woman" in the poem? Who is "the girl"?

2. List the images associated with each side of the person in the poem. What contrasts are made?
3. How does "the girl" behave? Why? Is she a hypocrite? If so, can you excuse her?
4. Reread the last two lines. How can these two comparisons work together? Are there similarities as well as differences between a handgrenade and goldenrod?

THE LOVER NOT TAKEN by Blanche Farley   [p. 623]

Unlike "My Last Duchess" and "My Ex-Husband," "The Lover Not Taken" and "The Road Not Taken" (p. 567) are quite different in tone. Though it is a parody of the Frost poem, Farley's "The Lover Not Taken" borrows lines and phrases but puts the speaker in a completely different situation, choosing a lover rather than a life path. The speakers' characters contrast, as well, in that the speaker in this poem seems to be selfish and superficial, while Frost's narrator is portrayed as deep. You may want to make overhead transparencies of the Frost poem and the Farley poem, and look at them side by side in class.

Questions for Discussion and Writing
1. Compare this poem to "The Road Not Taken" (p. 567). What is different in tone, character, form, and content? What effect do the differences have on how you read the Farley poem?
2. Underline or list phrases lifted and nearly lifted directly from the Frost poem. How does the new context affect your interpretation of the words?
3. What is the speaker's ultimate argument for the action she takes? How is it different from the decision of the Frost persona?
4. If "The Lover Not Taken" were not clearly a parody of the Frost poem, would it stand on its own as a good poem? Explain your opinion.

DIGGING by Seamus Heaney   [p. 624]

The speaker in this poem admires the work done by his forefathers, who were potato farmers. Their strength and skill and their connection to the earth make him nostalgic. Male virtues are venerated in the competition of cutting turf and in the way the grandfather tosses off his milk and returns to work without missing a beat. The speaker, a writer, has a pen instead of a spade to assert his manhood; the opening image of the pen as a gun supports this line of interpretation in an unsettling way. Other poems about writing: "Constantly Risking Absurdity" by Lawrence Ferlinghetti, "Theme for English B" by Langston Hughes, "Nuns Fret Not" by William Wordsworth.

Questions for Discussion and Writing
1. What does the speaker of the poem admire about his forefathers? Make a list of the qualities he seems to revere.
2. Do you have any feelings about carrying on the work of your parents or grandparents? Do you think most people do?

135

3. The speaker has chosen a profession very different from potato farming. He implies, though, in the last line, that it is similar. How is it the same?
4. How can you fit in the disturbing image in the first two lines with the rest of the poem?

ELEANOR RIGBY by John Lennon and Paul McCartney [p. 625]

The song consists of a series of images of loneliness, alienation, and meaninglessness. Eleanor Rigby and Father McKenzie live quietly desperate lives with neither human nor divine comfort. You may want to bring a tape of the Beatles song into class; the music poignantly supports the lyrics. Students who are dubious about their ability to understand a poem frequently feel comfortable interpreting popular song lyrics.

Questions for Discussion and Writing
1. How would you describe the overall tone or mood of the poem? Point out elements that enhance the mood.
2. Explain how each image relates to the theme of loneliness expressed in the refrain.
3. Does the poem support religion as providing hope for "the lonely people"? Give evidence for your answer.
4. How would you compare "Eleanor Rigby" to "Richard Cory"—both the Edwin Arlington Robinson poem (p. 562) and Paul Simon's song version (p. 627)?

THE DEATH OF MARILYN MONROE by Sharon Olds [p. 626]

Students need to understand what happened to Marilyn Monroe: she committed suicide by overdose at the age of 36 after many years of being a major sex symbol. Many commentators explain her suicide by the pressures of such fame and the relentlessness of the public gaze, which precluded a strong inner sense of selfhood. Some speculated that her death involved foul play by one of her powerful lovers who wished her silenced. Monroe was confined to being a fantasy woman rather than a real flesh and blood person, more public property than private human being.

Questions for Discussion and Writing
1. In the first stanza, why does the writer choose the specific physical details of Marilyn's body?
2. How would the ambulance men carry her "as if it were she" (line 9)? Is it not "she"? Why would they carry her this way, knowing she was dead?
3. Why do you think the men always went out for a drink or two after their duties? What purpose did this routine serve?
4. How did the various men respond to their experience? What responses to unusual experience does each man represent? In particular, consider the last man described. Why is the woman he listens to described as *ordinary*?

SEX WITHOUT LOVE by Sharon Olds   [pp. 626-27]

The main difficulty in reading this poem is construing the tone or attitude of the speaker. Our own preconceptions about sex without love get in the way of clearly perceiving what the speaker's point is. Some of the images have a positive bent—the ice skaters, dancers, great runners, and true religious. There is also an attractive realism to those who have sex without love. Other images, though, are negative, like "fingers hooked / inside each other's bodies." Perhaps the speaker herself is struggling with mixed feelings on the issue. Some readers believe that the poem takes place during a sex act, citing lines 8-10 as the point of orgasm.

Questions for Discussion and Writing
1. What other kinds of people are those who have sex without love compared with? Would you call these comparisons positive, negative, or mixed?
2. What do you think is the speaker's attitude toward people who have sex without love? What in the poem contributes to your opinion?
3. What ideas about love and sex are challenged in this poem?

RICHARD CORY by Paul Simon   [pp. 627-28]

The obvious thing to do with this song lyric is to compare it with E. A. Robinson's version, "Richard Cory." Listening to the Simon and Garfunkel recording will be useful in the comparison, for there the bitterness of this version is clear. The Cory of Robinson was actually a gentleman, while the Cory of Simon is a playboy sleaze. Even his charity seems designed to elicit thankfulness and admiration rather than to relieve suffering. The persona in the Simon version hates Richard Cory, while the persona in the Robinson version adulates him. Both speakers are puzzled by Cory's suicide, but for different reasons.

Questions for Discussion and Writing
1. Compare this lyric with the original by E. A. Robinson (p. 562). What are the differences between the personae and between the Cory figures in the two versions?
2. What difference in tone do you see between the Robinson and Simon versions of "Richard Cory"? Does the difference in time of composition (1896 and 1966) account for the change?
3. Choose a different poem from the nineteenth century or early twentieth century and write a modernized version, perhaps for a rock group to perform.

DREAMS by Nikki Giovanni   [p. 628]

This poem is quite straightforward if the references are clear. The Raelets and Majorie Hendricks are well-known, flamboyant rock and jazz singers. The quotations are from their songs. The wistfulness of losing childhood dreams and settling for less is emphasized by the last line, which is also the title of a famous song.

Questions for Discussion and Writing
1. What youthful hope did the speaker hold? What image do you think she had of herself when she daydreamed?
2. Why does the speaker believe that black people aren't supposed to dream?
3. What youthful hope or aspiration did you have to give up? Why did you give it up? Write an essay.

LIFE IS A NICE PLACE by Louise Glück   [pp. 628-29]

This poem provides an example of an extended metaphor: the comparison between life and a fancy party continues throughout the parenthetical interruption. The style of this part imitates a gushing Hollywood gossip, a style ironically superficial considering the depth of the real subject. The frame statement, "Life is a nice place to visit. But I wouldn't want to live there," can be interpreted several ways: that the narrator prefers to live in a fantasy world, that the narrator welcomes death, or even that life is too pleasing to endure for very long.

Questions for Discussion and Writing
1. Consider the bulk of the poem, the part within parentheses. What metaphor runs through this section? Imagine a character speaking these lines. What sort of character do you visualize?
2. Now look at the part outside the parentheses. What do people usually mean when they say "So-and-so is a nice place to visit, but I wouldn't want to live there"? How could you interpret such a statement when it's made about Life?
3. How do the capitalized characters Love and the Host add to the humor in the metaphor?
4. What do you think of the odd line division? What effect did it have when you first read the poem? Can you speculate on a reason for this line division?

MY MOTHER SEWS BLOUSES by Gina Valdés   [p. 629]

Students need to understand the garment industry in order to appreciate this poem. Along the U.S.-Mexican border, clothing factories are set up, and piecework is sent to the Mexican side to be done without union pay and U.S. safety controls (in other words, very cheaply). Final steps are taken on the U.S. side so that the garments can be considered U.S.-made. In the poem, the speaker's mother risks her vision for one dollar a blouse while thinking about going to night school, no doubt to upgrade her job. The hope seems pitifully futile, given her circumstances.

Questions for Discussion and Writing
1. Why do you think the mother is so poorly paid for her sewing?
2. Consider possible symbolism in the poem. What do we usually associate with the inability to see? What could the black lint symbolize?
3. Why is the woman "thinking about night school"? What effect will her current job have upon this goal? Does the poem suggest that she will succeed or fail? Explain.

FACING IT by Yusef Komunyakaa   [pp. 629-30]

Students must understand the visual situation in order to appreciate this poem. Describe or show pictures of the Vietnam Memorial in Washington, DC. Get people who have visited there to talk about the experience. The highly reflective surface of the Wall, on which the names of Vietnam dead are engraved, mirrors the people who are visiting the memorial as well as the scene behind them. The speaker in "Facing It" captures the odd sensory experience thus created when he says, "I'm stone. I'm flesh." Metaphorically, he is part of the Vietnam tragedy (the Wall) but also he is still alive.

Questions for Discussion and Writing
1. Explain the title of the poem. What is "It"?
2. In lines 15 and 16, why is the speaker "half-expecting to find my own [name] in letters like smoke"? Assuming that he is a Vietnam veteran, why is his name not there?
3. What happened to Andrew Johnson? What relation is he to the speaker?
4. From line 19 on, the speaker describes several images he sees reflected in the Wall. Can you explain the choice of these particular images?
5. What do you make of the error in perception at the end of the poem? Why are the woman and the boy present? How is their activity symbolic?

DAYSTAR by Rita Dove   [pp. 630-31]

A question about who in the class identified with the woman in the poem may start an interesting class discussion. Many of us wish for a solitary time in which we do not have to fulfill any of our roles, even freely chosen ones. Notice that the things the woman watches are utterly undemanding. The last stanza suggests that she does not welcome sex with her husband. Perhaps she feels that she is not real to him at the time ("nothing"), or perhaps she is avoiding the thought of conceiving another child. Though the night is usually associated with solitude, in this case the noon hour is: this irony may be the source of the title (the "daystar" is the sun).

Questions for Discussion and Writing
1. Did you identify with the woman in the poem? When, if ever, do you want solitude? Why? Why does the persona want it?
2. Who are Liza and Thomas? Are they important characters? Why does the writer refrain from identifying them? Why is the woman not identified by name, as they are?
3. What does the woman reply to Liza's question? What does her answer reveal about her?
4. What is happening in the last stanza? Why would the woman want to be "pure nothing" while having sex?
5. Can you explain the term "daystar," the title? Look the word up in the dictionary. The last line of the poem may provide a clue.

THERE ARE BLACK by Jimmy Santiago Baca [pp. 631-32]

The realities of prison life are expressed in this poem by an ex-convict. He focuses on the fact that both inmates and guards come from all races; the fact that the guards will keep their own people imprisoned and subject them to cruelty is especially brutal. The speaker understands the urge for power that makes a man a prison guard—the money and command that the same men could probably never find in other jobs open to them. He believes that they must harden their hearts, water down their blood, and turn off their minds in order to "seclud[e] themselves from their people."

Questions for Discussion and Writing
1. What is it about the prison guards that horrifies the speaker in "There Are Black"?
2. The speaker understands what motivates the guards to keep their jobs. What are their motivations?
3. What are the two types of convicts described in stanzas 5 and 6?
4. Do you think that this subject matter is appropriate for poetry? Why?

INDIAN BOARDING SCHOOL: THE RUNAWAYS by Louise Erdrich [pp. 632-33]

This poem tells the story condensed in the title. One night, the children hop a boxcar heading for their tribal home. They are not surprised to be found missing by the guard and caught by the sheriff before they reach their destination: the poem has a tone of calm resignation. The runaways have to scrub the sidewalks as punishment, but within the duty lie the marks they made when the cement was still wet, marks that confirm their identities. Throughout the poem, images of injury and violence provide the background, like the history of the children's people.

Questions for Discussion and Writing
1. Tell the story recounted in the poem. Why do the children run away? What means do they use? How do they get caught? What is their punishment?
2. Underline the images of injury and pain throughout the poem. Why are they appropriate, when no real violence befalls the runaways?
3. What do the children see when they scrub the sidewalk? Why do these impressions undercut the shame of the punishment? Will the children rebel again?

MY EX-HUSBAND by Gabriel Spera [pp. 633-34]

This is a humorous parody of Browning's "My Last Duchess" (p. 549). You may want to reproduce both poems on overhead transparencies and project them side by side for purposes of comparison. Spera wrote, "A good parody (as opposed to satire) recognizes the merits of the original, highlights distinctive stylistic elements, accentuates the inevitable failure of imitation, and leads to a greater appreciation of the original work. I think that's what makes it fun."

Questions for Discussion and Writing

1. Looking at this poem alongside of the original, Browning's "My Last Duchess" (p. 549), note the similarities. Make a list of parallels in the poems' form and tone. Then discuss parallels in content: what changes are made in the details of the situation?
2. What do the personae of the poems have in common? What does the persona of "My Ex-Husband" do rather than have the spouse murdered?
3. Is there a difference in the ways you respond to the personae? If so, how do you account for the difference?

SELECTED AUDIO AND VIDEO RESOURCES FOR TEACHING POETRY

The following list of audio-visual resources is not meant to be exhaustive. There are numerous videos and recordings that can be used to supplement and stimulate the study of poetry. Most of the distributors listed below will send catalogs that give details of their holdings. (For addresses and telephone numbers, see the Directory of Audio and Video Distributors found at the back of this manual.)

W. H. Auden
Recording: 1 cassette
Read by the poet
Available from Spoken Arts.

W. H. Auden Reading
Recording: 1 cassette
Available from Caedmon/HarperAudio

The Poetry of William Blake
Recording: 1 cassette
Available from Caedmon/HarperAudio

William Blake: Something About Poetry
Recording: 1 cassette, 22 min., 1969
Available from Audio-Forum

Gwendolyn Brooks
Video: 30 min., 1966
Brooks talks about her life and poetry.
Available from Indiana University Center for Media and Teaching Resources

Gwendolyn Brooks
Recording: 1 cassette, 29 min., 1989
Available from New Letters on Air

Robert Browning: My Last Duchess and Other Poems
Recording: 1 cassette
Available from Caedmon/HarperAudio

Treasury of George Gordon, Lord Byron
Recording: 1 cassette
Available from Spoken Arts

The Poetry of Countee Cullen
Recording: 1 cassette
Available from Caedmon/HarperAudio

E. E. Cummings: The Making of a Poet
Video: 24 min., 1978
Available from Films for the Humanities & Sciences

Poems of E. E. Cummings
Recording: 1 cassette, 60 min., 1981
Available from Summer Stream

Emily Dickinson: The Belle of Amherst
Video: 90 min., color, 1976
With Julie Harris
Available from The Video Catalog

Emily Dickinson
Recording: 1 cassette
Available from Recorded Books

Poems by Emily Dickinson
Recording: 2 cassettes, 236 min., 1986
Available from Audio Book Contractors

Dickinson and Whitman: Ebb And Flow
Recording: 2 cassettes.
Available from Audio Editions

Treasury of John Donne
Recording: 1 cassette
Available from Spoken Arts

Rita Dove
Recording: 1 cassette, 29 min.
Available from New Letters on Air

Poet Laureate Rita Dove
Video: 60 min., color
Available from Films for the Humanities & Sciences

Paul Laurence Dunbar
Video: 22 min., color, 1973
Available from Pyramid Film and Video

T. S. Eliot: Selected Poems
Recording: Read by the poet. 49 min.,
    1971
Available from Caedmon/HarperAudio

Robert Frost: A First Acquaintance
Video: 16 min., color, 1974
Examines Frost's life through his poems.
Available from Films for the Humanities
    & Sciences

Robert Frost Reads
Recording: 1 cassette, 55 min., 1965
Available from Audio-Forum

Allen Ginsberg
Recording: 1 cassette, 29 min., 1988
Available from New Letters on Air

Nikki Giovanni
Recording: 1 cassette, 1988
Available from New Letters on Air

The Poetry of Donald Hall
Recording: 1 cassette, 26 min., 1964
Available from Audio-Forum

Poetic Voices of Thomas Hardy
Video: 20 min., color
Available from Films for the Humanities
    & Sciences

**The Poetry of Gerard Manley
    Hopkins**
Recording: 1 cassette
Available from Caedmon/ HarperAudio

**A. E. Housman: A Shropshire Lad
and Other Poetry**
Recording: 1 cassette
Available from Caedmon/HarperAudio

Langston Hughes
Video: 60 min., color, 1988
Biographical sketch
Available from Filmic Archives

The Poetry of Langston Hughes
Recording: 2 cassettes.
Performed by Ruby Dee and Ossie Davis.
Available from Caedmon/HarperAudio

Langston Hughes Reads
Recording: 1 cassette, 50 min.
Hughes reads some of his most
    memorable poems.
Available from Filmic Archives

The Poetry of Randall Jarrell
Recording: 1 cassette, 67 min., 1963
Available from Audio-Forum

John Keats: Odes
Recording: 1 cassette
Available from Audio-Forum

Treasury of John Keats
Recording: 1 cassette
Available from Spoken Arts

Maxine Kumin: Progress Report
Recording: 1 cassette, 42 min., 1976.
Available from Watershed Tapes

The Poetry of Denise Levertov
Recording: 1 cassette, 37 min., 1965
Available from Audio-Forum

Audre Lord: Shorelines
Recording: 1 cassette, 53 min., 1985
Available from Watershed Tapes

Archibald MacLeish Reads His Poetry
Recording: 1 cassette
Available from Caedmon/HarperAudio

**Christopher Marlowe: Elizabethan
    Love Poems**
Recording: 1 cassette, 50 min.
Available from Spoken Arts

**Ralph Richardson Reads Andrew
    Marvell**
Recording: 1 cassette
Available from Audio-Forum

Edna St. Vincent Millay: Renascence
Video: 60 min., color
Directed by Vanessa Barth.
Available from Films for the Humanities
& Sciences

Poems of Edna St. Vincent Millay
Recording: 1 cassette, 60 min., 1981
Available from Summer Stream

I Am Pablo Neruda
Video: 28 min, b&w
Available from Films for the Humanities
& Sciences

Sharon Olds: Coming Back to Life
Recording: 1 cassette, 60 min.
Available from Audio-Forum

Wilfred Owen: The Pity of War
Video: 58 min., color, 1987
Available from Films for the Humanities
& Sciences

Linda Pastan: Mosaic
Recording: 1 cassette, 51 min., 1988
Available from Watershed Tapes

Marge Piercy: At the Core
Recording: 1 cassette, 58 min., 1976
Available from Watershed Tapes

Sylvia Plath
Video: 4 programs (30 min. each), color,
1974
Examination of the poet and her work
Available from New York State
Education Department

Sylvia Plath Reads
Recording: 1 cassette, 60 min., 1987
Available from Caedmon/HarperAudio

The Poetry of Adrienne Rich
Recording: 1 cassette, 36 min, 1968
Available from Audio-Forum

Theodore Roethke
Recording: 48 min., 1972
Available from Caedmon/HarperAudio

Anne Sexton Reads Her Poetry
Recording: 1 cassette
Available from Caedmon/HarperAudio

Shakespeare's Sonnets
Video: 150 min., color, 1984
In-depth look at 15 sonnets, with
readings
Available from Films for the Humanities
& Sciences

The Sonnets of Shakespeare
Recording: 2 cassettes
Read by John Gielgud
Available from Audio Editions

Treasury of Percy Bysshe Shelley
Recording: 1 cassette
Available from Spoken Arts

**W. D. Snodgrass: Calling from the
Wood's Edge**
Recording: 1 cassette, 58 min., 1986
Available from Watershed Tapes

William Stafford: Troubleshooting
Recording: 1 cassette, 50 min., 1984
Available from Watershed Tapes

Wallace Stevens Reads
Recording: 1 cassette, 60 min., 1987
Available from Caedmon/HarperAudio

Dylan Thomas: A Portrait
Video: 26 min., color
Available from Films for the Humanities
& Sciences

Dylan Thomas Reading His Poetry
Recording: 2 cassettes
Available from Caedmon/HarperAudio

The Poetry of John Updike
Recording: 1 cassette, 47 min, 1967
Available from Audio-Forum

Walt Whitman: The Living Tradition
Video: 20 min., color, 1983
Allen Ginsberg reads Whitman.
Available from Centre Productions

Walt Whitman
Recording: 1 cassette
Read by Alexander Scourby
Available from Filmic Archives

William Carlos Williams Reads His
Poetry
Recording: 1 cassette
Available from Caedmon/HarperAudio

Treasury of William Wordsworth
Recording: 1 cassette
Available from Spoken Arts

The Poetry of William Butler Yeats
Recording: 1 cassette
Available from Caedmon/HarperAudio

W. B. Yeats
Recording: 1 cassette, 49 min., 1953
Read by Stephen Spender
Available from Audio-Forum

Palgrave's Golden Treasury of English
Poetry
Recording: 2 cassettes
Available from Caedmon/HarperAudio

Victorian Poetry
Recording: 3 cassettes
Available from Caedmon/HarperAudio

Voices and Vision
Video: 13 programs (60 min. each),
color, 1988
Available from Annenberg/CPB
Collection

With a Feminine Touch
Video: 45 min., color, 1990
Readings by Valerie Harper and Claire
Bloom of poetry by women
Available from Monterey Home Video

GENERAL COLLECTIONS

Caedmon Treasury of Modern Poets
Reading Their Own Poetry
2 cassettes, 95 min.
Available from Caedmon/HarperAudio

English Romantic Poetry: Coleridge,
Shelley, Byron, Wordsworth
3 cassettes
Available from Recorded books

The Harlem Renaissance and Beyond
Video: 31 min, 1989
Available from Insight Media

Medieval and Elizabethan Poetry
Video: 28 min, color, 1989
Available from Films for the Humanities
& Sciences

Moyers: The Power of the Word
Video: 6 programs (60 min. each), color,
1989
Bill Moyers talks with modern poets
Available from PBS

PART IV   WRITING ABOUT DRAMA

Chapter 14   How Do I Read a Play?   [pp. 637-40]

Our advice in this chapter focuses on reading drama. A useful activity could be to have your students read a scene to themselves, using the suggestions in this chapter; then play a recording or video of professional actors doing the same scene. Discuss these questions:

> Was the actor's performance similar to your interpretation?
> Were there any readings that surprised you?
> Did the performance change any of your ideas about the scene?

If you show a video, you might also ask students to consider what effect the sets, lighting, costumes, gestures, and movements had on their understanding and response to the scene, reminding them to imagine these elements as they read the plays that are assigned.

Chapter 15   Writing About Dramatic Structure [pp. 641-90]

Although dramatic structure is in general quite similar to the structure of traditional short stories and novels, the terminology for describing it is somewhat more technical. Many instructors use these same terms in discussing structure in any literary work. Certainly by now your students will be familiar with most of these concepts.

Introducing Antigone

You may want students to read *Oedipus the King* (pp. 822-64) in conjunction with this play. The same principles of dramatic structure apply to both works. In fact, *Oedipus the King* is virtually unrivaled in the effectiveness of its dramatic structure, especially in its use of dramatic irony. You may want to supplement the brief summary of the Oedipus legend on p. 643 in the text with the somewhat longer version on p. 161 in this manual.

Analyzing Dramatic Structure [p. 680]

1. This opening section (lines 1-123) introduces the major conflict of the play and reveals this background information.
    *   The sisters are living under a curse (placed on their family because of their father's involuntary incest, we later learn).
    *   Antigone and Ismene have lost two brothers who killed each other in a recent battle during which the invaders, led by Polynices, were repelled.
    *   One of these brothers was buried with military honors but the other (who led the invaders) was left to lie in the field where he died.
    *   Creon, uncle to these two sisters and their dead brothers, is now the king.
    *   Creon has decreed that Polynices must not be buried, under penalty of death to anyone who tries.
    *   The girls' father, Oedipus, put out his eyes when he learned that he had unknowingly married his own mother.
    *   The girls' mother, Jocasta, hanged herself when she learned that she had unwittingly married her own son.

2. From the Chorus we learn the following:
    *   Thebes won the battle, repulsing at dawn the invaders who were roused to fight by Polynices.
    *   God favored the Theban warriors by sending a thunderclap when the first invading soldier scaled the wall.
    *   Again we are told that the brothers both died in combat.

3. The sentry serves to let the audience know that someone has attempted to bury Polynices, in defiance of Creon's law. This character also serves to emphasize the absolute power of the king by showing the fear he inspires in his followers. Clearly the

sentry and his fellow soldiers do not expect Creon to be just or fair. They know that he has a terrible temper and mistrusts everyone.

4. The major conflict involves the clash between duty to one's beliefs or conscience (Antigone's determination to bury her brother) and one's duty to authority and to the state (Creon's decree that Polynices be denied burial).

5. Antigone (whose name is the title of the play) is the protagonist. Our sympathies are always with her. Creon is the antagonist, causing the conflict by his unjust ruling. Although Antigone can accurately be called a heroine (she gives her life for what she believes to be right and holy), Creon is not precisely a villain because his intentions are not evil. Clearly misguided by pride and ambition to be a strong ruler, he does relent and try to save Antigone once he sees his wrongdoing.

6. Identifying the climax in this play is somewhat difficult because the plot takes several turns *after* the climax. But press your students to decide at what point the remainder of the action is predetermined (i.e., when clearly the die is cast). This turning point occurs when Creon declares that Antigone must die for not obeying his law. This act signals the turning point because the remaining actions result from this injustice.

   Some might reasonably argue that the climax occurs when Creon rejects the plea of Tiresias to spare Antigone and Tiresias then pronounces his curse. But since we do not know exactly when Antigone kills herself, Creon might have been too late even at this point to forestall the fateful chain of events leading to Antigone's death and his own downfall.

7. The climax does come unusually early in this play, but Sophocles maintains suspense by having Tiresias reason with Creon. The audience keeps hoping that Creon will relent in time to avoid the tragedy. Then the series of reported deaths surprises the audience—as well as Creon, who is shattered by losing his son and his wife in rapid succession.

8. The catastrophe in the extended denouement of this play begins with the report of Antigone's suicide, followed by Haemon's suicide, followed by Eurydice's suicide, the news of which prompts Creon's utter collapse. The outcome becomes inevitable once Creon has caused Antigone's death, thus depriving his son of his bride. Haemon's death causes Eurydice's suicide since she is thus deprived by her husband's willfulness of her last living son.

9. Your students might state the play's theme as "Pride goeth before a fall." Certainly, the major theme of this and many other Greek dramas warns against *hubris*, overweening pride, a character flaw which makes human beings think they know better than the gods. Also important in *Antigone* is the implication that one must stand up for one's beliefs and resist unjust laws. Antigone's refusal to allow Ismene to share her punishment underscores this idea, suggesting that because Ismene lacked the courage to stand up for her convictions, she should not be allowed to share Antigone's martyrdom.

10. Ismene's willing conformity—her timid "we are women, / we're not born to contend with men" and "I must obey / the ones who stand in power"—provides a sharp contrast with Antigone's brave defense of what she considers right and just. Ismene

simply accepts that the law was "made for the public good."

Haemon serves as a foil for his father, Creon. The young man boldly stands up to his father and voices reason in contrast to Creon's inflexible, authoritarian stance. His suicide upon finding his beloved Antigone dead suggests fidelity, tenderness, and sensitivity—traits entirely lacking in his father until Haemon's death.

11. Eurydice seems to be in the play primarily to show that, as Tiresias prophesied, everyone blames Creon for the deaths of the young people. Her suicide leaves Creon alone, and her dying curse places the guilt squarely on his head as "the murderer of her sons."

Additional Questions for Discussion and Writing

1. What ideas does the play *Antigone* express about duty and obedience? In what ways do these ideas conform or fail to conform to your own concepts of duty and obedience?
2. The Chorus expresses the values of the community. Is Antigone a danger to this community? How far do you believe a community should go to protect its values?
3. Both Creon and Antigone defend rights that they believe are sacred. What rights are in conflict? Is there any room for compromise?
4. Do you sympathize with Antigone or with Creon? What characteristics of each do you find admirable? Do you ever lose patience with either of them? Explain.
5. Is there any justification for Antigone's cold refusal to allow Ismene to share her martyrdom? Explain. Is Ismene entirely without courage?
6. How would you balance the claims of "ideas" and "character" in this play? In other words, are the issues more important than the people who are arguing them? Would either element alone suffice? Why or why not?
7. Creon says at the end, "The guilt is mine." Do you agree?
8. What is your judgment of Antigone as the tragic heroine? One critic has questioned her "total indifference to the rights of the city" and claims that no one in the play really praises her, except her fiancé. She herself says that if the gods allowed her to suffer death for her stand then she would know she was wrong. Was she wrong?
9. If you were Antigone, would you have stuck to your principles, or would you have given in? Explain your motivation.
10. In your opinion, what in this play could or should have been done differently, and by whom?
11. Can *Antigone* be read as a justification for civil disobedience? Explain.

Sample Student Paper [pp.685-90]

Since this student paper employs an approach to *Antigone* that your students might not have considered, you may want to let them respond to the "Questions for Discussion" [p. 690] after you have gone over with them in class the standard questions concerning the rhetorical components of the essay: Is the introduction effective? Is the thesis clearly stated? Are the paragraphs adequately developed? Are the sentences clear? Is the conclusion emphatic? Is the entire paper unified? Is the argument convincing? This last question should spark disagreement, which the discussion questions will allow you to explore.

Questions for Discussion [p. 690]

1. Since the writer focuses on the gender issue as her thesis, one could not say that she overemphasizes it. She acknowledges in her second sentence that she is not going to deal with "the more obvious conflict between the state and the individual." She deliberately chooses to discuss an aspect of the play that many readers might overlook.

2. Since the student was working within a 700-word limit for her essay, she was not able to include all of the evidence that might be used to support her thesis. During the argument between Creon and Haemon, Creon denigrates females: "never lose your sense of judgment over a woman / The warmth, the rush of pleasure, it all goes cold / in your arms, I warn you . . . a worthless woman / in your house, a misery in your bed" (723-26). The implication of his speech is that Haemon is interested only sexually in Antigone, and that once his ardor cools, she will make him miserable with her aggressiveness. Creon's contempt for women as mere sexual objects is first voiced crudely in lines, when Ismene expresses dismay that the king would condemn to death his own son's bride and Creon retorts, "there are other fields for him to plow" (642). Creon also tries to disparage Haemon's arguments by saying to the Chorus, "This boy, I do believe, is fighting on her side, the woman's side" (822-29) and calling him a "woman's accomplice!" (837) and a "woman's slave" (848).
   If the student had been given a less restrictive word limit, she might have discussed Eurydice as providing yet another example of the conflict between male and female. Although we know little about the marital relationship between Creon and Eurydice, we can be certain that she blames her husband for the deaths of her sons and curses him as their murderer. (Women, traditionally, have been opposed to war. Men make war, in which women's sons are killed.)

3. Antigone's purpose is more noble than mere sexual rivalry, but then, so is Creon's, supposedly. Although Antigone resents Creon, she clearly resents his power as a male: "Lucky tyrants—the perquisites of power! / Ruthless power to do and say whatever pleases *them*" (566-67). And in her final speech she places the blame for her death on men: "I alone, see what I suffer now / at the hands of what breed of men— / all or reverence, my reverence fore the gods!" (1032-34).

4. The student who wrote the essay naturally found the best evidence for her thesis ("The antagonist, Creon, is fighting to retain control over Antigone, not only as king over subject but also as man over woman") by analyzing the character of Creon. His misogynistic attitude forms the basis for her argument, since no other characters in the play appear openly anti-female. Her conclusion—that his fear of being beaten by a woman causes his rash action—is tied only by implication to his pride: "Creon's pride has made him blind to his mistake" (last sentence, next to last paragraph of the essay). She might well have stated this connection outright, thus emphasizing that her reading of the play supports and illuminates the usual interpretation. She argues that pride causes Creon's fall: her paper attempts to explain why he was so touchy, stubborn, and insecure in his pridefulness.
   As a matter of background information, you might want your students to know that during the period in Greek history before this play was written the state was governed by a matriarchy. Once women were ousted from control, it became expedient to keep them from regaining power. Scholars believe that the political threat that women perhaps posed underlies Sophocles' presentation of Creon as a tyrant unjustly persecuting an assertive woman of noble blood who shows qualities of

leadership. Antigone's insistence that the citizens are on her side suggests that she already has followers.

Video: *Antigone*. 88 min., b&w, 1962. With Irene Papas. In Greek with subtitles. Available from Insight Media and Filmic Archives.
    Antigone. 95 min., color, 1991. With Carrie O'Brien and Chris Bearne; directed by Arlena Nys. Available from Insight Media.
    Antigone. 120 min., color, 1988. Third part of the BBC production of the Theban Plays. With Juliet Stevenson, John Shrapnel, and John Gielgud. Adapted and translated by Don Taylor. Available from Films for the Humanities & Sciences.

Suggested Further Readings on Antigone
Brown, Andrew. *A New Companion to Greek Tragedy*. Totowa: Barnes, 1983.
Gellie, G. H. *Sophocles: A Reading*. Carlton: Melbourne UP, 1972. 29-52.
Linforth, I. M. *Antigone and Creon*. Berkeley: U of California P, 1961.
O'Brien, Joan V. *Guide to Sophocles'* Antigone: *A Student Edition with Commentary, Grammatical Notes, & Vocabulary*. Carbondale: Southern Illinois UP, 1978.
Roen, Duane H. "A Writing-to-Learn/Reader-Response Approach to Teaching *Antigone*." *Reader Response in the Classroom*. Ed. Nicholas Karolides. New York: Longman, 1992. 176-84.
Scodel, Ruth. *Sophocles*. Boston: Twayne, 1984. 43-57.
Segal, Charles. *Tragedy and Civilization: An Interpretation of Sophocles*. Cambridge: Harvard UP, 1981.
Winnington-Ingram, P. R. *Sophocles: An Interpretation*. Cambridge: Cambridge UP, 1980. 117-49.

Chapter 16   Writing About Character   [pp. 691-738]

What Is the Modern Hero?   [p. 691]

Discussion of both *hero* and *tragedy* (or *tragic*) will reveal rather loose and broad-ranging definitions of these terms. It might help to ask students to distinguish between *heroic* and *courageous* or *bold* (Are heroes ever *foolhardy?*) and between *tragic* and *sad* (or even *pathetic*). Some discussion of the limits and problems with abstract value words may also be necessary. Asking students to write out definitions of abstract terms—with examples or illustrations—and then to compare answers can be an enlightening, if sometimes perplexing, activity. Another useful prereading activity for this chapter is ask students to name a modern-day hero and defend or explain their choice.

Miller's definition of tragedy—"being torn away from our chosen image of what and who we are"—seems overly broad, one that can be applied to almost anybody. If Miller's concept is applied to the characters in *The Glass Menagerie*, it's possible to see most of them as displaced and at odds with the cosmos (or society). How useful, then, is this definition? Some readers may pity Laura but will not say that he is tragic. Even Amanda's single-minded determination, which is akin to Antigone's in some ways, seems, to some, more foolish and misguided than heroic or tragic. Perhaps there are no modern heroes.

Analyzing the Characters   [p. 735]

1. Some deceptions include Laura's dropping out of business school and pretending to continue; Amanda's pretense or hope that Laura is attractive and will have lots of gentleman callers; Tom's failure to pay the light bill and his keeping his plans to himself; Amanda's insincere sympathy for the "Christian martyrs" she solicits for magazine subscriptions; Jim's failure to tell anyone about his engagement until after he's built up some false hopes; Amanda's sentimental reminiscences about her past and her uncon- firmed claims about her children's extraordinary abilities; Tom's stories about where he goes at night; Amanda's refusal to say Laura is crippled; Jim's facile trust in night school courses as the road to success.

2. The scene could be played to bring out Tom's exasperation and discontent, Amanda's dominance and loquacity, and Laura's deference and gentle compliance.

3. Tom does not find fulfillment or satisfaction in his job. He yearns for adventure that ordinary life simply can't provide (as Amanda points out to him, people find adventure in their careers or "they do without it!"). Thus, he seems to fit Miller's concept by being torn away from his instinctual desires and forced to seek his adventure in alcohol and mindless escapism.

Statements that imply displacement or indignity:

Laura: And everybody was seated before I came in. I had to walk in front of all those people. My seat was in the back row. I had to go clumping all the way up the aisle with everyone watching! (Sc. VII)

Jim: You think of yourself as having the only problems, as being the only one who is disappointed. But just look around you and you will see lots of people as disappointed as you are. For instance, I hoped when I was going to high school that I would be further along at this time, six years later, than I am now— (Scene VII)

Tom: I'm starting to boil inside. I know I seem dreamy, but inside—well, I'm boiling!— Whenever I pick up a shoe, I shudder a little thinking how short life is and what I am doing!— (Scene VI)

Amanda: That innocent look of your father's had everyone fooled! He *smiled*—the world was *enchanted*! No girl can do worse than put herself at the mercy of a handsome appearance! (Scene V)

4. Antigone's heroism is different because she is sure of her destiny—her role in society. She pursues her obligation regardless of the consequences. She battles a hostile society on her own terms.

5. Tom probably feels guilty that he left Laura to live with their overbearing mother, especially since Laura always treated Tom with understanding and affection. Throughout the play, Tom seems to dismiss Laura and her problems, taking a "what can we do?" approach and focusing more on his own needs and desires. It may be that with the separation he has come to realize that he loves his sister and should have paid more attention to her.

6. Choices will vary, but it seems easiest to pick Tom because he finally does something to alter his life, to fight his feelings of displacement and indignity. He is also the narrator, so we have a more complete sense of his motives and development. We really don't know what happens to Laura, Amanda, and Jim—not in the same way we do with Tom.

Ideas for Writing [p. 736]

Use the first idea for responsive writing to get students to review the play and as prewriting for a critical analysis. Use the questions in the sixth idea for critical writing as the basis for small group discussions.

Exercise on Developing Paragraphs Specifically [p. 738]

Quotations to support generalizations:
1. Amanda is not deeply and completely self-deceived:

"My devotion has made me a witch and so I make myself hateful to my children!" (Sc. IV)

"I wasn't prepared for what the future brought me" (Sc. VI)
"Things have a way of turning out so badly. . . . Don't think about us, a mother deserted, an unmarried sister who's crippled and has no job!" (Sc. VII)

2. Human sexuality disturbs Amanda:

"I took that horrible novel back to the library—yes! That hideous book by that insane Mr. Lawrence. I cannot control the output of diseased minds or people who cater to them—BUT I WON'T ALLOW SUCH FILTH BROUGHT INTO MY HOUSE!" (Sc. III)

"Instinct is something that people have got away from! It belongs to animals! Christian adults don't want it!" (Sc. IV)

3. Characters in the play take both realistic and unrealistic action toward their goals:

Amanda takes some very real steps to prepare for the Gentleman Caller: "We can't have a gentleman caller in a pig-sty. All my wedding silver has to be polished, the monogrammed table linen ought to be laundered! The windows have to be washed and fresh curtains put up. . . ." (Scene V). But she also pins a lot of her hopes on wishes and dreams: "Laura, come here and make a wish on the moon! . . . A little silver slipper of a moon. Look over your left shoulder, Laura, and make a wish!" (Sc. V) Jim has some good ideas about the value of self-confidence, but he also believes that a night-school course in public speaking "fits you for-executive positions!"

4. Both times glass is broken in the play, the forces of masculinity and sexuality are involved:

Tom has just presented himself as a gambling, boozing rake. Then he tries unsuccessfully to fling his coat on and storm out:

"With an outraged groan [Tom] tears the coat off again, splitting the shoulder of it, and hurls it across the room. It strikes against the shelf of Laura's glass collection, there is a tinkle of shattering glass. Laura cries out as if wounded." (stage direction, Sc. III)

Jim takes Laura in his arms, telling her to relax as they dance. When she does begin to relax and enjoy it:

"[Jim] moves her about the room in a clumsy waltz. . . . They suddenly bump into the table. Jim stops." (stage directions, Sc. VII)

5. Tom Wingfield may live as much in his imagination as Amanda or Laura do in theirs:

"People go to the *movies* instead of moving! Hollywood characters are supposed to have all the adventures for everybody in America, while everybody in America sits in a dark room and watches them have them! Yes, until there's a war. That's when adventure becomes available to the masses! Everyone's dish, not only Gable's! Then the people in the dark room come out of the dark room to have

154

some adventures themselves—Goody, goody!—It's our turn now, to go to the South Sea Island—to make a safari—to be exotic, far-off!" (Scene VI)

" . . . my secret practice of retiring to a cabinet of the washroom to work on poems (Scene VI)

"I know I seem dreamy, but inside—well, I'm boiling!" (Scene VI)

Video: *The Glass Menagerie*. 134 min., color, 1987. Directed by Paul Newman. With Joanne Woodward, Karen Allen, John Malkovich. Available from Filmic Archives and Insight Media.

Audio: *The Glass Menagerie*. 2 cassettes. Dramatization performed by Montgomery Clift, Jessica Tandy, and Julie Harris. Available from Caedmon/Harper Audio.

Suggested Further Readings on The Glass Menagerie

Griffin, Alice. *Understanding Tennessee Williams*. Columbia: U of South Carolina P, 1995.
Hirsch, Foster. *A Portrait of the Artist: The Plays of Tennessee Williams*. Port Washington: Kennikat, 1979.
Jones, John H. "The Missing Link: The Father in *The Glass Menagerie*." *Notes on Mississippi Writers* 20 (1988): 29-38.
Levy, Eric. "'Through the Soundproof Glass': The Prison of Self-Consciousness in *The Glass Menagerie*." *Modern Drama* 36 (1993): 529-37.
Mann, Bruce. "Tennessee Williams and the Rose-Garden Husband." *American Drama* 1 (Fall 1991): 16-26.
Parker, R. B., ed. "*The Glass Menagerie*": *A Collection of Critical Essays*. Englewood Cliffs: Prentice, 1993.
Presley, Delma E. *The Glass Menagerie: An American Memory*. Boston: Twayne, 1990.
Stanton, Stephen, ed. *Tennessee Williams: A Collection of Critical Essays*. Englewood Cliffs: Prentice-Hall, 1977.
Thompson, Judith J. *Tennessee Williams' Plays: Memory, Myth, and Symbol*. New York: Lang, 1987.
Usui, Masami. "'A World of Her Own' in Tennessee Williams' *The Glass Menagerie*." *Studies in Culture and the Humanities* 1 (1992): 21-37.

Chapter 17   Drama for Writing: The Research Paper   [pp. 739-821]

The instruction in this chapter will introduce your students to cultural criticism as well as to the procedures for writing a paper using secondary sources. You will want to call their attention to Figure 17-1 (on p. 791), which lists the most useful guides to criticism of poetry, drama, and fiction. Although this chapter is called "Drama for Writing," the information is applicable to doing research in any genre, and we provide suggested topics for documented papers on poetry and fiction, as well as drama (on pp. 795-96).

We also now provide two sample student papers using secondary sources. The first example is a brief but full-scale research paper written by a student on the play included in this chapter, David Hwang's M. Butterfly. The second illustrates how a student used secondary sources to support her ideas about "The Lottery"; this paper provides a good contrast to the student essay on "The Lottery," which appears in Chapter 6—showing how students might make use of published criticism to develop and expand their analyses.

M. BUTTERFLY by David Henry Hwang   [741-85]

In his play, David Hwang critiques the sexual and racial attitudes that inform Western relations with Asia, captured most powerfully and seductively in the image of Puccini's Madame Butterfly. As Hwang explains in the "Afterword" to his play, the character of Butterfly has become a cultural stereotype of East-West relations: "speaking of an Asian woman, we would sometimes say, 'She's pulling a Butterfly,' which meant playing the submissive Oriental number" (95).

M. Butterfly explores the connection between the "Orient" of Western imagination and the political consequences that such images promote. The play's main character, the French diplomat Rene Gallimard, conducts his relationship with China in terms of Puccini's opera. In Madame Butterfly (1904), the American naval officer Pinkerton marries the Japanese geisha girl Butterfly; he then leaves for the U. S. promising to return. Butterfly waits for him, meanwhile bearing his child. When Pinkerton sends his American wife to collect the child, Butterfly realizes that he will never return—and she commits suicide.

When Hwang read of the French diplomat who had an affair with a Chinese actress, who turned out to be a spy—and a man—, the playwright concluded that the diplomat had fallen in love with a fantasy stereotype. By combining the diplomat's story with Puccini's plot, Hwang constructed the basic "arc" of his play: "the Frenchman fantasizes that he is Pinkerton and his lover is Butterfly. By the end of the piece, he realizes that it is he who has been Butterfly, in that the Frenchman has been duped by love; the Chinese spy, who exploited that love, is therefore the real Pinkerton" ("Afterword," 95-96).

M. Butterfly is also a highly political play. Hwang doesn't just contend that the sexist and racist stereotype of a "submissive Oriental number" fuels the fantasies of Western men about Asian women (as demonstrated by the profitable business of supplying

156

American and Europeans with mail-order brides from Asia); he also argues that this attitude has conditioned political relations between Asia and the West as well. In making this point, Hwang suggests that the debacle of the Vietnam War was related, in part, to cultural assumptions about the submissive nature of Asians in general. By fusing the erotic and political desire for domination in the character of Gallimard, the play presents a complex reading of the politics of race, gender, and sexuality in a brilliant theatrical production.

To help students understand the various levels of this play, you may want to give them the basic outline of Puccini's opera and discuss the romantic notions about Oriental women that it reinforced and fostered. Students will also benefit from knowledge about the true story the play is based on. It's important to note, though, that Hwang says he took his idea from a brief account in the *New York Times* ("France Jails 2 in Odd Case of Espionage": 11 May 1986) but did not do any further research into the incident. Students, like most people who read or see the play, will wonder how the French diplomat could not know that the "woman" he had fallen in love was really a man. It may help to remind them that Hwang did not invent this part of the story—nor the part about the child. The real-life diplomat, Bernard Bouriscot, continues to maintain that he did not know the true gender of the person he had the affair with.

Questions for Discussion and Writing

1. What does the stage look like in *M. Butterfly*, and what does it represent? (Notice that the initial description of the setting says that the play takes place "in recall," and that in Act 2, Scene 11, Gallimard says, "You have to do what I say! I'm conjuring you up in *my* mind!")
2. Gallimard says that he has "known, and been loved by . . . the Perfect Woman!" (1.3). What does he mean by this? In what way may he be right?
3. How does Puccini's opera *Madame Butterfly* function in this play?
4. Gallimard and some other characters address the audience directly and even interact with them (as when Marc flirts with the women in the audience). What do these breaks in theatrical convention suggest about this play? How do they contribute to the play's ideas about illusions and role-playing?
5. Gallimard says he was "not handsome, nor brave, nor powerful" (1.5), and he conjures up the image of a pinup girl from a sex magazine. What does this scene have to do with the play's main themes?
6. When Gallimard and Song first meet (1.6), they discuss the plot of *Madame Butterfly* and Song tells Gallimard, "It's one of your favorite fantasies, isn't it? The submissive Oriental and the cruel white man." Is Song right?
7. How does Song conduct her seduction of Gallimard without revealing "her" secret?
8. Does Gallimard believe what he sees, or does he see what he believes?
9. In 2.3, Gallimard gives Toulon some political advice about Vietnam. Later Toulon tells Gallimard that he is almost comically wrong in everything he says. How have gender issues affected Gallimard's political thinking?
10. What's the significance of the spelling of Renee's name? Compare Song and Renee. Why does Gallimard go to Butterfly in 2.6, instead of to Renee? Gallimard says that Renee "questions the role of the penis in modern society." Does Butterfly also question the role of the penis in modern society?
11. Song says that women's roles are played by men in the Peking Opera because "only a man knows how a woman is supposed to act" (2.7). What does Song mean? In what ways does the play confirm this point?

12. In the final scene between them (3.2), Song tries to get Gallimard to admit that he is still attracted to his "Butterfly," even though "she" is a man. What is the point of this scene?
13. Just before he kills himself, Gallimard dresses and makes up as Butterfly and says, "My name is Rene Gallimard—also known as Madame Butterfly." What is the point of this final switch of identities?
14. Is this play about international spying? odd and obsessive sexuality? political systems? or something else? Explain.
15. Does the fact that the play is based on an actual event make it more believable than it otherwise might be? Or is the plot just too improbable (even though it actually happened)? How does the playwright try to overcome the improbability of the story? Does he succeed?
16. Compare Song with Nora of *A Doll's House*. Analyze how the "women" in each play resist being defined by men.

Video: *M. Butterfly*. 110 min, 1973. An uninspired film version, with screenplay by Hwang, starring Jeremy Irons and John Lone. Available from Warner Home Video.

Suggested Further Readings on **M. Butterfly**

Cody, Gabrielle. "David Hwang's *M. Butterfly*: Perpetuating the Misogynist Myth." *Theater* 20.2 (Spring 1989): 24-27.
DiGaetani, John Louis. "*M. Butterfly*: An Interview with David Henry Hwang." *TDR: The Drama Review* 33.3 (Fall 1989): 141-53.
Eng, David L. "In the Shadow of a Diva: Committing Homosexuality in David Henry Hwang's *M. Butterfly*." *Amerasia Journal* 20.1 (1994): 93-116.
Haedicke, Janet V. "David Henry Hwang's *M. Butterfly*: The Eye on the Wing." *Journal of Dramatic Theory and Criticism* 7 (1992): 27-44.
Hwang, David H. Afterword. *M. Butterfly*. New York: New American, 1988. 94-100.
Rich, Frank. "*M. Butterfly*: A Story of a Strange Love, Conflict and Betrayal." *New York Times* 21 March 1988: C13.
Shimakawa, Karen. "'Who's to Say?': Or, Making Space for Gender and Ethnicity in *M. Butterfly*." *Theatre Journal* 45.3 (Oct. 1993): 349-61.
Skloot, Robert. "Breaking the Butterfly: The Politics of David Henry Hwang." *Modern Drama* 33 (1990): 59-66.
Street, Douglas. *David Henry Hwang*. Western Writers Series No. 90. Boise: Boise State U, 1989.
Wadler, Joyce. "For the First Time, the Real-Life Models for Broadway's *M. Butterfly* Tell of Their Strange Romance." *People Weekly* 8 Aug. 1988: 88-89+.
---. "The Spy Who Fell in Love with a Shadow." *New York Times Magazine* 15 Aug. 1993: 30-32+.

Ideas for Researched Writing [pp. 795-96]

You will probably want to go over these suggested topics with your class, brainstorming about how and where a student could begin research on each topic. A class trip to the library to determine what reference books are there and where they are located is of great help to students, if they have not already taken a course in library orientation.

General Advice for Helping Students Complete a Documented Papers

Most students find procrastination a major problem when they attempt to write using secondary materials. Setting a clear schedule with well-defined checkpoints along the way will help these students enormously. Here is a list of checkpoints you might want to have them meet. Assign your own dates.

1. Discuss chosen topic in conference with you—at least, those who are having trouble deciding on an approach.
2. Turn in thesis question or hypothesis for approval.
3. Turn in for checking a preliminary bibliography.
4. Bring to class for checking a substantial number of note cards—to be sure they are making progress
5. Turn in outline or plan for approval.
6. Pass open-book quiz on MLA style; a sample quiz is included next in this manual.
7. Bring a section of the rough draft along with note cards to class—or have them bring note cards and actually write a section in class—so that you can check how well they are integrating sources and how accurate their documentation is.

Also call your students' attention to the description of "A Student Reseacher's Process," p. 798, as well as to the suggestions about prewriting (p. 787), finding a thesis (p. 788), locating sources (pp. 788-90), taking notes (p. 790), developing a plan (p. 792), and writing before researching (pp. 792-93). These brief discussions reinforce the importance of following a process and emphasize the notion that good writing develops in stages

The Online Catalog [p. 789]

The library's computers provide an overwhelming number of sources and service options. With so many possibilities, it's important that students take an orientation course if they haven't already done so. You may want to arrange a tour or an orientation session with your school's librarian Many libraries can tailor their presentations to fit the needs of a specific assignment, so even students who already know how to use the online services can benefit from such a session Students will also have to spend some time with these data systems to find out how they work and how useful they are. But it's time well spent. Once students get the hang of it, they will be able to research a topic with astonishing ease and thoroughness.

Using the Internet [pp. 789-90]

The Internet and the Web give students access to a great deal of information that is often more current than anything available in printed sources, and the Web's hyptertext feature allows them to explore a topic quickly and thoroughly. Nonetheless, there are a couple of serious pitfalls in using the Web that you might want to point out.

First, it's difficult to know how to judge the vast array of information that's available. Students will find research reports, online journals, government publications;

but they will also find unsupported opinion, propaganda, inaccurate information, and tasteless junk. Anyone can publish on the Web; there is no editorial board to screen the material. So, researchers must apply sound judgment in evaluating each of their electronic sources, just as they would the print sources that they find in the library. Encourage students to check the information against other sources, and consider carefully the credentials—and the biases—of the person or organization supplying the data.

Second, searching on the Internet, especially on the WWW, can eat up a lot of valuable time. Because it's so easy to move from site to site through numerous interlinked sources, it's possible to spend hours browsing the Web. Students' time might be better spent reading their source materials, taking notes, and writing the paper. To avoid wasting time, students should always go to the Web for specific purposes, skim the sites first, and note the size and downloading time of a document before printing it out. (The slow downloading time on some equipment can consume a lot of time.)

Documenting Electronic Sources

For complete, authoritative explanations of the MLA style for citing sources from online sources and the World Wide Web, see the *MLA Handbook for Writers of Research Papers*, 4th ed., 1995 (for high school and undergraduate college students) and the *MLA Style Manual and Guide to Scholarly Publishing*, 2nd ed., 1998 (for graduate students, scholars, and professional writers). The MLA also provides guidelines and updates of information on their World Wide Web site (http://www.mla.org/).

Quiz on the MLA Documentation Style

The following brief test—or it could function as a worksheet—will bring to your students' attention the details essential to accurately using MLA documentation.

Part I. Write correctly spaced and punctuated Works Cited entries using the following fabricated sources:

1. A third edition of a book named Grammar Is Fun by Oliver M. Battleax. The book was published by the McGraw-Hill Book Company in New York, New York, in 1984.
2. An essay called Springsteen's Special Magic by Carla Mayhem in a collection of essays about rock and roll. The collection, edited by Spiro Agnew, is entitled Jump On It, Baby. It came out in May 1983, published by Macmillan Publishing Company in New York City. The essay on Springsteen appears on pages 24 through 28.
3. An article called Madonna as Social Icon that was published in Cultural Currents in the summer of 1991 in volume 7 of that periodical (meaning a scholarly journal or magazine). Written by Peaches Pretentious, the piece appeared on pages 27 through 32.
4. An article from the first page of section C in the New York Times of April 13, 1994. Entitled How to Train Your Bad Puppy, it was written by Thomasina Schnarre. It appeared on the New York Times Online database and was accessed through Nexis computer service on February 4, 1994.

Part II. Fill in the blanks.

The MLA style does away with_____in source documentation.
Instead, the author of the source and the appropriate_____number are
given within the paper, surrounded by_____. The author's name and
the page number are separated by a_____, not a comma. Just the page
number is cited if the author's_____is mentioned in your sentence. The
Works Cited list, at the_____of your paper, is organized according to
the_____.

ANTHOLOGY OF DRAMA

OEDIPUS THE KING by Sophocles [pp. 822-64]

This play is Sophocles' masterpiece and considered by many the greatest of classic Greek tragedies. Aristotle used it as a model for his definition of tragedy in the *Poetics*; Freud used it as evidence for his theory of the Oedipus complex. The story of Oedipus gripped Sophocles' imagination for thirty years, and he wrote three plays about it: *Oedipus the King, Oedipus at Colonus*, and *Antigone* (which is included in Chapter 15). Sophocles could have counted on his audience to know something of the legend of Oedipus: such knowledge allows readers and viewers to recognize and appreciate the series of dramatic ironies and foreshadowings contained in the play. You may want to distribute a summary of the Oedipus legend, such as the following, to your students:

> In Greek mythology, Oedipus was the son of Laius and Jocasta, king and queen of Thebes. Laius was warned by an oracle that he would be killed by his own son. Determined to avert his fate, he bound together the feet of his newborn child and left him to die on a lonely mountain. The infant was rescued by a shepherd, however, and given to Polybus, king of Corinth, who named the child Oedipus ("Swollen-foot") and raised him as his own son. The boy did not know that he was adopted, and when an oracle proclaimed that he would kill his father, he left Corinth. In the course of his wanderings he met and killed Laius, believing that the king and his followers were a band of robbers; and thus he unwittingly fulfilled the prophecy.
>
> Lonely and homeless, Oedipus arrived at Thebes, which was beset by a dreadful monster called the Sphinx. The frightful creature frequented the roads to the city, killing and devouring all travelers who could not answer the riddle that she put to them. When Oedipus successfully solved her riddle, the Sphinx killed herself. Believing that King Laius had been slain by unknown robbers, and grateful to Oedipus for ridding them of the Sphinx, the Thebans rewarded Oedipus by making him their king and giving him Queen Jocasta as his wife. For many years the couple lived in happiness, not knowing that they were really mother and son.
>
> Then a terrible plague descended on the land, and the oracle proclaimed that Laius's murderer must be punished. Oedipus soon discovered that he had unknowingly killed his father. In grief and despair at her incestuous life, Jocasta killed herself, and when Oedipus realized that she was dead and that their children were accursed, he put out his eyes and resigned the throne. He lived in Thebes for several years, but was finally banished. Accompanied by his daughter Antigone, he wandered for many years. He finally arrived at Colonus, a shrine near Athens sacred to the powerful goddesses called the Eumenides. At this shrine for supplicants Oedipus died, after the god Apollo had promised him that the place of his death would remain sacred and would bring great benefit to the city of Athens, which had given shelter to the wanderer.

.

Oedipus the King is concerned with the unpredictability, the power, and the relentlessness of fate. Oedipus tries hard to avoid his fate and alter his destiny, but instead he runs headlong into it. At the start of the play, Sophocles shows us Oedipus at the height of his powers; his determination to save his city is the central action. By beginning the plot near the end of the story, the playwright exploits the dramatic irony of the situation—the difference between what the audience knows and what the characters know. Step by step, Oedipus becomes acquainted with the facts of his past, and in a single day he falls from supremacy and fame to a self-inflicted humiliation.

Sophocles asks us to consider the moral issues behind human actions and to recognize the powers that operate on human affairs. Throughout the play Oedipus clashes with conditions and people, notably the plague, then Tiresias, then Creon. But the primary conflict is between Oedipus and the gods. Oedipus's fate is bound up with his character. He is neither wholly virtuous nor wholly blameless but is presented as a complex human being who offers the audience an intellectual and moral challenge. He is partly a victim of fate and the savagery of the gods, but his own spirited character leads him to his downfall.

Students may wonder what is "tragic" about Oedipus's fate and, given the prophecies of the oracle, what he could have done to avoid this fate. To some, the tragedy lies in the way that Oedipus's strengths—the qualities that enabled him to outwit the Sphinx—lead this time to his destruction. Oedipus's "flaw" is not a moral failing or a deed that he could have avoided; it is simply that he behaves like himself—intelligent, masterful, assertive, impatient, impulsive—and this leads him, as it always did in the past, to discover the truth he seeks. Only this time, the discovery of truth has ruinous consequences.

To underscore the irony of the tragic outcome, Sophocles plays with the opposition between sight and blindness. In dismissing the advice of the blind Tiresias not to pursue the truth, Oedipus is blind. At the end of the play, when at last he sees the truth, he destroys the organs which allowed him to deceive himself. Blinded, he now sees clearly.

Questions for Discussion and Writing

1. Do you think Oedipus deserves his fate? Why or why not?
2. In the opening scene what does the Priest's speech reveal about how Oedipus has been regarded as a ruler?
3. Identify instances of dramatic irony in the play. What is their function?
4. What do the confrontations with Tiresias and Creon tell us about Oedipus's character?
5. Explain the functions of the Chorus. What are the Chorus's views and beliefs, and how do they differ from those of Jocasta?
6. Trace the images of blindness and vision throughout the play. How are they related to the theme?
7. Why does Oedipus blind himself instead of committing suicide as Jocasta does? Why does Sophocles have Oedipus blind himself offstage? What would be the effect of having him perform this act in full view of the audience?
8. At the end of the play, what has Oedipus learned about himself? About the gods? About the quest for truth?
9. What's your assessment of Oedipus at the end of the play? Was he foolish? heroic? doomed?
10. Is it possible for twentieth-century readers to identify with Oedipus? What issues does he confront that are relevant to modern readers?
11. What is an "Oedipus complex"? Does this concept shed any light on the events in the play?

12. Write the storyline for a modern-day equivalent of this play.
13. Compare the "tragedy" of *Oedipus the King* with that in either *A Doll's House* or *The Glass Menagerie*.
14. How is the riddle of the Sphinx related to the other questions that Oedipus seeks to answer?
15. What do you think of Tiresias? Write an essay in which you analyze his character and his contributions to the play.
16. Write an essay in which you take one of the following statements as your thesis:
    The play is about human blindness. (Oedipus did not know who he was and was blind to the honesty of Creon and Tiresias.)
    The play is about the curse of honesty. (Oedipus's relentless desire to know the truth brings him to suffering.)
    The play is about a tragic situation. (If Oedipus abandons his quest, he fails his people; if he pursues his quest, he ruins himself.)
    The play is about injustice and undeserved suffering.

Video: *Oedipus the King.* 45 min., color, 1975. With Antony Quayle, James Mason, Claire Bloom, and Ian Richardson. Available from Films for the Humanities & Sciences.
    Oedipus the King. 120 min., color, 1987. First part of the BBC production of the Theban Plays. With Michael Pennington, John Gielgud, and Claire Bloom. Adapted and translated by Don Taylor. Available from Films for the Humanities & Sciences.

Suggested Further Readings on Oedipus the King

Bloom, Harold, ed. *Sophocles' Oedipus Rex.* New York: Chelsea, 1988.
Hogan, James C. *A Commentary on the Plays of Sophocles.* Carbondale: Southern Illinois UP, 1991.
Knox, Bernard M. W. *Oedipus at Thebes: Sophocles' Tragic Hero and His Time.* New York: Norton, 1971.
O'Brien, M. J., ed. *Twentieth-Century Interpretations of* Oedipus Rex. Englewood Cliffs: Prentice, 1968.
Segal, Charles. *Tragedy and Civilization: An Interpretation of Sophocles.* Cambridge: Harvard UP, 1981.
---. Oedipus Tryannus: *Tragic Heroism and the Limits of Knowledge.* New York: Twayne, 1993.
Senior, W. A. "Teaching Oedipus: The Hero and Multiplicity." *Teaching English in the Two-Year College* 19.4 (December 1992): 274-79.
Winnington-Ingram, R. P. *Sophocles: An Interpretation.* New York: Cambridge UP, 1980.

THE TEMPEST by William Shakespeare   [pp.865-929]

In *The Tempest* Shakespeare creates an idealized world of imagination, a place of magical restoration and reconciliation. Shakespeare's island is a visionary realm, where everything is controlled by the artist. Yet it's no escape from reality, for the island shows humans what they are and what they ought to be. Even its location combines the "real" world with an idealized landscape; it is to be found both somewhere and nowhere. According to the plot, it is located in the Mediterranean Sea. Yet there are suggestions of the New

World, the Western Hemisphere, where Thomas More placed his island of Utopia: Ariel fetches dew at Prospero's command from the "Bermudas" (1.2.230); Caliban at first reminds Trinculo of a "dead Indian" (2.2.33) who might be displayed before crowds eager to see such a monster from across the seas; and Caliban's god, Setebos, was worshipped by South American natives.

Prospero rules as the artist-king over this imaginary world, conjuring up trials to test people's intentions and visions to promote their renewed faith in goodness. To the island come an assortment of men who are separated by Prospero and Ariel into three groups: King Alonso and those accompanying him; Alonso's son, Ferdinand; and Stephano and Trinculo. Prospero's authority over them, though strong, has limits. As Duke of Milan he was inattentive to political matters and thus vulnerable to the political conniving of his younger brother Antonio. Only in this world apart, the artist's world, do his powers find their proper stage. His power may imitate the divine, but Prospero is no god. His chief ability, learned from books and exercised through Ariel, is to control the elements so as to create illusions. Yet even this power is an immense burden. Prospero has much to learn, like those he controls. He must subdue his anger, his self-pity, his readiness to blame others, his domineering over Miranda. He does these things through his art, devising games and shows in which his anger and jealousy are transformed into playacting scenes of divine warning and forgiveness toward his enemies and watchful parental austerity toward Miranda and Ferdinand.

Prospero creates an illusion of loss to test his enemies and to make them reveal their true selves. Only Gonzalo, who long ago aided Prospero and Miranda, responds affirmatively. He alone notices that his garments and those of his shipwrecked companions have miraculously been left unharmed by the salt water. Sebastian and Antonio react to the magic isle by cynically refusing to believe in miracles. Confident that they are unobserved, they seize the opportunity afforded by Alonso's being asleep to plot a murder and political coup. This attempt is not only despicable but ludicrous, for they are all shipwrecked and no longer have kingdoms over which to quarrel. Alonso, though also burdened with sin, responds to his situation with guilt and despair, for he assumes that his son Ferdinand's death is the just punishment for Alonso's part in the earlier overthrow of Prospero. Alonso must be led through the experience of contrition to the reward he thinks impossible and undeserved: reunion with his lost son.

Alonso's son, Ferdinand, must also undergo ordeals and visions devised by Prospero to test his worth, but more on the level of romantic comedy. Ferdinand is young, innocent, and hopeful—the perfect match for Miranda. Although Prospero obviously approves of his prospective son-in-law, he is not ready to lay aside the role of parental opposition. He invents difficulties, imposes tasks, and issues stern warnings against premarital lust. In place of the ceremonies of the church, Prospero must create the illusion of ceremony by his art. The marriage of Ferdinand and Miranda unites the best of both worlds: the natural innocence of the island and the higher law of nature achieved through moral wisdom at its best. In Ferdinand and Miranda, "nurture" is wedded to "nature."

At the lowest level of the social scale are Stephano and Trinculo. Their comic scenes join them with Caliban: he represents untutored nature, and they represent the unnatural depths to which civilized people can fall. In this way they parallel Sebastian and Antonio, who have learned in supposedly civilized Italy the arts of intrigue and political murder. The antics of Stephano and Trinculo mock the conduct of their presumed betters. In contrast with them, Caliban is almost a sympathetic character. His sensitivity to natural beauty is entirely appropriate to this child of nature. He is, to be sure, the child of a witch, and is called many harsh names such as "Abhorred slave" and "a born devil, on whose nature / Nurture can never stick" (1.2.354; 4.1.188-189). But he protests with some justification that the island was his in the first place and that Prospero and Miranda are interlopers. His very existence calls into question the value of civilization, which has shown itself capable of limitless depravity.

The play's ending is far from completely satisfying. Antonio never repents, and we cannot be sure what the island will be like once Prospero has disappeared from the scene. Ultimately, however, Shakespeare's play strives to celebrate humanity's highest achievement in the union of the island with the civilized world. Miranda and Ferdinand have bright hopes for the future. And even Caliban may be at last reconciled to Prospero's idea of a harmony between will and reason: Caliban vows to "be wise hereafter / And seek for grace" (5.1.298-299). Although Caliban is a part of humanity, Ariel is not. Ariel takes no part in the final union of human society. This spirit belongs to a magic world of song, music, and illusion that the artist borrows for his use but which exists eternally outside of him. With it the artist achieves powers of imagination, enabling him to raise a storm or call forth the dead from their graves. But these visions are illusory in the same sense that all life is illusory, an "insubstantial pageant" melted into thin air (4.1.150-155). Prospero the artist cherishes his own humanity and desires relief from his labors. Yet the art created by the artist endures, existing apart from time and place as does Ariel: "Then to the elements / Be free, and fare thou well!" (5.1.321-322). It's probably a romantic fiction to associate the dramatist Shakespeare with Prospero's farewell to his art, but it is an almost irresistible idea because we are so moved by the exultation and sense of completion contained in this leave-taking.

Questions for Discussion and Writing

1. What is the significance of the title? Does it apply only to the opening scene?
2. What is the "back story" for the plot of this play? Why are Prospero and Miranda on this "uninhabited" island? Where is the island? Who are the people on the ship, and why are they traveling near the island?
3. How are Ariel and Caliban similar? How are they different? Explain how they can be seen as parts or elements of Prospero's character.
4. What is Prospero's purpose in separating the shipwrecked party into three different groups? How do different individuals respond to the island? What do their varying responses tell us about their characters?
5. Describe Miranda. Is she a product of nature or nurture?
6. Why does Prospero treat Ferdinand harshly at first? How does Ferdinand fit into Prospero's plans?
7. How do you respond to Caliban? Is he a villain or a sympathetic character? What positive qualities does Shakespeare give to Caliban?
8. Prospero has been called an overbearing patriarch, a colonist, and even a racist. How do you evaluate the way he treats Ariel, Caliban, and Miranda?
9. Describe the natural world found on the island. Is it innocent or corrupt? How is it affected by the invasion of civilization?
10. Are there any really "bad guys" in *The Tempest*? If so, what makes them bad?
11. According to Gonzalo, what constitutes as ideal commonwealth (2.1.139-60)? How does Gonzalo's vision of a ruler's power compare with Prospero's? How does it compare with Sebastiano's and Stephano's ambitions for power?
12. Discuss Prospero's comparison of life to a stage (4.1.148-58). What does this play say about the relationship between illusion and reality?
13. What does this play say about freedom and servitude?
14. Trace the theme of usurpation through the play. What point does Shakespeare seem to be making about power and the acquisition of power?

15. What is Gonzalo's role or function in the play? Is he in any way a foil to Prospero?
16. Compare the illusions in *The Tempest* to those in *The Glass Menagerie.*
17. Compare Miranda to Nora in *A Doll's House.* To what extent is each one protected, victimized, or both by the men in her life?
18. Compare the representation and use of the supernatural in *The Tempest* to that in *Oedipus the King.*

Video: The Tempest. 76 min., color, 1963. With Maurice Evans, Richard Burton, Roddy McDowell, Lee Remick, and Tom Poston; directed by George Schaefer. Available from Films for the Humanities & Sciences.
The Tempest. 127 min., color, 1987. With Efrem Zimbalist, Jr., William H. Bassett, Ted Sorel, and Ron Palillo. Performed on a re-creation of the Globe Stage. Available from Filmic Archives.
The Tempest. 150 min., color, 1980. With Christopher Guard and Michael Hodern. BBC Shakespeare. Available from Time-Life Video and from Filmic Archives.
Tempest. 140 min., color 1982. With John Cassavetes, Gena Rowlands, Susan Sarandon, and Raul Julia. A New York architect abandons city life to live on a barren Greek island with his daughter. Available from local video distributors.

Suggested Further Readings on **The Tempest**
Berger, Harry, Jr "Miraculous Harp: A Reading of Shakespeare's *Tempest.*"
    Shakespeare Studies 4 (1969): 253-83.
Bloom, William, ed. *Caliban.* Major Literary Characters. New York: Chelsea, 1992.
--- *William Shakespeare's* The Tempest. Modern Critical Interpretations. New York:
    Chelsea, 1988.
Cantor, Paul A. "Prospero's Republic: The Politics of Shakespeare's *The Tempest.*"
    Shakespeare as Political Thinker. Ed. John Alvis and Thomas West. Durham:
    Carolina Academic P, 1981. 239-55.
Hunt, Maurice, ed. *Approaches to Teaching Shakespeare's* The Tempest *and Other Late
    Romances.* New York: MLA, 1992.
Palmer, D. J., ed. The Tempest: *A Casebook.* Rev. ed. Basingstoke: Macmillan, 1991.
Skura, Meredith. "Discourse and the Individual: The Case of Colonialism in *The
    Tempest.*" *Shakespeare Quarterly* 40 (1989): 42-69.
Thompson, Ann. "'Miranda, Where's Your Sister?': Reading Shakespeare's *The
    Tempest.*" *Feminist Criticism: Theory and Practice.* Ed. Susan Sellers. Toronto:
    U of Toronto P, 1991. 45-55.

A DOLL'S HOUSE by Henrik Ibsen [930-80]

Though it would not shock many people today, *A Doll's House* shocked its first audiences by rejecting socially sanctioned roles. Nothing could seemingly justify a wife's walking out on her marriage, away from her children, leaving a husband who abused her only mentally. When Ibsen is able to do so, he makes a powerful statement about personal freedom and development. We can understand Nora's transformation from a powerless child to an adult groping for a reason for existence and principles to live by.

In the first act, Nora is shown as a bubbling and happy childlike doll who depends on her husband to do the thinking. Torvald keeps her in this dependent state and repeatedly emphasizes her dependence by calling her "my little squirrel," "my little skylark," and "my pretty little pet." He foreshadows later difficulties when he says, "There's always something inhibited, something unpleasant about a home built on credit and borrowed money." He cannot allow her to grow up. Nothing will spoil his doll and model dollhouse if he allows no change in her.

Nora reveals the shallowness of her thoughts and her background as a rich and spoiled child when her old friend Christine shows up looking for work. Though Christine is careworn and desperately poor, Nora is unable to stop talking about her own good fortune. When Krogstad arrives to fill in the details of Nora's forgery, she still looks down on him, even though they have committed the same crime. By the end of the first act, Nora's happy bubble has been punctured, and we see the tension begin to grow.

Nora spends Act II urgently trying to retain her secure little world, but despite her best efforts, her forgery is destined to come to light. Her mind now operates in two modes. Her childlike thinking assures her that her husband will forgive her the small crime because she did it to save his life. This thought comforts her, and she is eager to see the confirmation of his love. But her slowly awakening adult mind tells her that Torvald is more worried about his own reputation than about her feelings.

Act III shows the beginning of a much healthier relationship between Christine and Krogstad than prevailed in the past. In contrast, the marriage of the Helmers is rapidly deteriorating. When Nora's forgery is finally revealed and her husband betrays his self-centeredness, she makes the break that will allow her to grow.

Questions for Discussion and Writing

1. Looking back on the first act, what foreshadowing can you see?
2. Why is it dramatically appropriate for Nora to borrow the money from Krogstad?
3. How many scenes are between only two people? How does Ibsen use contrasting pairs of characters?
4. Which characters provide background information? Do they help to develop the main characters?
5. What is the function of Dr. Rank? Does he expose Nora's naiveté and Torvald's callousness? Or does he offer a model for facing life and death without illusions? Does his courage inspire Nora?
6. What or who is the main antagonist? Is it a person, an environment, or a social force? Is there more than one?
7. This play follows traditional dramatic structure rather closely. What point would you identify as the climax?
8. Why do Torvald's arguments against Nora's leaving fail?
9. Is Ibsen attacking marriage? What else may he be attacking?
10. Do you find this play dated? Write an essay explaining why or why not.
11. What will become of Nora? Will she find happiness and fulfillment? Write an essay about Nora's future.
12. Write an essay in which you support this thesis: "A Doll's House concerns the trouble caused by clinging to illusions."

Video: *A Doll's House*. 89 min., b&w, 1959. With Julie Harris, Christopher Plummer, Jason Robards, Jr., Hume Cronyn, and Eileen Hacket. Available from MGM/United Artists Home Video.

A Doll's House. 105 min., color, 1973. With Claire Bloom, Anthony Hopkins, Sir Ralph Richardson, Denholm Elliott, Anna Massey, and Dame Edith Evans. Available from The Video Catalog and Films, Inc.

A Doll's House. 98 min., color, 1973. With Jane Fonda, Edward Fox, Trevor Howard, and David Warner. Available from Prism Entertainment.

Suggested Further Readings on A Doll's House

Fjelde, Rolf, ed. *Ibsen: A Collection of Critical Essays*. Englewood Cliffs: Prentice, 1965.

Clurman, Harold. *Ibsen*. New York: Macmillan, 1977. 108-18.

Hardwick, Elizabeth. *"A Doll's House." Seduction and Betrayal*. New York: Random, 1974. 33-48.

Shafer, Yvonne, ed. *Approaches to Teaching Ibsen's* A Doll House. New York: MLA, 1985.

Sprinchorn, E. M. "Ibsen and the Actors." *Ibsen and the Theatre*. Ed. Errol Durback. New York: New York UP, 1980. 118-30.

THE PROPOSAL by Anton Chekhov   [pp. 981-90]

This brief farce was written as a curtain-raiser; it does not pretend to great depths or even to great comedy. It is, however, a very funny play when skillfully performed. It is light and pleasant, something of a comedy of manners, lacking the serious edge of *Los Vendidos* or even *Death Knocks*. You might compare this play with a good situation comedy on television, since it derives its charm and appeal from being near enough to people like our neighbors and ourselves. Although we can identify to some degree with the characters, the exaggeration allows us to enjoy their foibles while telling ourselves that we are not nearly as silly.

The force of the comedy in a farce comes from the exaggeration of character and situation. As in *The Proposal*, a farce begins in commonplace, credible circumstances and surroundings, and then shifts gradually into improbability and even into nonsense. Although all comedy involves some deviation from the norm, a farce pushes the exaggeration to an almost grotesque point. The farcical exaggeration in this play can be seen in the fact that Lomov and Natasha are just as concerned about their meadowlands and their dogs as they are about making an acceptable marriage. Chekhov also presents a hypochondriac, constantly in seeming pain, talking rapidly and inconsistently--and the impact is humorous, not serious.

Much of the humor in this play is verbal, so reading it aloud may help to engage students in the comedy. The possibilities for physical humor are also numerous; it is, after all, a farce. You might help your students to visualize the action by discussing how the actions and movements, even the dress and gestures, of the characters could be exploited for comic effect. You might illustrate how an actor would "play" one of Lomov's imaginary heart attacks, for instance. Or ask students to act out some scenes, taking direction from the rest of the class.

Although the play's theme is less important than its humor, Chekhov does seem to suggest that this little slice of life before marriage is like many slices of married life. This suggestion comes out especially in the play's conclusion when Chubukov says, "And they lived happily every after!" This line may be ironic, but it also confirms the familiar stereotype of married life as a continuing battle for ascendancy.

Students may have difficulty identifying the social class of the characters. They are clearly landowners. Chubukov is described as "rich," and Lomov must be his equal, or nearly so: otherwise Chubukov would not consent to the marriage. In England these people would be called "gentry," but they are not aristocrats. They are members of the middle or upper-middle class. Their families seem to have owned land for generations and to have shared borders. Lomov's speech on page 982 reveals that the marriage is to be a middle-class union of convenience rather than a romantic one. Natasha is slightly on the wrong side of a good marriageable age for her time and place. At 25, she could do worse than her neighbor Lomov. Lomov is not much better off than Natasha, but he does have the greater freedom to be single that comes to men in a male-dominated society.

Suggestions for Discussion and Writing
1. What do we learn about Chubukov from the way he treats Lomov in the opening scene?
2. Why does Lomov want to marry Natasha? Why does she want to marry him? Does either of them have a good reason?
3. What do we learn about Natasha in the first encounter with Lomov (pp.982-84)? What impression does she make on Lomov?
4. Describe the relationship between Natasha and her father. What family traits do they have in common?
5. Do the traditional dramatic terms apply to this play? Is there a protagonist and an antagonist, a climax and a denouement?
6. What is a farce? How does it differ from other types of comedy? What is farcical about this play?
7. Compare this play to Allen's *Death Knocks* or to Valdez's *Los Vendidos*. In what ways are the plays absurd and farcical? Are the characters exaggerated in the same way? What serious statement, if any, do the plays make?
8. How would you adapt *The Proposal* for television? Who would you cast in the parts?
9. Write your own farcical scene in which a serious exchange between two people is constantly interrupted for some silly reason.

Video: Anton Chekhov: A Writer's Life. 37 min., color and b&w, 1974. A biographical portrait of the playwright. Available from Films for the Humanities & Sciences.

Suggested Further Readings on **The Proposal**
Eekman, Thomas A., ed. *Critical Essays on Anton Chekhov.* Boston: G. K. Hall, 1989.
Kirk, Irina. *Anton Chekhov.* Boston: Twayne, 1981.
Magarshak, David. *Chekhov the Dramatist.* New York: Hill, 1960.
Wellek, Rene, and Nonna D. Wellek. *Chekhov: New Perspectives.* Englewood Cliffs: Prentice, 1984.
Williams, Lee J. *Anton Chekhov the Iconoclast.* Scranton: U of Scranton P, 1989.

TRIFLES by Susan Glaspell [pp. 991-1000]

Susan Glaspell wrote this play at a time (1916) when women did not often write for the stage. The play's feminist point of view is also remarkable for its time. While the action centers on a murder investigation, the playwright skillfully introduces a second investigation, conducted by the two women who accompany the men inquiring into John Wright's death. At the beginning of the play Mr. Hale remarks that "women are used to worrying over trifles," but it just such trifles that are the substance of the women's investigation.

The men hunt in vain for clues to the murder; the women quickly find what the men have missed. Their discovery is the result of their feminine sensibilities, which enable them to recognize the importance of what they find—a bird with a broken neck. They realize that Wright must have killed it and that the bird's death was probably Mrs. Wright's motive for murdering her husband. Glaspell also introduces the idea that the truly "awful thing" was not the murder of John Wright but the lonely and isolated life his wife had been forced to endure. Because they neglected Minnie Wright, the women feel implicated and decide to hide the incriminating evidence.

The play emphasizes the essential differences between men and women in rural life. The men are insensitive to the nature of women's lives. More important, their adherence to the letter of the law precludes a merciful administration of justice. The two women, with their sense of a higher purpose, band together to protect another woman from the injustice of man's law when applied to women. (At the time this play was written, women were not allowed to vote or serve on juries.)

A year after Glaspell wrote this play, she rewrote it as a short story, titled "A Jury of Her Peers." Although the story is close to the play (after the first page, much of the dialogue is identical with that in the play), the women take more central roles earlier in the story than in the play. The story also takes us inside Mrs. Hale's mind to learn of her guilt for not having visited Mrs. Wright. The story seems to focus more on justice than on the "trifles" overlooked by the men. Perhaps this shift in thematic emphasis is why the author changed the title.

Questions for Discussion and Writing

1. Make a list of the events that occurred (or that you speculate might have occurred) before the play begins. Why did Glaspell choose to begin the play where she did?
2. Describe the atmosphere evoked by the play's setting.
3. How would you characterize Mr. Henderson, the County Attorney?
4. Several times the men "laugh" or "chuckle." What do these expressions of amusement convey about them and their attitudes?
5. Why does Glaspell include Mrs. Peters' speech about the boy who killed her cat (p. 999)?
6. What is the point of the women's concern about the quilt and whether Mrs. Wright "was going to quilt it or knot it"? What is the significance of the last line of the play? Why is it ironic?
7. What sort of person was Minnie Foster before she married? What do you think happened to her?
8. Susan Glaspell wrote a short story version of *Trifles* and changed the title to "A Jury of Her Peers." What is the significance of each title? Why do you think she changed the title? Which one do you prefer?
9. What is your reaction to the decision made by Mrs. Peters and Mrs. Hale to hide the dead bird from the men? What are their motives?
10. Could it be argued that this play is immoral? Write an essay in which you explain your answer to this question.
11. Write an essay comparing *Trifles* to "A Jury of Her Peers" [pp. 281-94 in the Anthology of Short Fiction]. Consider any differences in tone and emphasis between the two versions. Why do you think the author wrote a second version in another literary form?

Video: *A Jury of Her Peers*. 30 min., color, 1980. Filmed version of *Trifles*, directed by Sally Heckel. Available from Films Inc. and Michigan Media.

Suggested Further Readings on **Trifles**

Ben-Zvi, Linda. "'Murder, She Wrote': The Genesis of Susan Glaspell's *Trifles*." *Theatre Journal* 44 (1992): 141-62.

---. *Susan Glaspell: Essays on Her Theater and Fiction*. Ann Arbor: U of Michigan P, 1995.

Dymkowski, Christine. "On the Edge: The Plays of Susan Glaspell." *Modern Drama* 31 (1988): 91-105.

Mael, Phyllis. "*Trifles*: The Path to Sisterhood." *Literature/Film Quarterly* 17 (1989): 281-84.

Mustazza, Leonard. "Generic Translation and Thematic Shift in Susan Glaspell's *Trifles* and 'A Jury of Her Peers.'" *Studies in Short Fiction* 26 (Fall 1989): 489-96.

Quinn, Laura. "*Trifles* as Treason: Coming to Consciousness as a Gendered Reader." *Reader Response in the Classroom*. Ed. Nicholas Karolides. New York: Longman, 1992. 187-97.

Smith, Beverly A. "Women's Work—Trifles? The Skill and Insights of Playwright Susan Glaspell." *International Journal of Women's Studies* 5 (1982): 172-84.

Stein, Karen. "The Women's World of Glaspell's *Trifles*." *Women in American Theatre*. Ed. Helen Chinoy and Linda Jenkins. New York: Crowell, 1981. 251-54.

Zehfuss, Ruth E. "The Law and the Ladies in *Trifles*." *Teaching English in the Two-Year College* (February 1991): 42-44.

FLORENCE by Alice Childress [pp. 1001-10]

This brief play with a small cast is perfect for reading aloud in class. A good way for the whole class to prepare for an oral reading would be to ask students to write out their analyses of each character and describe how each should be portrayed. You can also ask them to think of performers from television and movies who would be right for the various parts.

At first glance this play may appear to be little more than a slight, static depiction of southern racism in the late 1940s. But a deeper analysis reveals a powerful, well-crafted drama about issues and feelings that are still very much alive in the U.S. The play contains forceful symbols and symbolic gestures that project its main thematic message: that blacks must not turn over to white liberals the responsibility for nurturing young, black dreamers but must encourage their children to fight to reach their fullest potential in spite of racial biases.

The signs that divide the railway waiting room constitute an important set of symbols. "Colored" and "White" signs hang over the doorway entrances to each side; the division is further emphasized by the using the word "ladies" and "gentlemen" on the restroom door signs for whites. These titles, which suggest grace, culture, or wealth, do not appear on the restroom doors for blacks, an implication that black men and women are a cut below white ladies and gentlemen. Moreover, Childress expands this symbolism by having the Porter tell Mama that should she need to use the restroom, she must use the colored men's because the other is out of order. It is illegal for Mama to step into the "White ladies" restroom, so she will have to demean herself and risk having her privacy invaded in the colored men's restroom. The out-of-order restroom becomes a symbol of the black woman's historical burden in America, that of struggling to keep together the family that the system of slavery plotted to destroy. This play on words hints that for

Colored women, there is no room for rest. On another level, Childress's symbol suggests that the American societal structure is out of order, nonfunctioning for African Americans. Childress mirrors a society that is—and will remain—out of order as long as people are judged by the color of their skin.

In addition to the prominent signs that bar whites and blacks from crossing lines, a low railing, dividing the waiting room, serves as a physical and emotional barrier between the races and is the key symbol for developing the play's central idea. Conversations and actions are structured around this dividing line; Childress moves both the black and white characters toward or away from this low railing to suggest racial constraints. She ingeniously demonstrates that the railing prevents both blacks and whites from crossing into each other's territory. On one level, the bar symbolizes the need for blacks to fight against the restrictions of racism and to cross the line to secure those privileges in life that belong not just to whites but to all human beings. On another level, the railing suggests that segregation breeds ignorance: when whites are barred from firsthand knowledge about blacks, they are forced to imagine, which leads to creating the kind of stereotypes that pervade Mrs. Carter's attitudes and opinions.

Questions for Discussion and Writing

1. Why is the play named after a character who never appears?
2. How would you describe the relationship between Marge and her Mama?
3. What is the difference between Marge and her sister Florence? Could they be compared to Sadie and Maude in Gwendolyn Brooks's poem by that title (pp. 600)?
4. What is the role of the Porter in the play?
5. How would you describe Mrs. Carter? Do you know any people like her?
6. How would you characterize Mama? Why does she react to Mrs. Carter the way she does? Why does she grab Mrs. Carter's wrist and call her "Child!"?
7. How does Mama change in the course of the play? What causes her to change?
8. What is the significance of the divided stage and the separate restroom signs? What do these symbols contribute to the themes of the play?
9. What happened to Florence's husband? Why does Childress include this detail?
10. Is this play outdated? What details tell you that it was written in 1950? Compare the treatment of racial and social issues in this play to that of *A Raisin in the Sun* (pp. 1011-1066 in the drama anthology), which was written almost a decade (eight years) later.
11. Write an essay in which you argue that the ideas and issues presented in *Florence* are still relevant today.
12. How would you update this play? Rewrite the encounter between Mama and Mrs. Carter (pp. 1004-09), placing it in a contemporary setting and using current language.

Suggested Further Readings on Alice Childress

Betsko, Kathleen, and Rachel Koening. *Interviews with Contemporary Women Playwrights.* Taylors: Beech Tree, 1987.

Brown-Guillory, Elizabeth. "Alice Childress: Pioneering Spirit." *SAGE: A Scholarly Journal on Black Women* 4.2 (Spring 1987): 66-68.

Hey, Samuel. "Alice Childress's Dramatic Structure." *Black Women Writers (1950-1980).* Ed. Mari Evans. Garden City: Anchor, 1984. 117-28.

Jennings, La Vinia Delois. *Alice Childress.* New York: Twayne, 1995. 20-26.

Maguire, Roberta. "Alice Childress." *The Playwright's Art: Conversations with Contemporary American Dramatists.* Ed. Jackson R. Bryer. New Brunswick: Rutgers UP, 1995. 48-69.

A RAISIN IN THE SUN by Lorraine Hansberry   [pp. 1011-66]

This play tells the story of a family's attempt to move from an all-black neighborhood to the white suburbs, a struggle that Hansberry's own parents fought all the way to the Supreme Court. Before the Hansberrys were granted the right to live in the house they had purchased, they were harassed and threatened daily. The play was first produced in 1959; its action takes place before the Civil Rights Movement of the 1960s. Abortion was also against the law in this country at that time, meaning that Ruth's decision about her pregnancy could lead to a physically dangerous and illegal operation.

The play portrays the "American Dream" of working hard, saving your money, buying your own home, and having the kind of space and privacy that will permit you to live with dignity and pride. Although this theme seems to emphasize middle-class values and consumerism, Hansberry wrote her play to explore these issues and to demonstrate that the needs of black families parallel those of white families but also involve conflicts that most white families do not experience.

Hansberry's play is painfully honest. It shows that Walter Younger is affected by the same lust for possessions (and the power they can confer) that affects many Americans. He is also caught up in the old pattern of male dominance over women, although the women in his life do not tolerate his chauvinistic behavior. Mama opposes her son's plan to buy a liquor store--because it will further corrupt her own community and because she wants the security and identity that she feels her family deserves. In the end, Walter finds the strength to think of his family rather than his own selfish concerns. He refuses the offer of the Clybourne Park Improvement Association, not to express a desire to own a better house but to demonstrate that the Youngers are not socially inferior and that they have the right to live wherever they choose.

Questions for Discussion and Writing
1. What is the significance of the title? It's a phrase from a poem called "Harlem" by Langston Hughes. Look up the poem and explain why you think Hansberry chose this phrase for her title.
2. Compare and contrast the dreams of Walter, Mama, Beneatha, and Ruth. Which one of these characters do you find most admirable?
3. Who is the play's protagonist? Who (or what) is the antagonist? Is the central conflict within the Younger family?
4. Why are Joseph Asagai and George Murchison in the play? What perspectives of the black experience in the United States do they represent? How do their views relate to the problems of the Younger family?
5. How would you answer the charge that this play celebrates consumerism and material values? Does the play promote the idea that blacks should want to be just like whites?
6. Is the play dated? Have the conflicts that it presents been resolved?
7. Look up the word "assimilation" or "assimilationism" in a good college dictionary. Does the term apply to the Youngers?
8. What conflicts between men and women do you see in this play? How do the gender conflicts in this play compare to similar conflicts in other works you have read recently?
9. Write a scene or story that shows the Younger family ten years later. What has happened to their dreams? Where are they living, and what are they doing?

Video: *A Raisin in the Sun.* 128 min., b&w, 1961. With Sidney Poitier, Claudia McNeil, and Ruby Dee. Available from RCA/Columbia Pictures Home Video.

A Raisin in the Sun. 171 min., color, 1988. American Playhouse production with Danny Glover, Starletta DuPois, Esther Rolle, and Kim Yancey. Available from DVC, Inc.

Lorraine Hansberry: The Black Experience in the Creation of Drama. 35 min., color, 1975. Includes clips of her plays. Available from Films for the Humanities & Sciences.

Suggested Further Readings on A Raisin in the Sun

Ashley, Leonard R. "Lorraine Hansberry and the Great Black Way." *Modern American Drama: The Female Canon.* Ed. June Schlueter. Rutherford: Fairleigh Dickinson UP, 1990. 151-60.

Baraka, Amiri. "A Critical Reevaluation: *A Raisin in the Sun*'s Enduring Passion." *A Raisin in the Sun* and *The Sign in Sidney Brustein's Window.* Ed. Robert Nemiroff. New York: New American Library, 1987. 9-20

Brown, Lloyd W. "Lorraine Hansberry as Ironist: A Reappraisal of *A Raisin in the Sun.* *Journal of Black Studies* 4 (March 1974): 237-47.

Carter, Steven R. *Hansberry's Drama: Commitment and Complexity.* Urbana: U of Illinois P, 1991. 19-66.

Cheney, Anne. *Lorraine Hansberry.* Boston: Twayne, 1984.

Miller, Jeanne-Marie. "Black Women in Plays by Black Playwrights." *Women in American Theatre.* Ed. Helen Chinoy and Linda Jenkins. Rev. ed. New York: Theatre Communications, 1987. 256-62.

Washington, J. Charles. "*A Raisin in the Sun* Revisited." *Black American Literature Forum* 22.1 (Spring 1988): 109-24.

DEATH KNOCKS by Woody Allen   [pp. 1067-72]

This brief two-person play seems little more than a humorous sketch, but it poses some interesting questions about a serious subject (death) in a style that is both disarming and engaging. Students may be familiar with Allen's movies, which may be a good place to begin a discussion of the aims and methods of his brand of comedy. An examination of the comic effects in this play should lead to an understanding of how comedy depends upon the recognition of some incongruity of speech, action, or character. The incongruity may be verbal (as with a play on words), or bodily (as with pratfalls and physical antics), or satirical (as with the discrepancy between fact and pretense displayed by a braggart or pompous fool). Allen uses all of these elements of incongruity, but employs them more skillfully and less crudely than many other contemporary comedians do. *Death Knocks* is not a farce-comedy, like Chekhov's *The Proposal*, or a social satire, like Valdez's *Los Vendidos*, although it shares some of the same goals and comic techniques with both of these plays.

As with most good comedy, Allen's sketch is about a very serious topic indeed: the human tendency to avoid confronting mortality. The reference to "Faust" reminds us of how many plays and stories, both serious and humorous, there are about people who try to bargain with or cheat death (or the devil). Allen's take on the subject is especially effective because Nat Ackerman seems to have found a way to outwit death, although in order to make the premise work, the playwright has to portray death as a clumsy nebbish who loses at cards. The concept is attractive, but not entirely convincing. Still, the play can be fun and provoke some interesting reactions.

Questions for Discussion and Writing

1. What is the pun in the title? What does the title suggest about the play's tone and comic approach?
2. At one point Death says "I'm one of the most terrifying figures you could possibly imagine." Is that the way he's depicted in this play? How does Allen's characterization match or contradict traditional portrayals of death.
3. Nat Ackerman says to Death "You look a little like me"; later Death says that "Each one has his own personal way of going." What concept of death and dying is Allen developing with these details?
4. Why does Nat believe it should not be his time to die? To what degree is he convincing, and what strategies does he use to delay Death?
5. Death mentions "Faust," a famous fictional character who sells his soul to the devil for borrowed time on earth. What other stories do you know about people who tried to delay or bargain with death? How do people in our society try to put off death?
6. Compare Allen's ideas about facing death with those presented in "On Tidy Endings" (p. 1081).
7. Compare and contrast Allen's personification of Death that of Emily Dickinson's (pp. 554-55). How would you personify death?
8. Compare the comedy in *Death Knocks* with that of *The Proposal* (p. 981) and *Los Vendidos* (p. 1073).
9. Write a sketch in which you present a humorous confrontation between a human being and a personified abstraction (like Fear or Temptation or Greed or Vanity).

Suggested Further Readings on Woody Allen

Blansfield, Karen C. "Woody Allen and the Comic Tradition in America." *Studies in American Humor* 6 (1988): 142-53.
Jacobs, Diane. *Magic of Woody Allen*. London: Robson, 1982.
Lax, Eric. *Woody Allen: A Biography*. New York: Knopf, 1991.
McCann, Graham. *Woody Allen: New Yorker*. London: Polity, 1990.
Reisch, M. S. "Woody Allen: American Prose Humorist." *Journal of Popular Culture* 17 (1983): 68-74.
Yacowar, Maurice. *Loser Take All: The Comic Art of Woody Allen*. New York: Ungar, 1979.

LOS VENDIDOS by Luis Valdez   [pp. 1073-80]

In 1964 Valdez founded El Teatro Campesino ("The Farmworkers' Theater") to assist the grape boycott and farmworker strike in Delano, California. The company devised a form of drama which they called *actos*, short satirical plays that portrayed the oppression of the field workers. According to Valdez the *actos* were used to "Inspire the audience to social action. Illuminate specific points about social problems. Satirize the opposition. Show or hint at a solution. Express what people are feeling."

Los Vendidos is one of Teatro Campesino's most acclaimed and enduring *actos*. It presents a range of stereotypes that Anglo culture applies to Chicano experience: farmworkers, urban tough guys, revolutionaries, and the "new" Mexican-American yuppie. In the surprise ending, however, the yuppie turns on the secretary, and the "Used

Mexicans" turn out to be in charge of the shop—Honest Sancho is their front. Although *Los Vendidos* is no less political than the earlier *actos*, the focus is no longer on striking farm workers. It is on the Chicano's relationship to Anglo culture. Furthermore, this play seems less concerned with offering a solution than with showing contrasting kinds of Chicanos, although it is clear where Valdez's sympathies lie.

The play's title sums up the conflicts inherent in the Mexican-Americans' dual experience. "Los Vendidos" can be translated two ways: "those who are sold" (like the Mexicans in Sancho's lot, who are "used" and exploited by Anglos) and "the sellouts" (like Sancho and Miss Jimenez, who have sold out their cultural identity). This duality is reinforced by the play's mixture of Spanish and English—the two languages that Chicanos use to define themselves and to relate to the Anglo world. In other words, the play operates on the border between the two cultures, demonstrating through exaggerated comedy the complex social and political negotiations that Mexican-Americans engage in today.

Questions for Discussion and Writing
1. What is the meaning of the play's title? Who are the "sellouts" that the title alludes to?
2. What stereotypes of Mexican-Americans does the play present? Are these stereotypes offensive? Why does Valdez use them?
3. What change occurs in the end of the play? Does this change clarify or explain the reason for using stereotypes?
4. Do you think the play is a satire? Why or why not?
5. Did you find the play dated? entertaining? offensive? Explain your reactions.
6. How would different audiences respond to this play? Would Mexican-Americans be offended or delighted? Would Anglos enjoy this play? Do you think Valdez wants to make his audience uncomfortable?
7. What social or political messages does the play convey? Do the politics interfere with the play's dramatic effectiveness?
8. In 1971, the group performing the play changed its ending by having the men decide to use the money to build a community center. What do you think of this ending? Does it increase or diminish the play's effectiveness?
9. Explain how you might adapt *Los Vendidos* to fit another minority group.
10. Compare this play's treatment of racial issues with that of *Florence* or *Raisin in the Sun*. Which approach do you prefer?
11. How is the comedy of *Los Vendidos* similar to or different from the comedy of *Death Knocks*?
12. Compare this play's treatment of cultural stereotypes to that of *M. Butterfly*. Is the purpose the same in both?

Video: *Luis Valdez and El Teatro Campesino*. 26 min., color, 1991. Interview. Available from Films for the Humanities & Sciences.

Suggested Further Readings on Los Vendidos
Cardenas de Dwyer, Carlota. "The Development of Chicano Drama and Luis Valdez' *Actos.*" *Modern Chicano Writers: A Collection of Critical Essays.* Ed. Joseph Summers and Tomas Ybarra-Frausto. Englewood Cliffs: Prentice, 1979. 160-66.
Hernandez, Guillermo. *Chicano Satire: A Study in Literary Culture.* Austin: U of Texas P, 1991.
Huerta, Jorge A. *Chicano Theater: Themes and Forms.* Ypsilanti: Bilingual Press, 1982.
Kanellos, Nicolás. *Hispanic Theatre in the United States.* Houston: Arte Público, 1984.

Morton, Carlos. "An Interview with Luis Valdez." *Latin American Theatre Review* 15 (1982): 73-76.
---. "The Teatro Campesino." *Tulane Drama Review* 18.4 (Dec. 1974): 71-6.
Morales, Ed. "Shadowing Valdez." *American Theatre* 9.7 (Nov. 1992): 14-19.
Valdez, Luis, and El Teatro Campesino. *Actos*. San Juan Bautista: Menyah, 1971.

ON TIDY ENDINGS by Harvey Fierstein   [pp. 1081-97]

This play, the final part of a trilogy entitled *Safe Sex*, depicts the confrontation between the homosexual lover and the former wife of a man who has died of AIDS. It was adapted as the Home Box Office television "Tidy Endings" in 1988, co-starring Stockard Channing and the author (in the part of Arthur). Although AIDS is central to the plot, the play is not really *about* AIDS. It does not deal with such issues as mandatory testing or public spending on AIDS research. Rather, it focuses on the problem of how the living deal with death of a loved one. As Fierstein said in an interview, "This is not a play about disease, it's about life."

In many ways the plot in "On Tidy Endings" follows the structure of Greek drama: it begins near the end of the story and slowly reveals the conflict (and its background) through explosive bits of dialogue. On the surface the play is all exposition; it seems to be almost entirely about the past. Although nothing much seems to happen, the real "action" in the play occurs in dramatic confrontations between Marion and Arthur. Both characters loved the deceased (Collin) deeply, both are hurt by his death and by the behavior of others, and both have some understanding of each other's feelings and situation. But both also have a great deal to learn. And it is this painful, sometimes humorous education that constitutes the primary action in this drama.

Much of the dialogue in the play is jocular, and that may strike some readers as inappropriate. After all, AIDS and all the grief associated with it are scarcely laughing matters. But, of course, one way that humans have of dealing with extreme grief is through laughter. Many of Arthur's jokes are defensive—and sometimes hurtful. He uses humor to express his anger and frustration. He also makes jokes as a way to defuse and resolve conflict. Dealing with the shifting moods in the play may require some careful analysis.

Questions for Discussion and Writing
1. How would you describe the relationship between Marion and her son (Jim)? Consider the way each responds to Collin's death and to the other's response to Collin's death.
2. What do you think of Marion? How believable is her concern for Arthur?
3. How do you respond to Arthur? What do you learn about his relationship with Collin through his conversation with Marion? How would you describe his attitude toward Marion? Do you think he's justified in lashing out at her?
4. June says, "Arthur got plenty already. I'm not crying for Arthur." What does she mean? What did Arthur gain and lose from his relationship with Collin and from Collin's death?
5. June is not necessary to the plot. Why is she in the play? In what ways is she a foil to Marion?

6. Arthur says that Marion should have told Jimmy the real reason his father decided to leave. Do you agree? Explain.
7. What are your impressions of Collin? At one point Marion calls him "one of the most special human beings there ever was" and Arthur says he would have done anything to keep Collin alive. What do you think of these assessments?
8. What does the title mean? What is implied by a "tidy" ending or by "tidying up loose ends"? Is the ending of this play "tidy"? Could the title be ironic?
9. What do you think was Fierstein's purpose in writing this play? Did he want to inform, persuade, or entertain his audiences? Is this a protest play?
10. What does the play say about the way human beings face death?
11. What do you think of the humor in the play? Does it seem out of place? Or does it serve a legitimate dramatic purpose?
12. What do the main characters learn about themselves by the end of the play? What did you learn about AIDS and its effects on individual and family lives?

Suggested Further Readings on On Tidy Endings

Cohen, Jodi R. "Intersecting and Competing Discourses in Harvey Fierstein's 'Tidy Endings.'" *The Quarterly Journal of Speech* 77.2 (May 1991): 196-208.

Gross, Gregory D. "Coming Up for Air: Three AIDS Plays." *Journal of American Culture* 15.3 (Summer 1992): 63-67.

Oliver, Edith. Rev. of "Safe Sex." *The New Yorker* 63 (20 April 1987): 75.

Simon, John. Rev. of "Safe Sex." *New York* 20 (20 April 1987): 66-67.

PART V   THE EDITING PROCESS

A HANDBOOK FOR CORRECTING ERRORS (p. 1101)

Remember to advise your students to consult the Handbook when they revise their papers. You may want to assign various exercises to individuals who have particular problems, or occasionally to the whole class if, for instance, the majority of them are writing comma splices or making modifier mistakes.

Exercise on Comma Splices   [pp. 1107-08]

1.   Clyde is constantly revising his essays; thus he turns in fine finished papers.
     [Students could use a period and a capital letter on *thus* if they prefer.]

2.   Your analysis is flawed in several ways; because you need to rewrite it, let's discuss your problem.
     [Or preferably, a period after *ways* and a capital letter on *you*.]

3.   You have written an excellent analysis, Bertha; you should read it to the class.
     [Or a period after *Bertha* and a capital letter on *you*.]

4.   Monroe complains that he never understands the stories; yet he only reads through them once, hastily.
     [Or a period after *stories* and a capital letter on *yet*.]

5.   Plot is the main element in this story, as far as I can tell; characterization is scarcely important at all.
     [Or a semicolon after *story* and a comma after *tell*.]
     [Or a period after *story*, a capital on *as*, and a comma to replace the semicolon after *tell*.]
     [Or a period after *tell* and a capital on *characterization*.]

Exercise on Faulty Predication   [p. 1109]

There are, of course, many possible corrections. Here are some:

1.   As the tone of the jingle changes, the characters singing it dance.

180

2. Broken hearts and forgotten dreams supply the lyrics to country music.

3. Applying the psychological approach to the modern novel can yield significant insights.

4. The works of Chicano poets reflect the culture of their Aztec forebears.

5. The women's movement has caused increased respect for Wharton's fiction.

Exercise on Pronoun Errors [p. 1116]

1. The policeman yelled at Walter Mitty, irritating Mitty very much.

2. Good dramatists always respect the intelligence of their audiences.

3. A perfectly clear story can be made obscure by the abstract words and vague terms used by a literary critic.
[Or A perfectly clear story can be made obscure by a literary critic using abstract words and vague terms.]

4. Rereading the story and underlining key words will help you analyze it better.

5. Both optimists and pessimists will always be able to find examples of poetry to support their own point of view.

Exercise on Shifts in Person [p. 1117]

In Willa Cather's short story, "Neighbor Rosicky," we see a comparison between the debilitating life of the city and the harsh life of the country. Yet we notice a difference in the quality of these lifestyles. Through Rosicky, Cather shows us the stagnant, draining effects of urban life, which serve to enhance the birth-death-rebirth theme of the story. Rosicky, we can easily observe, is a gentle, loving, and tender person. Through the trials of city living and country living, he has gained knowledge about the meaning of true happiness. We see him, in his gentle, unobtrusive manner, try to share his enlightenment with those around him. If we observe closely, we notice that even a minor character, Dr. Ed, is affected by Rosicky's example. By examining this relationship, we see Cather put forth a plea for tasting the simple pleasures our lives have to offer. Education, wealth, and career cannot guarantee us happiness. Cather wants us to realize that the enjoyment of our lives makes living worthwhile.

Exercise on Shifts in Tense [p. 1118]

1. Dudley Randall's shocking images include "a stub, a stump, a butt, a scab, a knob" as he describes the possible victims of mercy killing.

2. When Dickinson wrote, "To ache is human—polite," she made a statement about the nature of politeness as well as humanity.

3.   The relationship between the ideal lovers in Donne's poem is illuminated by a comparison between the two legs of a compass, whose interdependence is emphasized.

4.   In "Design," Frost pondered the possible meanings of a chance meeting of a spider, a flower, and a moth and made the apparent coincidence seem ominous.

5.   The first line of Donald Hall's poem sets up the paradox the persona expresses: he finds his own mortality brought home to him by his new baby, an "instrument of immortality."

Exercise on Modifier Mistakes [pp. 1119-20]

1.   Without a doubt, Antigone's faith sustained her in her struggle with Creon.

2.   After Haemon attempts to kill his father, the son's sword becomes the instrument of his own death.

3.   In her heart, Ismene feels Antigone is right.

4.   Thinking the edict is good enough for the populace, Creon has no illusions about their stupidity.

5.   In the opening scene, Antigone wants to bury her brother Polynices.

6.   Championing unwritten universal laws, Antigone turns into an enemy of the state in Creon's eyes by burying Polynices.

Exercise on Irregular Verbs [p. 1121]

1. chosen   2. begun   3. waked, wakened   4. laid   5. Drunk

Exercise on Using Active Voice [p. 1122]

1. The play dealt with the problem of male impotence.

2. Shocking sexual revelations embellished the story line.

3. Silly, outrageous rhymes and puns make limericks lively and amusing.

4. Several mistaken identities complicate the comedy's plot.

5. The playwright reveals the main conflict in the second act.

6. Too many strange symbols have obscured the meaning.

7. An inattentive reader might misinterpret the ending.

Directory of Audio and Video Distributors

For further information, consult the *Educational Film & Video Locater,* published by R. R. Bowker.

American Audio Prose Library
P.O. Box 842
Columbia, MO 65205
800-447-2275

Annenberg/CPB Collection
P. O. Box 2345
South Burlington, VT 05407

Audio Book Contractors
P. O. Box 40115
Washington, DC 20016
202-363-3429

Audio Editions
P. O. Box 6930
Auburn, CA 95604-6930
800-231-4261

Audio Forum
Jeffrey Norton Publishers
96 Broad St
Guilford, CT 06437
203-453-9794
800-243-1234

Caedmon/Harper Audio
P. O. Box 588
Dunmore, PA 18512
717-343-4761
800-242-7737

Caedmon Records
1995 Broadway
New York, NY 10023
212-580-3400

Carousel Film & Video
260 Fifth Ave.
Suite 405
New York, NY 10001
212-683-1660
800-683-1660

Centre Productions
1800 30th St.
Suite 207
Boulder, CO 80301
303-444-1166
800-886-1166

Corinth Films
410 East 62 Street
New York, NY 10021
212-421-4770

Coronet/MTI Film & Video
P. O. Box 2649
Columbus, OH 43216
614-876-0371
800-321-3106

DVC, Inc.
P. O. Box 30054
Indianapolis, IN 46230
800-828-0373

Filmic Archives
The Cinema Center
Botsford, CT 06404
800-366-1920

Films for the Humanities & Sciences
12 Cerrine Road
Monmouth Junction, NJ 08852
609-275-1400
800-257-5126

Films Inc.
5547 Ravenswood Ave.
Chicago, IL 60640
312-878-2600
800-323-4222

Indiana University Instructional Support
    Services
Franklin Hall, Room 0001
Bloomington, IN 47405
812-885-2853

Insight Media
2162 Broadway
New York, NY 10024
212-721-6316
800-233-9910

Learning Corporation of America
  See Coronet/MTI Film & Video

Listening Library
1 Park Ave.
Old Greenwich, CT 06870
203-637-3616
800-243-4504

MGM/United Arts Home Video
1350 Avenue of the Americas
New York, NY 10019
212-408-0600

Michigan Media
University of Michigan Media
        Resources Center
400 Fourth Street
Ann Arbor, MI 48109
313-764-5360

Monterey Home Video
28038 Dorothy Drive
Suite 1
Agoura Hills, CA 91301
818-597-0047
800-424-2593

New Letters on Air
University of Missouri at Kansas City
5100 Rockhill Rd.
Kansas City, MO 64110
816-235-1168

New York State Education Department
Center for Learning Technologies
Media Distribution Network
Room C-7, Concourse Level
Cultural Education Center
Albany, NY 12230
518-474-1265

PBS Video
1320 Braddock Place
Alexandria, VA 22314
703-739-5380

Perspective Films and Video
65 East South Water St.
Chicago, IL 60601

Prism Entertainment
1888 Century Park East
Suite 1000
Los Angeles, CA 90067
213-277-3270

Pyramid Film & Video
P. O. Box 1048
Santa Monica, CA 90406
800-421-2304

RCA/Columbia Home Video
3500 W. Olive Ave.
Burbank, CA 91505
818-953-7900

Recorded Books
270 Skipjack Rd.
Prince Frederick, MD 20678
310-535-5590
800-638-1304

Spoken Arts
801 95th Ave. N
St. Petersburg, FL 33702
813-578-7600
800-726-8090

Spoken Arts Records
310 North Ave.
New Rochelle, NY 10801
914-636-5482

Summer Stream
P. O. Box 6056
Santa Barbara, CA 93160
805-962-6540

Time-Life Video
Customer Service
1450 East Parham Rd.
Richmond, VA 23280
800-621-7026

The Video Catalog
P. O. Box 64267
St. Paul, MN 55164-0267
800-733-2232

Warner Home Video
40000 Warner Blvd.
Burbank, CA 91522

Watershed Tapes
Dist. by Inland Book Co.
P. O. Box 120216
East Haven, CT 06512
203-467-4257
800-243-0138

Wireless Audio Collection
Minnesota Public Radio
P. O. Box 64454
St. Paul, MN 55164-0454
800-733-3369

USEFUL REFERENCE WORKS

Brunel, Pierre, ed. *Companion to Literary Myths, Heroes, and Archetypes.* Trans. Wendy Allatson and Judith Hayward. London; New York: Routledge, 1996.

Cirlot, J. E. *A Dictionary of Symbols.* 2nd ed. Trans. Jack Sage. New York: Barnes & Noble, 1995.

Cooper, J. C. *An Illustrated Encyclopaedia of Traditional Symbols.* New York: Thames and Hudson, 1990.

Frazer, Sir James and George W. Stacking. *The Golden Bough: A Study in Magic and Religion.* 1922. Rpt. New York: Penguin, 1998.

Gassner, John, and Edward Quinn, eds. *The Reader's Encyclopedia of World Drama.* New York: Crowell, 1969.

Gibaldi, Joseph, and Herbert Lindenberger. *MLA Style Manual and Guide to Scholarly Publishing.* 2nd ed. New York: MLA, 1998.

Guerin, Wilfred L., et al. *A Handbook of Critical Approaches to Literature.* 2nd ed. New York: Harper, 1979.

Harmon, William, and C. Hugh Holman. *A Handbook to Literature.* 7th ed. Upper Saddle River: Prentice, 1996.

Lazarus, Arnold, and H. Wendell Smith. *A Glossary of Literature and Composition.* Urbana IL: NCTE, 1983.

Lentricchia, Frank, and Thomas McLaughlin. *Critical Terms for Literary Study.* 2nd ed. Chicago: Chicago UP, 1995.

Magill, Frank N., ed. *Critical Survey of Short Fiction.* 7 vols. Englewood: Salem, 1981-93.

McMahan, Elizabeth, Robert Funk, and Susan Day. *The Elements of Writing About Literature and Film.* New York: Macmillan, 1988.

Shaw, Valerie. *The Short Story: A Critical Introduction.* London: Longman, 1983.

Tresidder, Jack. *The Hutchison Dictionary of Symbols.* Oxford: Helicon, 1997.

Walker, Barabra G. *The Woman's Encyclopedia of Myths and Secrets.* San Francisco: Harper, 1983.